W9-CUN-444

CHICAGO BREAKDOWN

MIKE ROWE

DRAKE PUBLISHERS INC
New York — London

A 784. 756
R879c

E757   64

Published in 1975 by
Drake Publishers, Inc.
381 Park Avenue South
New York, New York 10016

Library of Congress Cataloging in Publication Data
    Chicago breakdown.

    Includes index.
    1. Negro music — History and criticism. 2. Blues
(Songs, etc.) — United States — History and criticism.
I. Title.
ML3556.R7   784   74-22597
ISBN 0-87749-813-X

Printed in the United States of America.

1234567890

CONTENTS

Acknowledgements

Blues research must be counted among the great growth industries of the '60s and, with much of it centred on Chicago, there has been a large amount of published material to draw upon. This book, then, represents the culmination of the efforts of collectors and researchers too numerous to credit individually; but some must be singled out for special mention. Thus all enthusiasts of Chicago blues are indebted to those first researchers who laid the foundations for the serious study of the music; to Paul Oliver, the intrepid French collectors Jacques Demetre and the late Marcel Chauvard, and Belgian enthusiast George Adins, who were visiting the Chicago clubs before I'd ever heard of Elmore James or J. B. Lenoir; to Neil Paterson, Don Kent and Pete Welding, who sent some of the earliest reports on the Chicago scene; and to Simon Napier and Mike Leadbitter who published much of the material in *Blues Unlimited*, thus providing a focal point for the research.

Many people helped specifically with this book and I am grateful to Tony Russell for the extensive use of his interviews with Floyd and Moody Jones and Johnny Williams, to John J. Broven for the loan of his correspondence with J. B. Lenoir, to Willie Leiser, and to Mike Leadbitter for the discography, numerous snippets of information and in particular his superb article based on Gayle Dean Wardlow's research on Elmore James. In Chicago I am grateful for the use of photographs and material collected by Jim and Amy O'Neal for *Living Blues* magazine. For my own interviews I was helped enormously by Ron Watts and Chris Trimming, who allowed me generous access to the artists they promoted on European tours, and in the United States by Frank Scott, who encouraged me when my energy (never great) was flagging (which was all too often).

Ralph Bass of Chess-GRT in Chicago was enormously helpful and allowed us full run of the master files and tapes of the many unissued recordings. This filled in many of the gaps.

I am also grateful to Cliff G. Massoth of the Illinois Central Railroad Public Relations Department, who was kind enough to answer my questions and through whose courtesy the I.C. Railroad information and photos appear, and to the officials of the Illinois Department of Public Health's Bureau of Vital Records in Springfield. But my greatest debt is of course to the singers themselves, who with unfailing patience answered all my impertinent questions with great good humour and kindness.

For the use of their rare unpublished photographs I am immensely grateful to Mrs. Letha Jones, Homesick James, Rev. Moody Jones, James Gregory and George Paulus. For the other photographs my thanks go to Valerie Wilmer for the cover, Sylvia Pitcher, Bill Greensmith, and Simon

7

Napier of *Blues Unlimited* and the other copyright holders. For the maps I am indebted to Martin Steenson and for providing me with several hard-to-get books I want to thank Bob Yates. Many friends outside the blues world helped too. Richard Wilcox spent a great deal of time copying the many, tattered, original photos. For the drudgery of typing and presenting the manuscript I am especially grateful to Janice O'Callaghan and Jean Fitzpatrick, to Sean O'Callaghan who master-minded the operation, and to Pia Di Mora. In Chicago Kevin and Netta Gormley very generously allowed us the complete run of their apartment and provided us with a base for operations.

To Tony Russell and my publishers I owe a huge debt for their patience and assistance and for affording me the opportunity to write this book. I also owe a great debt to my wife Barbara, who researched all the references and suffered my bad temper when my inability to communicate the great beauty of the music overcame my usual calm disposition. To her my thanks, my apologies and my promise to return the flat to its intended function of a dwelling rather than a depository for records, books, magazines, tapes, photos and the flotsam of two years research.

Mike Rowe, London, 1973.

Picture Credits

Photographs reproduced by kind permission of the photographers, copyright holders or owners, as listed: Georges Adins 127R; Arhoolie Records 24-5; Brad Barrett 169; *Blue Unlimited* 19L, 66, 136L, 164T, 166R; Pete Brown 16; Henri Cartier-Bresson (courtesy Conway Picture Library) 10, 36, 37, 38, 42T, 213L; *Cash Box* 60R, 91, 124L, 139, 149L&R, 150; Chess Records, 9, 42B, 64, 65, 82, 83, 132L&R, 146; Jimmy Dawkins 127L, 109L; Jacques Demetre 13, 97, 121, 154, 166L, 185; Willie Dixon 62, 107; David Evans 19R; John Godrich 44L; Bill Greensmith 51L, 55B, 71, 81, 93R, 94L, 107L&R, 117L&R, 122L, 159R, 175L&R, 198; Jim Gregory 196; Illinois Central Railroad 29, 33; Mrs Letha Jones (courtesy *Living Blues*) 72, 134, 144, 202, 203; Rev. Moody Jones 50, 55TR, 58T&B; James LaRocca (courtesy *Blues Unlimited*) 136R; *Living Blues* 55TL (courtesy Snooky Pryor), 68 (courtesy Homer Harris), 184L, 190L; Danny Lyon 27; Mrs Lillian McMurry 143; Rick Milne 90; Max Moore 140; Paul Oliver 78T, 85, 104-5, 110R, 194; George Paulus 79, 124R, 125, 133, 161, 162, 176, 178; Sylvia Pitcher 118, 181TL, 181B; *R&B Monthly* 110L; Mike Rowe 23, 46, 48, 53R, 60L, 69, 78B, 94R, 98L&R, 102, 111, 114, 122R, 147, 152T (courtesy Eddie Taylor), 152B, 156, 164B, 168, 171L, 173L&R, 187, 190R, 208L, C&R, 209C&R, 213R, 214; Tony Russell 44R, 53L, 93L, 184R, 186; Frank Scott 73, 193; Jim Simpson 171R; Big Boy Spires (courtesy Don Kent) 129; Sunnyland Slim 95; Sandy Sutherland 181TR; Alan Thompson & Dave Luxton 86; Dimitri Vicheney 159L; Pete Welding 51R; Homesick James Williamson 41, 77, 108, 199, 201. The diagram on page 210 is based on an original in Cayton & Drake, *Black Metropolis* (see Sources, page 215).

Foreword / 'What's He Singing?'

At one o'clock on a Saturday morning in April 1948 Aristocrat Records of Chicago released its second Muddy Waters record in the time-honoured manner of all young and struggling record companies—the new issue being hustled from the trunk of a car to their 180 outlets on the South Side—to porters, Pullman conductors, beauty shops, barber shops and even to some record shops. It was either a reluctant issue, Leonard Chess of Aristocrat needing to be convinced of its commercial appeal, or part of the frantic stockpiling of material that the independent labels engaged in to beat the recording ban of 1948.

Muddy had cut the sides, *I Can't Be Satisfied* and *I Feel Like Going Home*, at the RCA Victor studios in the previous autumn and they had since laid on the shelf. Certainly the songs were very different from the jump blues and sophisticated vocals which Chess had set out to record and with which Aristocrat was enjoying some success. They were very different even from Muddy's first record *Gypsy Woman*, a fairly undistinguished blues with guitar and piano accompaniment. *I Can't Be Satisfied*, in contrast, was a romping country blues with a strangled vocal and whining bottleneck guitar that increased the excitement to fever pitch. 'What's he singing? I can't understand what he's singing', Chess had complained at the rehearsal, and it was only at the insistence of Leonard's red-headed partner Evelyn that Muddy was allowed to record it. 'I think he's got something', she said. Len Chess remained unconvinced but finally he issued it as Aristocrat 1305 and awaited his customers' reaction. He didn't have to wait long. The initial pressing was sold out by 2 o'clock that Saturday afternoon. Muddy recalls that he went to the Maxwell Radio Record Co. at 831 Maxwell Street next morning and found they wouldn't let him buy the two copies he wanted, even at the $1.10 they were charging for the 79¢ record! 'But I'm the man who made it!' he protested in vain, and finally he had to settle for the one copy and, later, send his wife back for another.

Chess realised he'd stumbled on to something and had a hit on his hands. He was astute enough to see that with this record the Chicago blues had once again changed course; in fact it marked the beginning of an era of country-orientated blues of great creativity and richness which was to persist for the next decade and reach a peak of excellence in the early '50s.

1 / The Prewar Blues

The early '50s were remarkable for the last resurgence of the country blues—a style that had been largely superseded by the urban blues of the late '30s and '40s. By 1950 the wheel had again turned full circle, for there was a return to the boom years of the '20s when blacks left the South in a great wave of migration, bringing with them their musical inheritance the country blues.

But how shall we define the country blues? In the classic form a singer usually accompanied himself on guitar, his voice and instrument weaving a complex pattern as he frequently extended or contracted the 12-bar verses, the guitar underlining or taking up where the voice left off and becoming an extension of the voice itself. He sang his own songs or blues loosely based on traditional themes but there was an astonishing variety in this basically very limited form.

Originally the lack of communications and isolation of rural communities in the South had fostered various musical styles, each peculiar to a particular region or locality. Naturally any young black learning to play a guitar or harmonica would learn from the local musicians and thus the style was perpetuated. Musicians were plentiful for there was little else in the way of recreation and most families included a singer or guitarist of sorts. The most accomplished of them would be in demand for picnics and house-parties and obviously had the greatest influence both on the up-and-coming generation of singers and in creating the local style.

It's convenient to postulate a regional theory of blues and to describe the various styles in terms of the state boundaries as though they were completely contained within them for example, Mississippi blues, Texas blues, Georgia blues—whereas it would be more accurate to define a style by a county or sometimes a village even. In Mississippi the heaviest cotton-producing area, the Delta, was also the centre of the greatest blues activity in the state, and the term 'Mississippi blues' is used interchangeably with 'Delta blues'. But the geographical definition of the Delta is as approximate as that of its music. Charters describes it as 'an inland delta, the land flooded over by the Yazoo River and the rivers that flow into it from the north, the Tallahatchie and the Sunflower' and by this strict definition only Tunica, Coahoma, Leflore, Sunflower, Yazoo and Humphreys counties are in the Delta. Other authorities would be more generous and include all the counties west of Highway 49 as far as the Mississippi River from Tunica in the north to Issa Quena in the south: that

Downtown Chicago and the River, from a set entitled "The American Scene", photographed in Summer 1948 by Henri Cartier-Bresson.

is, a rough crescent of land bounded by Memphis, Vicksburg and Greenville.

Thus by Mississippi blues we generally mean the harsh, rhythmic Delta style of Charley Patton, Son House and Robert Johnson, which would have little in common with the Senatobia school of Skip James and even less with the so-called South Jackson style of delicate two-guitar accompaniments exemplified by Tommy Johnson and Ishman Bracey. But in as much as each form comprises the same elements, and it is only a preponderance of one or the other that gives each its characteristic sound, the regional theory is a useful generalisation.

Thus the Mississippi blues are characterised by intense, emotional singing and highly rhythmic guitar accompaniment, often in the bottle-neck style. It's not too fanciful to imagine this dark and dramatic music being torn only from the Delta earth while the sun-scorched barrenness of Texas gave rise to the high, keening voice and interminably extended guitar lines of the Texas blues. In contrast the blues from Georgia and the Carolinas (the South Atlantic blues style) with their beautiful melodies, regularly picked guitar patterns and lower emotional range seem cultivated from a lush and fertile soil. Perhaps topography rather than latitude and longitude played the important part in the fashioning of the country blues?

When the singers first moved northwards they carried with them their own musical inheritance and from their records of the late '20s and early '30s these local traditions can be detected. Most of these records were made on field trips to the South by the recording companies or by Southern artists brought to Chicago or New York to record, and the salient feature of blues recording up to World War II was that it was limited to a handful of companies, all of which were based in the North. Thus the entrepreneurial drive came from the North to record Southern artists for what was principally a Southern market. In the boom years of 1927-30, for example, OKeh of New York would make repeated field trips to Atlanta, Georgia and San Antonio, Texas, while the sister label Columbia would make similar but usually separate tours, recording in Atlanta, Dallas, Texas, and New Orleans. Victor of New Jersey also visited Atlanta and especially Memphis, Tennessee. Vocalion, a label of the Brunswick-Balke-Collender Company of Chicago, also recorded in Memphis, as well as Atlanta, Dallas and New Orleans, while Gennett made a lone trip to Birmingham, Alabama. Only Paramount, which enjoyed the earliest success of them all, was content to send for its very popular artists, Blind Lemon Jefferson and Blind Blake, to record in its Chicago studios.

Trite Like That

Some blues singers had already settled permanently in the North and not surprisingly their records were the first to show a distinct urban influence.

Vocalion recorded Leroy Carr in Indianapolis in June 1928 and Tampa Red in Chicago in September of the same year and their first releases, Carr's *How Long, How Long Blues* and Tampa's *It's Tight Like That* were immediately successful. Both artists were living in the North– Leroy Carr had moved to Indianapolis from Nashville, Tennessee, and Tampa Red to Chicago from Florida. The new departure was not only the piano-guitar instrumentation, which added a more sophisticated dimension to the style, but also a change of mood. Gone was the shouted urgency of the lone guitarist, to be replaced by Leroy's wistful sadness and Tampa's sly cheerfulness. The addition of the piano was a direct result of the music moving from the fields to the bars for there was usually a piano on club premises. Not only was the piano more likely to be heard above the noise of drinking and dancing but its presence ensured ready entertainment, since the pianist, unlike the more mobile guitarist, was always limited by the fixed nature of the instrument and had actively to seek out a piano to play. It was natural that a guitarist looking for work in the clubs would team up with a resident pianist and generally he was glad to do so, for with another instrument to carry the bass and rhythm the guitarist was freer to concentrate on his singing. In this way the pianist Leroy Carr formed a close association with the guitarist Scrapper Blackwell while Tampa Red teamed up with the pianist Georgia Tom.

As a result of working in such pairs greater limitations were imposed on both, for their timing had to conform and each had less flexibility. Piano

Tampa Red. Chicago, 1959.

disciplines were already beginning to curb the rough country zeal of the blues guitarist and this trend towards a more uniform blues sound was the first effect of the transition of the blues from the country to the city. And it would have accelerated even more rapidly had not the whole fabric of American society been rent by an event of the most far-reaching social and economic consequence.

Even as the United States basked in the false sunshine of the unprecedented prosperity of the '20s storm clouds were gathering on the economic horizon. With the stock market crash of October 1929 the deluge was on. Business confidence shattered, production plummetted, factories closed and men were laid off; the twin spectres of unemployment and hunger haunted bemused America. The poor were the hardest hit, of course, and America s poor, black and white, were to be hit hard through the Depression years of 1930 to 1933. The migration flood was stemmed to a trickle as the Northern factories closed their gates.

That the production of blues records suffered was not remarkable; what was remarkable is that any were issued at all, and the 'race record' companies must be counted among the super-optimists of the time for persisting in trying to sell luxury items to the most economically hard-pressed section of the country. In 1932 sales of phonograph records were only just over 5% of the 1927 figure and race records' total sales were down to 60,000. And this figure was only achieved by drastic price cutting from 75¢ to 25¢ or 35¢ each. Paramount failed in 1932, the parent company of the Gennett group of labels went into liquidation in 1934, and Columbia was in serious financial straits. A new company, the American Record Company, had entered the field with unique ill-timing in 1930 with a range of cheap labels each tied to a specific chain-store outlet; these were known as the 'dimestore' labels. Subsequently, with Brunswick and Vocalion, they were bought out by Consolidated Film Industries. Rationalisation took place throughout the record industry by a process of take-over and merger until by 1934 there were only two companies seriously competing for the tiny race market: ARC-Brunswick, through ARC's dimestore labels and Brunswick's Vocalion, and Victor (which had been taken over by RCA), through its new race label Bluebird, started in 1933.

Victor were more fortunate in their timing for by 1934 the worst of the Depression was over and America was getting back on her feet again. The gradual return to prosperity coincided with the launching of another new race catalogue, the Decca 7000 series. Recording in New York and Chicago with Mayo Williams, the man responsible for Paramount's early success, as talent scout, Decca was quickly established. Once again the blues record market was expanding and Decca, with Bluebird and Vocalion, set out to fill the demand.

But things had changed since the '20s; the demand was now for the sound of the Chicago-based artists like Tampa Red, Bumble Bee Slim and

Big Bill Broonzy. There was much less need for field trips to the South, and when these were taken the object was to record as much as possible from the artists in the shortest time. The boundaries of the music thus contracted as more records were issued by fewer artists. The end of the Depression years marked the beginning of the intense development of the urban blues proper, the seeds of which had been sown by Leroy Carr and Tampa Red just before the slump. It also marked the beginning of what could be properly called the Chicago blues.

Already there was a lifetime's difference, musically, between the country blues of, say, Blind Lemon Jefferson and the Chicago singers. Lemon's parched voice and sparse guitar were sullen in comparison with Tampa's gay, infectious double entendre or Big Bill's ingratiating exuberance or even Leroy's quiet introspection. The urban blues were altogether more sophisticated—lighter in texture with the emotional power turned down and the beat turned up. Tampa's first offering might easily have been titled *Trite Like That*, and the songs that followed were frequently just that. It was probably a reaction to the trauma of the Depression years that the emphasis was more on entertainment, but there had always been a duality to the blues function. The very act of singing of one's sorrows provided a partial release from them but at the same time such singing also provided entertainment. To the mass black audience the function of the blues was becoming more and more blurred and never before had there been such a confusion of the twin roles.

At any period the nature of the blues is always the result of the mood of the black masses, but the blues sound does not necessarily react as the sensitive barometer of black taste but more as the commercial interpretation of that feeling. Thus, while the black public may well have found that a lively, noisier and more exciting music was to its liking, the inevitable result of commercial pressures was a stereotype, the individuality smoothed out by the deliberate policy of record companies aiming at the same sound and launching artists who sounded like their competitors' best-sellers.

By 1935, before the advent of exclusive contracts, the most popular artists were recording for more than one label, sometimes under pseudonyms, sometimes not. This was another reason for the overall sameness of the records, but new singers were appearing in the race lists too. As well as the ever popular Big Bill, Tampa Red, Bumble Bee Slim, Memphis Minnie and Peetie Wheatstraw there were new names like Jazz Gillum, Washboard Sam, Johnny Temple, Bill Gaither, Jimmy Gordon—all artists who sang in the then prevailing blues style. There were still singers, however, who stood out against the Chicago-dominated scene and sang in a maverick country style; singers like Bo Carter, whose gentle, melodic double entendre songs were very popular on the Bluebird lists. Also from Mississippi but playing in the harsh Delta tradition was Joe Williams, an artist destined never to lose his Mississippi background in a musical career

JO WILLIAMS   Bluebird Record

reaching to the present day. Sleepy John Estes' individual and completely personal style was similarly untouched by current fashion and his blues were to provide an antidote to much of the music in the Decca catalogue.

Another artist who was enormously popular was Walter Davis from Grenada, Mississippi, probably the most original of them all with his deeply moving singing and lyrical piano style. Davis was to have nearly 90 records issued in a recording career of 22 years. Most of his songs were at the same unvarying tempo with a low-keyed sadness that was immensely touching. This mood permeated his up-tempo songs of a leering bawdiness and even those of other artists where he was merely an accompanist.

July 1935 saw Blind Boy Fuller from Carolina making his first visit to the recording studios in New York. With Buddy Moss, who had recorded for ARC two years previously, Fuller was to become one of the main exponents of the East Coast style. Already the blues output of the two main recording centres, Chicago and New York, was beginning to parallel musically the traditional migratory patterns, a process that was to accelerate greatly through the postwar years.

Blind Boy Fuller was not the only country singer to find success in the late '30s, for the young Mississippi singer Robert Johnson was recorded by ARC in 1936 and 1937. Some months later he was dead, poisoned by a woman or alcohol. Johnson's emotion-charged singing and poetic imagery stamp him as an artist of enormous stature and his songs and his bottleneck guitar style make him the most important influence on the post-war blues despite his tragically short recording career.

The Melrose Mess

But in Chicago Bluebird was beginning to grab most of the blues market with what Sam Charters characterised as the 'Bluebird Beat'. It might have been called with even more justification the 'Melrose Mess', for it was a white businessman, Lester Melrose, who was really responsible for shaping the Chicago sound of the late '30s and the '40s. Melrose was born in Olney, Illinois, in 1891 and after working as a fireman on the Baltimore & Ohio Railroad, as a store assistant and in a grocery store venture, interrupted by service overseas in World War I, he and his brother Walter opened a music store on Cottage Grove in 1922. Early success came with their publishing compositions by King Oliver and Jelly Roll Morton and in 1926 Lester sold out his half-share in the music publishing business to start out on his own as an agent. 1928 saw him recording the Hokum Boys (Tampa Red & Georgia Tom) for Paramount; 1930, Big Bill Broonzy for Paramount and Gennett. February 1934 found him anxious to take up where he had left off in the Depression, and he put out feelers to RCA Victor and Columbia which immediately resulted in contracts to record artists on their behalf. Melrose has said, 'From March 1934 to February 1951 I recorded at least 90 per cent of all rhythm-and-blues talent for RCA Victor and Columbia records,' and a glance at the names of Melrose's artists will show just how effectively he had the blues recording scene tied up: Big Bill Broonzy, Tampa Red, Jazz Gillum, Washboard Sam, Walter Davis, Big Joe Williams, Sonny Boy Williamson, Memphis Minnie, Roosevelt Sykes, Johnny Temple, Lonnie Johnson and many others. It's interesting to note that when he recorded the dreary Big Three Trio in 1946 they included the bass player Willie Dixon who was to become the Melrose of the postwar years.

But Melrose had more than a large stable of blues artists under his control. Since only a few of them had regular accompanists most of them would play on each other's records and thus Melrose had a completely self-contained unit which made great sense economically, if less artistically. The instrumentation was generally constant: singer accompanied by guitar, piano, bass and drums, with occasional saxophones or harmonica. Melrose had effected the greatest rationalisation in blues recording. Whereas the major companies had clumsily sought to record artists who sounded like each other, the Melrose machine provided them with artists who *were* each other! The final stage of this musical incest was completed when they started recording each other's songs. Broonzy and Washboard Sam were the most prolific songwriters of them all and their importance as lyricists cannot be overstressed.

To be fair to Melrose, not all the music he recorded came off the production line. Some of the singers worked in pairs with an accompanist and recorded together for many years. Big Bill had a regular pianist, Black Bob, in the mid '30s, and then later Josh Altheimer, while Tampa Red worked with the pianist Major Merriweather, better known as Big Maceo, in partnerships which were broken up only by death. The house-band only accompanied those singers who didn't have a regular group. Artists who couldn't or wouldn't play with a band Melrose wisely recorded alone or with a minimum of support. One such artist was Tommy McClennan.

Tommy was a short, very dark man from Yazoo City, Mississippi, and his acquisition as a recording artist speaks volumes for Melrose's tenacity. Big Bill relates how he warned Melrose against going down to Mississippi to fetch Tommy, who worked on a farm about 15 miles out of Yazoo City. As a Northern white man Melrose would be particularly unwelcome on a farm of five or six hundred blacks and would be regarded with great suspicion, if not hostility. Melrose wouldn't listen though Bill warned he might get hurt. When he came back empty-handed after being run out of town he told Bill, 'Get hurt, get hurt, Hell, they nearly killed me, and they would have done it if I hadn't run like hell! I'll certainly never go down there again.' So Bill had to go and fetch Tommy. Five feet seven and weighing 130 pounds, what Tommy lacked in stature he made up in sheer aggression. With fierce growls of 'Play it right' he cowed his bass-player into submission on more than one record. Bill used to tell a story of Tommy insisting on singing the word 'nigger' in his big song *Bottle Up And Go* at a party on first arriving in Chicago. He left by the window with the remains of his guitar round his neck. Tommy sounds as if he was a lot of fun.

McClennan was 31 years old when he cut his first session in Chicago. His blues were shouted with a ferocity that assailed the listener and like most Mississippi artists he used traditional tunes and themes, playing guitar with the typical rhythmic intensity of the Delta bluesman. Sometimes, though, he could surprise with a song as beautiful and delicate as *Baby Please Don't Tell On Me*.

His popularity was such that Bluebird recorded his close friend, the mysterious Robert Petway, who played and sang in a style that was virtually indistinguishable from McClennan's. Neither recorded again in the postwar years, although McClennan was living at 22nd and State in 1951 and was still to be seen in the clubs.

Another uncompromising country singer whom Melrose actively sought out was Booker Washington White, or Bukka White, as he was known on record. Melrose had recorded Bukka for Vocalion in 1937 and his one release had proved successful enough for Vocalion to request another and Sonny Boy played together the effect was heightened so much that it even overcame comparatively cheerful themes. For instance, *Joe Louis And John Henry Blues*, which commemorated the one-round success of the new folk-hero Joe Louis six months previously, sounds as mournful as anything else from the session.

From Sonny Boy's 1940 session we catch a glimpse of things to come. The accompanists were Joshua Altheimer from Pine Bluff, Arkansas, on piano and Fred Williams on drums, both from Big Bill's band, and the sound was very different. Pushed along by Williams's steady, taut drumming and Altheimer's solid, percussive piano Sonny Boy blew the most exciting harp yet. The beat had become much more pronounced and the accompanists were laying down the solid foundation for the future Chicago blues.

Sadly Joshua Altheimer died that year, on 18 November, only 30 years old, and Sonny Boy's main accompanying pianist on record was to be Blind John Davis, the Bluebird house pianist who denied any real interest in blues. Another of Sonny Boy's pianists with almost the same reservation was Eddie Boyd, who nevertheless played superbly on the July 1945 session when the classic *Elevator Woman* was recorded. This was a gay and jaunty blues and everybody knew what Sonny Boy meant went he sang

> Elevate me mama, mama five or six floors on down
> You know everybody tells me you
>> must be the elevatingest women in town.

Sonny Boy had something. He didn't have a dark, dramatic blues voice but he was easily the most expressive of any of the singers then recording. Happy or sad, Sonny Boy reached out from the grooves to his listeners and his pleasures or his sorrows became theirs. His personality shone through his songs as he nudged his audience with ingenuous asides or explanations, as in *Bluebird Blues*. This is a tender love song in which he exhorts the bluebird with no little politeness to take a message to his fiancée. It is made all the more personal by the mention of her name, and her house on Shannon Street in Jackson, Tennessee. The message itself is curiously stilted:

> Now Bluebird when you find Miss Lacey Belle I want you to please
>> give her my best regards.

He starts the final verse:

> Now Bluebird she may not be at home but please knock on
>> her door

and as if anticipating that this may raise some doubts about her fidelity in his listeners' minds he carefully explains in the last line:

> Well that she might be right across the street visiting her
>> next-door neighbour you know.

The punning significance of the bluebird as the traditional love-bird and also the name of the company for which he was making the record adds a further dimension to the song's meaning.

Lacey Belle, his wife, crops up frequently in Sonny Boy's lyrics and only rarely does he stray to 'Suzanna' or 'Miss Stella Brown', but in *Jiving The Blues* he does attempt a gentle seduction in a typically self-effacing manner. He talks over Altheimer's rolling piano as he tries to persuade the girl to dance:

> I don't care nothing about your engagement ring
> Oh come on now at least you can talk with me you know
> J-Just let me tell you something you know
> Oh I don't want to marry no way . . .
>
> Oh you ain't coming at all huh?
> Oh I know you don't love me, you love somebody [else]
> But I just want to talk with you . . .
>
> I-I wish I'd met you much earlier you know how it is
> Maybe I'm a little too late
> But I just want to show you how to Susie-Q
> Come on . . .

Sonny Boy's women are not always treated in such a light-hearted manner for in the brilliant *Dealing With The Devil* he sings:

> I got the meanest women you most ever seen
> She sleeps with an ice-pick in her hand man and she fights all
>   in her dreams
> I been dealing with the devil
> My woman don't love me no more.

Equally ferocious was Sonny Boy's attitude to World War II and the enemy:

> I want to drop a bomb and set the Japanese city on fire (x2)
> Now because they are so rotten I just love to see them die.

From the same session, *Check Up On My Baby Blues* is more oblique. With Mussolini substituted for the Japanese, Sonny Boy's motives for fighting have more to do with protection of his woman than any high patriotic zeal:

> I got to check up on my baby, I got to see how my baby
>   been getting along
> Now I go and fight for our country, that'll keep Mussolini from
>   treating my baby wrong.
> [spoken] Mussolini got scared and cut out didn't he?

Sonny Boy's songs range from intense, slow blues like the very moving *My Black Name Blues*, through rocking good-time blues like *Elevator Woman* to light inconsequential jivy numbers such as *Mellow Chick Swing* and nonsense like *Polly Put The Kettle On*—all fired by that majestic harp-playing.

Not only his songs but also the warm Tennessee voice gives the clue to his personality, and it comes as no surprise to learn that he was one of the best-loved singers of all time. Stories of his generosity are legion. Big Bill

said, 'He would give you anything he had, he would give the shirt off his back to a friend . . .' Homesick James uses almost the same words: '. . . Take his shirt off and give it to you if it would help you, you know.' Billy Boy Arnold says that when he met him

> He told me and my cousin that if we ever needed anything to come and ask him. 'Don't steal', he told us. 'Please don't steal, come and ask me for what you need'.

Sonny Boy always had a lot of hangers-on.

> He was 'bout one of the finest fellers I know . . . He worked to help the people with somethin' to eat and somethin' to drink. When pay-day come he didn't have anything—he had *no* pay-day. He was just good—he bought everything they wanted to drink; everything they wanted to eat. He was good to the crowd around him. That's all he did, was work for them.'

Eddie Boyd and Sunnyland Slim put the other side of Sonny Boy:

> He was a good fellow but his attitude when he's drinking, for a person that don't know him, they would think he was a vicious man. And he was harmless as a lamb.
> Sonny Boy stayed sharp, had plenty of women and was dangerous to fool with if you made him mad. But you loved him just the same.

Affable and generous, he drank heavily like most of the other singers. Big Bill once said you had to be tongue-tied to sing the blues but he meant it metaphorically. Sonny Boy however did have a slight speech impediment which one can detect in the spoken passages of *Jiving The Blues*. But it all but disappeared in his singing, emerging as his tendency to garble the verses, making them often difficult to understand.

One of the trends of the late '30s that Sonny Boy sidestepped, or

Big Bill and Sonny Boy.

mercifully Melrose didn't attempt with his sessions, was the addition of trumpet or clarinet to the basic instrumentation. It was probably Melrose's early experience of jazz recording that led him to such experiments with Washboard Sam, Memphis Minnie, Big Bill, Tampa Red and others, but whilst the addition of, say, clarinettist Arnett Nelson strongly emphasised the good-time music of Washboard Sam, the use of unsuitable instruments behind other artists so diluted the blues feeling that the records today sound as dated as any slang from the '30s.

No doubt Sonny Boy's harp-playing kept such unwelcome visitors at bay; it was in his hands that the harp became the blues instrument *par excellence*. He accompanied other Bluebird artists too, usually those who had recorded with him like Robert Lee McCoy, Yank Rachell and Big Joe Williams. And it was a Joe Williams session in December 1941 that gave the next hint of the sound of the Chicago blues that were to follow. This was the first time on record that Sonny Boy had accompanied Big Joe's singing and he played immaculately, embellishing the melody and matching Joe's guitar note for note in an improvisational tour de force. The interplay between Joe's voice and guitar and Sonny Boy's harp-playing was not to be equalled until the records of Muddy Waters with Little Walter ten years later.

Bluebird was well on top by 1942 but when the United States entered the war shellac rationing was introduced and all the companies cut back on their race releases. Bigger problems were to come for the American Federation of Musicians was getting worried about the effects of jukeboxes on the livelihoods of their members and finally in July 1942 the union's president, J. C. Petrillo, ordered a complete ban on all commercial recording. The studios closed and remained closed for two years.

The two main features of black life in the United States were segregation and migration; the former providing the impetus for the latter. Musically, while segregation created the blues, migration spread the message. The migrants had respectable antecedents in the first slaves who had escaped to the North but with the increasingly heavy migration after the Civil War many Negroes could point to the example of their own parents, brothers, aunts or uncles who had left for the industrial cities of the North. Segregation was not the sole cause of migration, for equally large numbers of whites also left their native states; migration was the last remedy poor people had available to overcome their economic circumstance; but for blacks segregation was an added spur to leaving.

The causes of migration are often described in terms of 'push' factors, which encourage people to leave, or 'pull' factors, which attract people to a particular place. The figures (Table 1) for the net loss through migration from the South show that the great peaks occur when the 'push' factors are strongly reinforced by the 'pull' factors.

Table 1	Net Loss Through Migration From The South
1900-10	180,500
1910-20	453,800
1920-30	773,400
1930-40	347,500
1940-50	1,597,000
1950-60	1,457,000

The first great Northward migration started about 1915 (this is disguised slightly by the decennial nature of the US Census figures above) when Southern agriculture was in a parlous state, the cotton crops having been ravaged first by the boll weevil and then by a series of floods. At the same time the war in Europe cut off European immigration on which Northern industry depended, just at the time when the United States' entry into the war stimulated production and the need for labour was greatest. With jobs available and nobody to fill them the Northern businessmen actively encouraged recruitment of black workers from the South. After the war immigration from Europe picked up again and there was some black redundancy but when immigration was restricted by legislation in the early '20s blacks were holding on to the gains made in employment. The 1930-40 figures, which include the Depression years, when people stayed on the farms if they possibly could, show a great fall in migration, although in 1935-40 migrants were again leaving the South in large numbers. The next great peak was from 1940 as World War II stimulated

the US economy to such heights that blacks left the South in droves. In 1940-50 Mississippi alone lost one quarter of its total black population. The 'pull' factors are very clearly illustrated by comparison of the Negro median wage per annum which for 1949 was $2254 for Detroit, $1919 for Chicago and only $439 for Mississippi. Migration appears two-dimensional in nature, for as well as the more obvious movement away from the South there has been the movement from the country to the city. Of course this Northward trend is almost overwhelmingly a movement to the cities but what is significant is that by 1960 even in the South there were more blacks living in the towns. Table 2 shows this very clearly:

Table 2	Negro Population Distribution	
	1900	*1960*
South	**89.7%**	**59.9%**
Urban	15.4	35.0
Rural	74.3	24.9
Rest of U.S.	**10.3**	**40.1**
Urban	7.2	38.2
Rural	3.1	1.9

In 1900 77.4% of the black population lived in the rural areas while the urban proportion was 22.6%. In 60 years the rural proportion has dropped to 26.8% while the urban black population has risen to 73.2%. In so far as the black population has more than doubled in that time, from 8.8 millions to 18.9 millions, there were more blacks living in urban areas outside the South by 1960 than there had been living in rural areas in the whole of the United States in 1900. The true picture is thus of a movement from farm to factory and the change in the nature of the blues was a reflection of this change in circumstances.

If the quantitative aspects of migration account for the country blues giving way to the city blues, the qualitative aspects explain the resulting sound of the city blues, for there was a definite geographical pattern of migration. That there were three main centres of attraction for the Southern migrants is shown by Table 3, which is an analysis of the estimated net gains of migrants in the host states of the North and West:

Table 3	Estimated Net Migration of Negroes		
	North East	North Central	West
1900-10	101,600	55,800	19,700
1910-20	194,300	244,100	28,400
1920-30	357,000	364,000	37,500
1930-40	175,800	127,800	49,000
1940-50	483,000	632,000	323,000
1950-60	541,000	558,000	332,000

Note: that these totals do not agree exactly with the figures for Table 1 is probably owing to the estimation techniques and sampling error. (From C25-73 Historical Statistics of the U.S.)

The poles of these areas of attraction were, respectively, the cities of New York, Chicago and Los Angeles, although the westward migration was not really significant until the war years of the '40s. What was significant and particularly fascinating, bearing in mind the regional blues traditions, was the similar geographical backgrounds of the blacks within each region and city. For there was nothing haphazard about migration; the host states were virtually determined by the migrants' most direct route north or, later, west. The effect was that migrants from any given Southern state would generally tend to settle in a specific Northern state or group of states. The US Census employs such groupings in its analysis and divides the United States into nine areas: New England, Mid Atlantic, East North Central, West North Central, South Atlantic, East South Central, West South Central, Mountain and Pacific.

Table 4			Non – White Residents in 1950				
Birth State	Total	M.A.	E.N.C.	W.N.C.	S.A.	E.S.C.	W.S.C.	Pacific

Birth State	Total	M.A.	E.N.C.	W.N.C.	S.A.	E.S.C.	W.S.C.	Pacific
S.A.	6,125,050	810,945	262,290	8,740	4,882,210	60,780	18,125	28,105
E.S.C.	3,634,040	91,980	604,445	89,670	104,760	2,569,950	108,770	52,715
W.S.C.	2,954,750	25,165	169,690	85,170	15,965	36,775	2,323,380	263,510

Note: The figures are for Non-white and thus include very small numbers of Indians, Chinese, Japanese etc.

Illinois Central passenger train of the '40s.

Of the 1,242,840 non-whites alive in 1950 who had left the South Atlantic states of Delaware, Maryland, District of Columbia, Virginia, West Virginia, North Carolina, South Carolina, Georgia and Florida 810,945 were living in the Mid Atlantic states of New York, New Jersey and Pennsylvania. And over 60% of them would have come from just two states, Georgia and South Carolina.

By far the largest proportion, over 56%, of the E.S.C. migrants (from Kentucky, Tennessee. Alabama and Mississippi) had settled in the E.N.C. states of Ohio, Indiana, Illinois, Michigan and Wisconsin with the heaviest influx to Illinois, Michigan and Ohio, (over 80% of them coming from Mississippi and Alabama).

The W.S.C. states of Arkansas, Louisiana, Oklahoma and Texas provide the most migrants to the Pacific states of California, Washington and Oregon. (But this was in fact a trend that only started during World War II; previous movement had been heaviest to the E.N.C. and W.N.C. states, at least from Arkansas and Louisiana).

Table 4 shows the position by 1950—but have these trends been constant for previous decades or have there been complete reversals of migration patterns? It's instructive to compare the distribution of migrants over the three great periods of population movement, 1910-20, 1920-30 and 1940-50. Tables 5a and 5b have been compiled from the same source as Table 4, and consider only the migrants who left from the South. The figures refer to the minimum net migration, ignoring intercensal deaths of migrants.

Table 5a   Destination of Southern Non-White Migrants (1940-50)

Destination	S.A.	%	E.S.C.	%	W.S.C.	%
North East (N.E., M.A.)	241,830	71.1	44,750	12.3	13,275	3.9
North Central (E.N.C., W.N.C.)	80,585	23.7	278,855	76.7	104,055	30.5
West (Mountain, Pacific)	17,700	5.2	39,845	11.0	223,615	65.6

Table 5a shows clearly the geographical nature of migration during the '40s. From the South Atlantic states 71.1% chose to move directly north to the North East. The same pattern is observed for the East South Central states, 76.7% of their migrants being claimed by states directly north. Of the West South Central migrants, faced with the choice of moving north or west, the majority chose to move west. The distribution can be compared for each of the three previous decades of heaviest migration in Table 5b:

Table 5b

Birth States	Destination	1910-20	1920-30	1940-50
South Atlantic	North East	62.6	69.2	71.1
	North Central	34.8	29.8	23.7
	West	2.6	1.0	5.2
East South Central	North East	14.0	12.3	12.3
	North Central	83.2	85.9	76.7
	West	2.8	1.8	11.0
West South Central	North East	7.5	4.4	3.9
	North Central	71.1	62.1	30.5
	West	21.4	33.5	65.6

Thus the trend for South Atlantic blacks to move to the North East has intensified, the proportion steadily increasing from 62.6% over 1910-20 to 69.2% from 1920-30, reaching 71.1% from 1940-50, mainly at the expense of the North Central states, which show a corresponding decrease from 34.8% to 23.7%. The westward movement is not at all significant in any decade.

The North Central states lost a little of their appeal for the E.S.C. migrants as the move to the West gathered momentum during the war and early postwar years but with the overwhelming majority (76.7%) still preferring to move due north.

The significant change is in the pattern for the West South Central states, where the North Central and West proportions show a complete reversal. From 1910-20 the North Central share was 71.1% to the West's 21.4% but by 1940-50 the proportion of westward migrants had jumped to 65.6% pushing the North Central share down to 30.5%.

The statistics so far have shown that the urban black population of the North East, North Central and Western states is drawn from the South mainly according to strict geographical patterns. This much is evident from the US Census groupings but these figures still mask the differential migration from states within the same censal groups. If these groups are further broken down into their constituent states and the relative migration rates compared, the geographical rules are seen to be drawn with an even greater rigidity. Taking the E.N.C. states as a whole, their greatest number of migrants has always come from the E.S.C. states; but, considering them individually, the two most easterly states, Ohio and Michigan, show more migrants from the South Atlantic group. In fact by 1930 Georgia had supplied most migrants to Ohio and Michigan, Kentucky to Indiana, and Mississippi to Illinois.

Table 6   *E.S.C & W.S.C. Negro Migrants to E.N.C. States (1930)*
Birth Place

| | E.S.C. | | | | W.S.C. | | | |
Residence	Ky.	Tenn.	Ala.	Miss.	Ark.	La.	Ok.	Tex.
Ohio	27,177	19,222	34,366	7,588	3,377	2,096	739	1,667
Indiana	25,317	13,728	6,205	7,428	2,819	1,630	436	854
Illinois	17,280	34,844	24,958	50,851	16,425	19,867	2,315	6,669
Michigan	6,627	12,478	20,216	9,869	5,931	3,988	1,451	2,914
Wisconsin	487	810 ˙	569	1,236	559	402	157	286

Negroes in the United States 1920–1932, U S Dept of Commerce Bureau of the Census.

From Table 6 it is seen that the greatest migration from the West South Central states is to Illinois, the most westerly of the North Central states, But of the W.S.C. states migration is significantly higher from Arkansas and Louisiana, since the more westerly states, Oklahoma and Texas, were providing more migrants to the West Coast (e.g. the figure for Texas migrants to California was 14,314, higher than to all the E.N.C. states combined).

By concentrating on migration from the South we have ignored the small number which moves back from the North and also the much larger number which moved to neighbouring states. For, while more migrants from Kentucky and Alabama went to Ohio, and more from Tennessee went to Illinois, than to any other state, Arkansas turns out to be the most popular stopping-place for Mississippi migrants. Similarly Texas for Louisiana and Oklahoma for Texas out-migrants.

Table 7 State of Birth	Residence of E.S.C. Born Negroes (1930) Residence	Proportion of Birth State
Kentucky	Ohio	9.3%
	Indiana	8.7
	Illinois	5.9
Tennessee	Illinois	6.5
	Ohio	3.6
	Missouri	3.1
Alabama	Ohio	3.0
	Mississippi	2.2
	Illinois	2.2
Mississippi	Arkansas	4.7
	Illinois	4.1
	Tennessee	3.9

Migration to the North or West was not necessarily the long haul it would seem, for often the migrants would break their journey, staying in intermediate states for a while before moving on. Memphis and St Louis were popular resting places for Mississippi blacks en route to Chicago, as can be seen from the large number of Mississippi migrants who moved to Tennessee and Missouri (see Table 9).

'The Illinois Central Railroad Brought The Blues To Chicago'

Short-haul or long-haul, there was nothing magical about the diverse migration patterns, for humans, unlike birds, do not migrate by instinct. They took the most direct routes: the highways and especially the railroads. The Texas and Pacific would take blacks west from Arkansas or Dallas, Texas, or the Santa Fe from Houston. Georgia migrants could choose the Southern to take them to Mid-Atlantic states or they could go north to Ohio on the Louisville and Nashville. The Carolinas were served by the Atlantic Coast Railroad. But the one line that ran almost due north for nearly a thousand miles, taking in the whole of the Delta blues country, was the Illinois Central from New Orleans to Chicago. And this is why the overwhelming number of blacks from Mississippi and Tennessee, and large numbers from Louisiana and Arkansas too, went to Chicago.

From 1940-50 the main I.C. lines from the South were New Orleans to Chicago via Jackson, Mississippi and from Greenville, Mississippi to Chicago. Another heavy passenger traffic line to Chicago was from

A Southerner's first sight of Chicago: the Central Station.

Birmingham, Alabama. The favourite trains of the period were 'The Creole', 'The Louisiane' and 'The Southern Express' and travel time to Chicago varied from 12 hours to 24 hours depending on the point of departure. 'The Louisiane', for example, left New Orleans at 8.30 am and arrived in Chicago 8.30 am the following day. In 1940 the fares were $16.95 from New Orleans, $15.35 from Jackson and $11.10 from Memphis.

> If you get to Chicago before I do
> Won't you tell 'em about me
> Everything that you know
> Everywhere that you go
> You be in Chicago baby
> Won't you tell 'em about me
> (Pinetop, *Tell 'Em About Me*)

Chicago has a very long Negro history; local tradition even has it that the first settler on the site of Chicago in 1790 was a black trader; but the mid-19th century dates the real beginnings of Chicago's black population, when fugitive slaves from the South and freed men from the North East made their home there. The black population in Chicago grew from 232 in 1850 to 30,150 by 1900 but the spectacular increases were to occur during and after World War I. The effect of this massive influx was to increase the black concentration in certain parts of the city. Allan H. Spear has written:

> In the late nineteenth century, while most Negroes lives in certain sections of the South Side, they lived interspersed among whites; there were few all-Negro blocks. By 1915, on the other hand, the physical ghetto had taken shape; a large, almost all-Negro enclave on the South Side, with a similar offshoot on the West Side, housed most of Chicago's Negroes.

The South Side black belt was a narrow strip, a few blocks wide, bounded by the railroad yards and factories just west of Wentworth Avenue and the stately homes east of Wabash Avenue. It stretched south from 22nd Street to 39th Street by 1900. The two centres on the West Side were along Lake Street between Ashland and Western and on the Near West Side in the old immigrant area of Halsted and Maxwell Streets.

With the influx of Southern migrants drawn by Chicago's stockyards, steel-mills, foundries and packing-plants the black belt had to expand but the South Side could only move south or east. To the west the railroad yards and plants limited the housing available, but the area east of State Street with the broad avenues of Wabash, Michigan and South Park Grand Boulevard contained fine, substantial houses which had been owned by Chicago's wealthy. The white residents were moving out to the suburbs on the North Side and as they moved out blacks from the one- or two-storey wooden-frame houses west of State Street moved in, leaving the old centre of the black belt, between State and Wentworth, a hideous slum. But the new areas began to deteriorate too. Spear quotes from the *Chicago Defender* when he writes: 'A few years later the district was characterised by "men and women half clothed hanging out of a window", "ragtime piano playing . . . far into the night" and "shooting and cutting scrapes".' What had happened was the direct result of Chicago's special tolerance of lawlessness and vice. The authorities tolerated prostitution but attempted to confine it to certain areas, which meant that they always centred it in the black belt away from the business section or the white residential areas. With the ending of legalised prostitution in 1912 the red-light district was left firmly established between Wabash and Wentworth and, as the migration continued, Wabash and Indiana began to decline and with them Prairie, Calumet and South Park Avenue. To escape again from the slum, black families moved south to Cottage Grove and, by 1920, south of 55th Street into Woodlawn. By 1930 Bronzeville (as the black belt was dubbed by the *Bee*, a black newspaper) was a narrow rectangle from 16th Street to 67th Street, and Chicago's black population had grown to 233,903 or nearly 7% of the total. Table 8 shows this remarkable growth:

Table 8	Negro Population of Chicago	% of Total	% Increase	% Increase due to migration
1900	30,150	1.8	-	-
1910	44,103	2.0	46	-
1920	109,458	4.1	148	140
1930	233,903	6.9	114	95
1940	277,731	8.2	19	16
1950	492,265	13.6	77	55
1960	812,637	23.6	65	(c.13)

Whilst World War I created job opportunities for blacks in the steel-mills, stockyards and food-processing plants of Chicago, industry was expanding enormously and many of the Northern cities could offer employment prospects to rival Chicago. But Chicago enjoyed certain special advantages over, for example, Detroit or Cleveland. As the terminus of the Illinois Central Railroad it was the most easily accessible city for blacks from Tennessee, Mississippi, Louisiana and Arkansas. Moreover Chicago intruded into every southern black man's daily life as the home of the great crusading black newspaper, the *Defender*. And not only was the *Defender*, widely read in the South, a Chicago newspaper, but under the editorship of Robert S. Abbott it was actually exhorting Southern blacks to leave the farms and make Chicago their home. For completely different reasons blacks were actively welcomed and courted by Big Bill Thompson, Chicago's Republican mayor, who saw the black vote as fodder for his political machine and a bulwark against the Irish working-class domination of the Democrats. Another reason why Chicago was on everybody's lips was that it was the address of the great mail-order firms of Sears Roebuck and Montgomery Ward, which supplied the special needs of all isolated rural communities in the United States. So it was natural that Chicago should become one of the first choices for blacks thinking of moving north.

All these factors stimulated migration to Chicago initially for by 1900 Chicago had a greater proportion (78.7%) of out-of-state migrants than any other Northern city, the largest numbers coming from the border states of Kentucky (14.8%), Tennessee (10.8%) and Missouri (7.4%). Mississippi was in seventh place with 3.8%. The influence of the Illinois Central Railroad was to be the most dominant factor, however, for by 1920 Mississippi had moved into second place, behind Tennessee, and ten years later it was the leading state for migrants, providing 38,356 or 16.3% of Chicago's black population. Tennessee was in second place in 1930, closely followed by Georgia, Alabama, Louisiana and Arkansas. Chicago in

Over page: *cigarette and liquor prices, clothes styles and storefront displays are all captured in Cartier-Bresson's 1948 views of two Chicago stores.*

fact had more Mississippi-born residents than any other town outside of Mississippi in 1930. The figures for selected cities are interesting:

Table 9	Residence of Mississippi-Born Migrants (1930)		
	No. Born in Mississippi	Total Negro Population	%
Chicago	38,356	233,903	16.3
Memphis	35,301	96,524	36.5
St. Louis	19,627	92,485	20.9
New Orleans	7,382	128,966	5.7
Detroit	6,904	118,621	5.8
East St. Louis	3,863	11,530	33.5
Gary	3,379	17,881	18.9
East Chicago	1,147	5,080	22.6
Los Angeles	1,707	38,369	4.4
New York	969	272,952	0.03

(Negroes in the United States 1920-1932)

From 1935-1940, when migration was again on the increase, there were 14,739 non-white newcomers to Chicago (although from other evidence this figure seems far too low) and the totals were listed by their state of residence in 1930. Again the state providing most of the migrants was Mississippi with 3,105 or 21.0% and the leading seven states provided nearly 70% of the total:

Table 10	Non-White Migrants to Chicago (1935-40)
Residence in 1930	
Mississippi	3,105
Arkansas	1,695
Tennessee	1,624
Alabama	1,110
Missouri	1,043
Louisiana	796
Georgia	752
other	4,614

As the breakdown is by residence at the last census date it's probable that the Mississippi-*born* total is even higher, considering the heavy migration from Mississippi to Arkansas and Tennessee (Table 7) and Missouri (i.e. St Louis—Table 9). Against this must be offset the heavy migration to Mississippi from Alabama which would exaggerate the Mississippi figure somewhat and correspondingly depress the Alabama-born total. But the trends are obvious enough for the '40s; migration was still heaviest and increasing from Mississippi with a spectacular increase from Arkansas. The totals were also broken down by Male, Female, Urban, Rural sub-divisions in this fascinating survey from the 1940 Census to show that more women migrated than men (probably just a feature of the imbalance of female and male in the total black population), and that of the 14,739 migrants 2,035 came from a Rural Farm background and 1,886 from Rural Non-Farm areas. The corresponding figures for Mississippi are 911 from Rural Farm and 701 from Rural Non-Farm. Thus of the 2,035 migrants to Chicago

Chicago slums, 1948.

from purely farm backgrounds nearly one-half came from Mississippi alone.

The '40s saw a huge jump in the number of Mississippi blacks settling in Chicago. Unfortunately the 1950 US Census does not provide a state-by-state breakdown of the background of Chicago blacks, but the composition would not be markedly different from that of Illinois, for by this time the Chicago non-white population accounted for 77% of the Illinois non-whites. Of the Illinois migrant population of 448,380 the leading state was Mississippi with 136,960. The second, Tennessee, provided only 47,605, and Arkansas moved into third place with 44,150. The only states to show a significant increase on the 1930 proportions were Mississippi with a 169.3% increase and Arkansas with 168.1%. From the best estimate, the net intercensal migration to Chicago for the years 1940-1950 was 154,000, and something like one-half of these migrants were born in Mississippi.

'They Had It Pretty Rugged Getting In'

Migrants of course are not abstract statistical units but flesh and blood and Spear vividly describes their arrival in Chicago.

Men in worn, outmoded suits carrying battered luggage, and women clutching ragged, barefooted children crowded into the Illinois Central Station on Twelfth Street looking hopefully for a familiar face. Park Row–the little drive running from Michigan Avenue to the station–was solidly packed with people. There the migrants mingled with local Negroes who came down every Sunday to meet a friend or a relative or just to see who had arrived. If there was no one to meet them, the newcomers seldom knew where to go. They might ask a Red Cap to direct them to the home of a friend–unaware that without an address the porter could be of little help in a city as large as Chicago. Or they might employ one of the professional guides who, for a fee, would help them find lodging. Some of the guides were honest, others were little more than confidence men. Travellers Aid and the railroad police tried to help the migrants and prevent exploitation; but for the newcomer without friends or relatives the first few days were often a terrifying experience.

Probably most of the migrants had relations in Chicago by the '40s–certainly this was true of those from Mississippi as the singers confirm. 'I have had a lot of relatives here in Chicago and I just wanted to be around them' (J. B. Lenoir). Or Jimmy Rogers: 'I had an uncle, a great uncle who lived here in Chicago . . .' Sometimes the reasons are startling: 'My daddy was a police[man]-and they beat him up–he sent me a ticket to come up here. That's how, how I got up here' (Eddie Taylor). Sometimes they just left; Muddy Waters explains: 'My mind led me to Chicago'; but they didn't all travel by the I.C. train. Johnny Shines tells how they all chaffed Little Walter:

> [Baby Face Leroy] and Johnnie Jones walked up from Mississippi . . . Little Walter wouldn't let it touch him y'know but Leroy and Johnnie Jones, all three of them walked from St Louis to Chicago. Little Walter wouldn't let it touch him, 'No man I don't walk that far!'

Shines laughs easily at the memory. 'They said they walked from St Louis to Chicago and Walter's feet were swolled up like two loaves of bread!' It was a typical exaggeration of Baby Face's which Homesick gently corrects:

> They had it pretty rugged getting in . . . I don't think they really walked! Because Johnnie did tell me one time–said that him and Baby Face Leroy y'know had rode the train so far y'know they didn't have any money. Had to get off at St Louis or somewhere in the southern part of Illinois. He say that they stop, had to work the cornfields or something, y'know pulling corn . . . loading trucks, something like that.

Life was going to be pretty rugged in Chicago, too, but, with good prospects of day-time employment and the wide-open club scene beckoning, they flocked to Chicago with hopes and heads held high.

3 / Sweet Home Chicago

Chicago was always a 'wide-open town' with an unsavoury reputation born of its brash beginnings as an Indian trading post in the 1830s, but by the 1920s, through political administrations such as that of the cowboy mayor Big Bill Thompson, who embraced the 'open town' philosophy as an ideal to be striven for, Chicago had established a notoriety which it hasn't since been able to shake off. The Volstead Act of 17 January 1920 banning the manufacture, sale or consumption of liquor heralded an era of unprecedented opportunity for the gangs to profit from an unpopular law. Illicit drinking dens sprang up everywhere in the United States but nowhere more so than Chicago where, in imaginative collusion with the civic authorities and business, the gangs set about supplying public demand.

Prohibition had as dramatic effect on the blues as it did on jazz, but while the jazzmen played for what was essentially a young and well-off white audience in the more palatial cafés and dance halls, the bluesmen played at semi-private house-parties in the black districts, though Johnny Temple remembered playing with Charlie McCoy for John, one of the Capone brothers. An institution which received a great boost from Prohibition was the rent party, where admission charged covered the cost of food and moonshine whiskey, the profits being used ostensibly to pay the rent. Pianists especially were in great demand and the '20s mark the rise of the piano blues and boogie-woogie.

The fourteen years of Prohibition spanned the halcyon days of the prosperous '20s right through to the depressed '30s, but what was left after repeal was a network of crime organised on the lines of big (and very big) business. The musical result was the establishment of a lusty and vigorous club scene that asserted Chicago's claim to be the home of the blues.

Most of the clubs were on the South Side, with a few scattered along the thin black finger of the West Side settlement of Lake and Madison Streets. The main arteries of the South Side were State Street, which is the East-West co-ordinate of Chicago's geometric house-numbering system, and Michigan and Indiana Avenues. The North-South divider is Madison Street with all the numbered streets south of Madison. Lonnie Johnson's first club date in Chicago, in 1930, was at the Three Deuces on N. State Street on the near North Side. That Lonnie worked easily in either a blues or a jazz environment is shown by the fact he had Baby Dodds on drums. But the early '30s saw Lonnie working on the South Side at joints on 51st Street, the Boulevard Lounge and for about five years at Square's, 931 W 51st. Homesick James moved to Chicago permanently in 1934 and lived with Sonny Boy, who had just preceded him, for about six weeks, until he

Jimmy Walker and Homesick James at the Square Deal Club, mid-'30s.

got a job in a steel mill. Soon afterwards Homesick was working with Horace Henderson's mixed group at Circle Inn, 63rd and Wentworth, and at the inappropriately named Square Deal Club, 230 W. Division Street, with the pianist Jimmy Walker. They played for five or six hours, mostly Blind Boy Fuller and Memphis Minnie numbers, for three dollars each. This was always the pattern, for, with the long-established artists like Big Bill, Tampa Red and Memphis Minnie playing regularly at the bigger clubs, it was very hard for newcomers to break into the scene, although most of the well-known singers were always willing to lend a hand to the young hopefuls from the South. Big Bill especially was remembered for his kindness to up-and-coming artists; Homesick says, 'That guy was just like a brother.' Bill also helped J. B. Lenoir and J. B. never forgot: 'Big Bill he take me as his son . . .' and Muddy too: 'Big Bill had been around a long time in Chicago when I came up in '43 so he helped me to get my start.' They would get their start by sitting in with the good-natured Big Bill, Lonnie Johnson or Sonny Boy and some other bar-owner would hear or hear of them and book them into his club. Many of the clubs were so small that they were just bars with a counter along one wall, some table seats along the other wall, and very little room for dancing and even less for the band. Most of their names are forgotten; sometimes just a name, like the Beehive or Subway, is remembered or just an address, like the 35th and State Club, where Tampa Red played. All the clubs from this era have vanished, some claimed by urban renewal, others renamed or converted for

other purposes, and we can only guess at the fate of such as the Club Claremont at 39th and Indiana, where Kokomo Arnold worked, or the Club Georgia at 45th and State, and George Wood's Tempo Tap at 31st and Indiana, where Sonny Boy Williamson could be heard. One of the most famous clubs was Ruby Lee Gatewood's Tavern at the intersection of W. Lake and N. Artesian Avenue, affectionately known as 'The Gate', where nearly all the name artists played. Big Bill had worked there regularly from the mid-'30s and Memphis Minnie was famous for her 'Blue Monday' parties there. In 1941 Big Bill was at the Gatewood Tavern and at the 1410 Club, 1410 Roosevelt Road, with Memphis Slim as his regular pianist; Memphis Minnie was at the White Elephant, 528 E. 43rd Street; and the very popular Sonny Boy Williamson was at the Triangle Inn, named after its location at the three-way intersection of Racine, 14th and Blue Island. Some of the plusher night-spots were well known outside Chicago's black community; the Rhumboogie, El Grotto and Club Trianon, on Cottage Grove, were famous, as was Mike DeLisa's Club at 47th and Dearborn, which featured Memphis Minnie for a long time during the '30s. But it was in the joints, the low-class bars that the blues were really rocking. The 708 Club was a favourite with the bluesmen because, with the bandstand *behind* the bar, the musicians were protected from an audience that gave the South Side its reputation for 'Saturday night tavern brawls, Sunday morning visits to the Provident Hospital emergency room and Monday morning appearances in the Fifth District Police Court at 48th and Wabash, "the busiest police station in the world".'

Johnny Shines, a Memphis singer who had moved to Chicago in 1941, remembers the wild club scene he found there, and Memphis Minnie in particular:

> Any men that fool with her she'd go for them right away. She didn't take no foolishness off them. Guitar, pocket-knife, pistol, anything she get her hand on she'd use it; y'know Memphis Minnie used to be a hell-cat. Y'know her and Son Joe, Roosevelt Sykes used to work together . . . boy! They'd have some of the terriblest rows but Memphis Minnie be the winner every time—she'd have it her way or else! When I knew her in Chicago she was drinking a lot of gin. I went out where they were playing at one night . . . it was called White Elephant . . . and they bought me so much gin—oh boy- gin was just everywhere. Gin was dropping out of my ears that night. I went home, the gin got hot, I run a bath of cold water . . . I didn't get *in* it—I *aimed* to get in it and missed the tub and fell on the floor and that's where they found me at next morning—laying on the floor and had to be at work 7 o'clock the next morning . . . at the Santa Fe Car Shop.

Left: *The High Life Inn was standing in 1948, but no memories of it have yet been collected from musicians.* Below: *Sonny Boy and Lacey Belle Williamson, with the young Muddy Waters* (left) *and Eddie Boyd* (centre, standing).

Johnny had been working with Eddie Boyd, a Clarksdale, Mississippi, pianist who had only just arrived in Chicago, at Big Jerry Johnson's, Lake and Leavitt, on the West Side. Most of the artists sought work in pairs, as Shines explains:

> This place [the White Elephant] closed down and reopened in the name of Don's Den—a fellow by the name of Don Simmonds, he opened the place and Memphis Slim called up to come out there . . . so if Eddie Boyd and I come out there we'd probably get the job . . . so the guy was picking who he wanted . . . y'know he wanted a piano player and a guitar player . . . so Minnie and Joe was there and a lot of piano players . . . guitar players I can't remember. Anyway it ended up Eddie didn't get the job playing piano—Curtis got the job playing piano and I got the job playing guitar with Curtis Jones. That's how Eddie and I got split up 'cause the guy was picking who *he* wanted, he wasn't picking pairs . . . This was in '42 . . . and Curtis and I worked out there a long time for Don Simmonds, long time. Curtis y'know get them good feelings, get to playing *Marie* and *Danny Boy, Trees* and *Stardust*. [Laughing] I couldn't play none of it! But he had a ball trying—oh boy, but he had a good time trying.

Eddie Boyd then went to play with Sonny Boy Williamson at the Triangle Inn with a group that included Lee Cooper on guitar, Alfred Elkins on bass and Alfred 'Fat Man' Wallace on drums. Eddie played with Sonny Boy through the '40s at the Triangle, Club Georgia and the Flame Club, until the latter's death in 1948. He relates one almost prophetic incident about Sonny Boy in the Flame Club:

Two popular and well-loved figures of the '40s, Big Maceo and Memphis Minnie.

He was drunk and be staggering and he stepped on a guy's foot, guy about my size. So he wouldn't say pardon or sorry or nothin'. Cause number one thing, he would feel embarrassed when he do these things. So this guy had a long knife, he tried to hit him right between the shoulders. I took a chance and knocked this guy's hand up. And I said, 'Now don't get mad at me, but he don't mean you no harm; he's harmless, he's just drunk! I told him [Sonny Boy] about it the next day when he got sober and he had tears knowing that he come that close to be killed.

Sonny Boy perhaps was too gentle, for the Flame Club's usual incumbents, Tampa Red and Big Maceo, had temperaments more in keeping with the clientele. As John Sellers says:

Don't say nothin' to them! They would raise a big mess! They would want to square it up all over the place. Ready to fight—especially Tampa Red—he used to be a mess in *his* day!

This description seems to fit Tampa, a softly-spoken, proud little man, but maybe Maceo's arguments were musical ones, for like other blues pianists he had a good grasp of music theory, as Big Bill recalled:

We used to argue and fall out with each other, but no licks were ever passed. He knew more about real music than I did but I knew more about the real blues and the arguments was because he would tell me to make the right chord.

Bill's reply was characteristic: 'The blues didn't come out of no book and them real chords did.'

Big Maceo was born Maceo (or Major) Merriweather on 30 or 31 March 1905 and he sang of Texas as his home, though his wife thought he was born in Atlanta, Georgia. His family had moved to Detroit by the '40s—an uncle, Robert Merriweather, also a pianist, still lives there—and Maceo probably came to Chicago about 1944, where he lived with his wife Lucille and daughter at 4706 S. Parkway, making frequent trips back to Detroit.

Unlike other pianists, he did not let his musical knowledge impair his blues feeling; he played nothing but the blues. He would have been referred to slightingly by Blind John Davis as one of the 'double-time guys' for his thunderous piano style, which sounded as though the whole 245 lbs of his frame was transmitted directly through his finger-tips, so powerful was the sound of hammered treble figures over a rock-steady eight-to-the-bar bass. The directness and energy of his piano playing, with little light or shade, contrasted perfectly with his singing, his smoky-brown voice investing the songs with a depth unequalled by most of his contemporaries. His songs were mostly his own, frequently 16-bars, with always interesting lyrics. *Texas Blues, County Jail Blues* and the beautiful *Poor Kelly Blues* were fine songs but he is best remembered for the superb and much recorded *Worried Life Blues*, his first record. It borrowed the verse from Sleepy John Estes' *Someday, Baby* but the rest of it was

FEE RECEIPT NO.

720735

STATE OF ILLINOIS — DEPARTMENT OF PUBLIC HEALTH

CERTIFIED COPY OF A DEATH RECORD

ORIGINAL	MEDICAL CERTIFICATE OF DEATH	STATE FILE NO. 11142

DECEDENT'S BIRTH NO.:

STATE OF ILLINOIS 38.588 DIST. NO. 3104 REG. NO.

1. PLACE OF DEATH a. COUNTY Cook , ILLINOIS	2. USUAL RESIDENCE (Where deceased lived. If institution: residence before admission). a. STATE Illinois b. COUNTY Cook
b. CITY (If outside corporate limits, write RURAL and give township or road dist.) OR TOWN CHICAGO c. LENGTH OF STAY (In this place) 9 YRS.	c. CITY (If outside corporate limits, write RURAL, and give township or road dist.) OR TOWN Chicago
d. FULL NAME OF HOSPITAL OR INSTITUTION (If not in hospital or institution, give street address or location) 4706 South Parkway	d. STREET ADDRESS (If rural, give location) 4706 South Parkway

3. NAME OF DECEASED (Type or Print) a. (First) Maceo b. (Middle) c. (Last) Merriweather	4. DATE OF DEATH (Month) Feb. (Day) 26 (Year) 1953

5. SEX Male	6. COLOR OR RACE Negro	7. MARRIED, Married (Specify)	8. DATE OF BIRTH 3-31-1905	8a. AGE (In years last birthday) 47	If Under 1 Year Months Days	If Under 24 Hrs. Hours Min.

10a. USUAL OCCUPATION (Give kind of work done most of working life, even if retired) UNKNOWN	10b. KIND OF BUSINESS OR INDUSTRY UNKNOWN	11. BIRTHPLACE (State or foreign country) Georgia ATLANTA	12. CITIZEN OF WHAT COUNTRY USA

13. FATHER'S NAME Kit Merriweather	14. MOTHER'S MAIDEN NAME Unknown

15. WAS DECEASED EVER IN U. S. ARMED FORCES? (Yes, no, or unknown) (If yes, give war or dates of service) No	16. SOCIAL SECURITY NO. Unknown	17. INFORMANT (Hospitals follow Special Instructions on this item) a. Signature Lucille Merriweather
		b. Address 4706 SOUTH PARKWAY c. Relationship to the deceased WIFE

18. CAUSE OF DEATH
I. DISEASE OR CONDITION DIRECTLY LEADING TO DEATH*
*This does not mean the mode of dying, such as heart failure, asthenia, etc. It means the disease, injury or complication which caused death. ENTER ONLY ONE CAUSE PER LINE for (a), (b), and (c)

INTERVAL BETWEEN ONSET AND DEATH

Direct cause (a) Myocarditis with Thrombosis of Heart
Morbid conditions, if any, giving rise to the above cause (a), stating the underlying cause last. due to (b)
due to (c)

II. OTHER SIGNIFICANT CONDITIONS
Conditions contributing to the death, but not related to the disease or condition causing death

19a. DATE OF OPERATION	19b. MAJOR FINDINGS OF OPERATION	20. AUTOPSY? YES ☐ NO ☒

21a. ACCIDENT SUICIDE HOMICIDE (specify)	21b. PLACE OF INJURY (e.g. in or about home, farm, factory, street, office bldg., etc.)	21c. (CITY, TOWN, OR TOWNSHIP)	(COUNTY)	(STATE)
21d. TIME (Month) (Day) (Year) (Hour) OF m. INJURY	21e. INJURY OCCURRED While at ☐ Not While at ☐ work at Work	21f. HOW DID INJURY OCCUR?		

22. I hereby certify that I attended the deceased from 12-5 , 1952 to 2-20 , 1953, that I last saw the deceased alive on 2-20-53 , 19 , and that death occurred at 7:58 a.m. m. from the causes and on the date stated above.

23a. SIGNATURE Thos W. Dixon	23b. ADDRESS AND PHONE NO. 417 E 47th	23c. DATE SIGNED 2-27-53

BURIAL—REMOVAL (date) FEB. 28 , 1953

RECEIVED FOR FILING ON: 2-27-53

DISPOSITION	Cemetery LOCAL	Signed:	SUB REGISTRAR
	Location DETROIT MICHIGAN	LOCAL REGISTRAR:	DEPUTY REGISTRAR
FUNERAL DIRECTOR	Firm Name METROPOLITAN FUNERAL PARLORS Address 4445 South Parkway	Address Norman T. Broadway , ILLINOIS Reserved for State Office
	Signature Theo B. Caine License Number F-128	

VS&R 200 DEPARTMENT OF PUBLIC HEALTH—Bureau of Statistics

I HEREBY CERTIFY THAT the foregoing is a true and correct copy of the record of death as made from the original certificate of death for the decedent named therein and that this certificate was established and filed with the Department of Public Health in accordance with the statutes of Illinois.

MAY 30, 1972

SPRINGFIELD

Franklin Yoder

Franklin D. Yoder, M.D.
Director of Public Health
State Registrar

Maceo's:

> Oh Lawdy Lawd, oh Lawdy Lawd
> It hurts me so bad for us to part
> But someday baby I ain't going to worry my life anymore
>
> So many nights since you been gone
> I been worried and grieving my life alone
> But someday baby I ain't going to worry my life anymore.

Sometimes he used traditional themes, like *Big Road Blues* or his version of *44 Blues* (an almost mandatory piece for a pianist), which was titled *Maceo's 32-20*. Even Maceo's music, heavy and unrelenting from his first session in June 1941, increased in power in the early postwar years, when he recorded the romping and very exciting *Kid Man Blues*, instrumentals with vocal comments like *Texas Stomp* and *Detroit Jump*, fine blues like *Winter Time Blues*, and the ultimate in his piano art, the classic *Chicago Breakdown*, a boogie-woogie solo of enormous power and drive. Sadly this 1945 recording was the last that Maceo made at the height of his powers; he was paralysed from a stroke in mid-1946, and, though he recovered, never again did he play with the same authority.

Big Maceo's place in the development of the Chicago piano blues is vitally important; taking over from the late Josh Altheimer, his influence can be traced through his successors, Little Johnnie Jones, Henry Gray and Otis Spann.

Jew Town

Working in the clubs sounds a rugged way of making a living, but there was the still harder, but to singers from the South very familiar, life of the street-singer. The clubs were for the established artists or those who were beginning to make a name for themselves; the new singers flocking to Chicago, if they didn't have the helping hand of a Big Bill or a Sonny Boy to introduce them, had to make it on their own by playing at house-parties or on the streets, and the largest audience a street musician could reach was to be found at the Maxwell Street market area. This open-air market, so designated by a city ordinance of 1912, extended over a few blocks on the near West Side off S. Halsted Street, the focal point being Maxwell, Peoria, Sangamon and Newberry Streets. This was the old immigrant area of Chicago, and the singers always called it 'Jew Town'. It has been scheduled for urban renewal and much of it has already been torn down, but there still remains much of the excitement and life it has seen. The wares range from the usual cheap or old clothing through second-hand furniture, TV sets, ancient radios, Italian ice-cream, used car-tyres, and Southern home-cooking to the more exotic snake-oil medicines and love-charms. This was the meeting place for all the newly arrived singers and the centre of the amateur blues activity of Chicago. The singers picked their way through the crowded streets to set up in front of the houses off the main thoroughfare. Here it was that Little Walter first blew harmonica in Chicago, that Floyd Jones sang and played guitar with Snooky Pryor and Moody Jones, that Johnny Young played mandolin with his guitarist cousin Johnny Williams. The young Chicagoan Jimmie Lee Robinson remembers:

> I played with all of them on Maxwell Street; Daddy Stovepipe, Little Willie Foster, I worked with him in Vi's Lounge; John Henry, Porkchops (Eddie Hines), Baby Face Leroy, Johnny Shines, Lazy Bill Lucas . . .

Jimmie Lee first started playing with Blind Percy.

> I started playing on the streets with this blind man, in churches and things like that. Then I worked for a bit with a mandolin player, can't remember his name. Then there was a man named Louis, they called him Heart—he still lives in Jew Town, he don't have any legs now. Every time he used to see me he told me, 'Boy, I'm gonna buy a guitar and an amplifier for you to play on.' I didn't know whether to believe or disbelieve him. So finally one day he came over and said, 'I've bought this guitar for you.' And he'd bought me a Silvertone guitar and a Gibson amplifier. Then I'd play on Maxwell Street every Sunday and he'd collect the money. He could play one or two songs on the harp, and I'd play behind him, and make it sound real good. We'd go from club to club and we'd get 25 or 30 dollars a night in each club. We did that up until about 1949.

'I heard the voice of a porkchop' . . . left, *Maxwell Street Jimmy;* centre, *Johnny Embry;* right, *Eddie 'Porkchop' Hines.*

Scabbin'

Jimmy Rogers describes this last activity:

> The first musician that I met here was a fella they call him
> Stovepipe. During the time I was living on Lake Street—1752 West
> Lake Street—and Stovepipe he knew the city just like a book, you
> know—all on the South Side, West Side, North Side—all over so I
> would follow him around—we'd call it scabbin'—you know. You hit
> here, you set up with asking this guy that owns the club if he
> wouldn't mind you playing a few numbers—quite naturally it was
> good for his business, he would say okay. You'd play a number or
> two, they'd like it—you'd pick up a buck here, a buck there, you
> know. One club was 708 E. 47th Street—we'd play there during the
> time I was scabbin'. That's called the 708 Club and on the North
> Side I can't recall the clubs over there now—and I played at a place
> on Roosevelt Road called Tom's Tavern.

But it wasn't all blues on Maxwell Street—Daddy Stovepipe, whose real
name was Johnny Watson, preferred to play *The Tennessee Waltz* or *South
Of The Border* and Little Walter first played waltzes and polkas before
coming under the influence of Big Bill and Tampa Red.

Jimmy Rogers must have been one of the few bluesmen who didn't play
on the street:

> I didn't ever play on the street—I would see those guys there—I'd
> say, these guys is wailin' good, I'd stand around, you know—I would
> stand around and look at them—and some of them asked me to but
> I never did sit in.

Others who did sit in were to be the first on the recording scene, for the
lifting of the Petrillo ban ushered in a new era of recording activity and the
breaking of the monopoly enjoyed by the major companies and Bluebird
in particular. In the same way that the hiatus of the Depression years
stimulated a demand for a new sound, the halt in recording from 1942-4
coincided with a desire for a different type of blues again. When recording
recommenced Bluebird was quick into its stride with sessions by the old
favourites Tampa Red, Washboard Sam and Sonny Boy Williamson, while
Columbia continued with Big Bill and Memphis Minnie, but this time there
was competition from the new independents, Savoy of New York, Modern
of Los Angeles and King of Cincinnati, soon to be followed by thousands
more. The lifting of the ban, the ending of shellac rationing and the
comparative prosperity of the early postwar years all conspired to bring
about the birth of numerous small record companies striving to break the
dominance of the majors and cash in on the boom. Under-capitalised,
ineptly and naively managed as many of the new labels undoubtedly were,
they enjoyed one great advantage over Bluebird and Columbia, although it
is doubtful if they realised it at the time. The new companies were forced
to look for new talent, since all the big-name artists were under contract to
the majors and, by happy chance, new artists with new styles reflecting

One-Leg Sam Norwood, from Crystal Springs, Miss.

new attitudes were just what the black public wanted. For in many ways it was a new audience, the enormously heavy migration of the '40s having shifted the balance of the black population of the Northern cities to a predominantly Southern one with a short history of city life. And the new artists whom the small companies sought were also newly arrived from the South and shared the same background. Many of these singers were to be found on Maxwell Street. Johnny Williams, Floyd Jones and his cousin, Moody Jones, remember some of them. As well as One-Leg Sam (Norwood), who lived at Elizabeth and Madison ('As good a chordin' man on the guitar as ever lived. He couldn't pick no guitar but he could chord it!') there was Daddy Stovepipe ('he followed shows') and his partners, cornet-playing Tom Stewart and percussionist Porkchop. Then there were guitarists Robert 'Earl' Foster (Little Willie Foster's cousin), Blind Johnnie and Greyhaired Bill (Johnson), a relation of Robert Johnson. 'He say he gonna play till he died and that's what he did. He wouldn't quit.' There was even a Fiddlin' Joe (Williams) who was already an old man back in the '40s, and of course Blind Percy (Robinson). 'He used to go with my sister,' says Moody and Floyd adds, 'I roomed with his mother, man!' As Johnny Williams puts it:

> There be musicians lined all up and down the street. So this was where the music world began, right there on Maxwell Street, among us. Which was mostly where they turned pro, right from there on Maxwell Street every Sunday.

With such a wealth of talent one company at least didn't have to look any further than its own doorstep. But in fact it was the singers themselves that provided the incentive and persuaded Bernard Isaac Abrahams of Maxwell Radio Record Co. to record them. Only two records were issued on his quaintly named Ora-Nelle label and they could not have been very

Little Walter's debut; and Johnny Young, featured on Ora Nelle's other issue.

profitable. Musically and historically, though, they are fascinating, being probably the first Chicago recordings of the new postwar country blues artists and introducing four new singers, one of whom, Little Walter, was to achieve worldwide success. On one side of Ora-Nelle 711 Little Walter (or Little Walter J, as the label has it) sang a rather ordinary up-tempo number, *I Just Keep Loving Her*, backed by Othum Brown (a guitarist from Richland, Mississippi), and blew harmonica in a manner which made plain his debt to Sonny Boy Williamson. On the reverse Othum sang, accompanied by Walter's harp, the beautiful *Ora-Nelle Blues*. From the lyrics it appears that Othum's woman Ora-Nelle provided the new record company with a name!

> You know you told me baby once upon a time
> You said if I'd be yours baby you'd be mine
> But that's all right
> Hey, hey that's all right
> You know then I begin to wonder who's loving my baby tonight
>
> Cried last night baby you know I cried all night before
> Cry this time baby you know aint gonna cry no more
> But that's all right
> Hey, hey that's all right
> You know then I begin to wonder who's loving Ora Nelle tonight.

The theme is more familiar as *That's All Right*, the song that launched Jimmy Rogers's recording career just three years later. Othum is said to have died soon after but no trace of his death appears in the Cook County or Illinois files. He may even be still living in Tennessee or New York. We'll never know if he got the song from Rogers, who claims it as his own, and says that he sang it first down in Mississippi. He vaguely remembers Othum but not Othum's record, which is curious, since Jimmy's first record too was made for Ora-Nelle, but sadly wasn't issued. With Little Walter again on harp it was a fine version of the old Sleepy John Estes Decca recording *Liquor Store Blues*. Strangely enough Ora-Nelle recorded another version by Sleepy John himself. Another superb unissued item was by a Texas singer, Boll Weevil, who was possibly Ernest Lewis; but their second and last record to be released was by the mandolin-guitar duo Johnny Young and Johnny Williams.

Mandolinist Johnny Young was born in Vicksburg, Mississippi, on 1 January 1917, but his musical interest was not stirred until the family moved to Rolling Fork in the Mississippi Delta. He was 12 years old when he started to play harmonica but under the tutelage of an uncle, Anthony Williams (who played guitar, mandolin, violin and banjo), he switched first to guitar and then finally to mandolin. He rapidly became proficient on the instrument, picking up a lot of his style from such local musicians as the Chatman brothers (the Mississippi Sheiks). While still in his teens he made the rounds of house-parties which he would play for five or six dollars a night. After a brief return to Vicksburg, where he played at the Blue Room with his cousin Henry Williams, each alternating on guitar and mandolin, Johnny moved to Chicago in 1940. By 1943 both he and Muddy Waters were playing with John Lee 'Sonny Boy' Williamson at the Plantation, 31st and Giles, and in Gary, Indiana, at The Spot. Johnny retired briefly from the music scene but 1947 found him working on Maxwell Street with another guitarist cousin, Johnny Williams, or in the company of harmonica-player Snooky Pryor and guitarists Floyd and Moody Jones.

The Ora-Nelle side *Money Taking Woman* is superb. Against an exciting mandolin accompaniment Young bellows the vocal:

Left: *Johnny Williams, who has given up blues to become a minister.* Right: *Floyd Jones, who plays on.*

Here I stand all out my hand
Me and my baby gonna raise some sand
She's a money taking woman, money taking woman
She's a money taking woman and she takes it all the time

She takes my money, calls me dad
She holds her hand out and never give it back
She's a money taking woman . . . [etc.]

Now here we stand, toe to toe
I'm gonna give you this money, ain't gonna give you no more
She's a money taking woman . . . [etc.]

On the other side Johnny Williams sings the equally primitive *Worried Man
Blues* in a deep, strong voice to his own rushed guitar and Young's
mandolin accompaniment.

Johnny Williams was born in Alexandria, Louisiana, 15 May 1906 but
was raised in Houston, Texas. Leaving there about 1917 when his mother
died he came to Belzoni to live with his uncle Anthony and it was there in
the Delta that he learned the guitar. The man who taught him his chords
was Robert Foster—Little Willie Foster's cousin—but he met all the singers
around at that time: the Chatman Brothers, Pet and Can, as well as
Charley Patton, with whom Anthony Williams used to play.

He moved to Chicago in 1926 and met Big Bill and Tampa for the first
time but the Depression years saw him back home in Belzoni. In 1933 he
met Elmore James, Rice Miller, the original 'Howling Wolf' and, in
Marianna, Arkansas, Robert Johnson, who was on the road travelling with
a jug player. Five years later Johnny moved back to Chicago and by 1943
he was playing in the clubs. Until then he had been playing 'sentimental
music' but meeting Floyd Jones and the other new men he realised that 'if
you didn't play some blues you's gonna starve to death.' This was when he
decided to put everything into his music, which had been only a minor
interest up to that time. In the evenings he played the blues while working
days in a packing-house. Then in 1945 he lost a finger in a meat grinder at
work and he gave up the guitar for a year until one Sunday on Maxwell
Street he saw Blind Gray.

A man with this thumb cut off and this finger. And he only played
with the three fingers. So I said now if this guy can play like that I
said I can too! So I went back and started all over again. So
eventually got to where by that finger being gone it didn't bother
me.

There were other entrepreneurs who had their eyes on the Maxwell
Street musicians and Ora-Nelle found itself rivalled by even shorter lived
recording ventures. Chester Scales, who had a record shop on the North
Side, recorded Snooky Pryor and Moody Jones in 1948, and the record
appeared on Planet. The Snooky and Moody record was probably the only

Studio portraits show Snooky Pryor and Moody Jones in their heyday. Stockyard Blues *was Floyd Jones's first record.*

blues issue on Planet but it was an important one. The tall, thin Snooky sang and played harmonica very much like Sonny Boy Williamson while 'Big' Moody Jones played boogie riffs on guitar in a highly rhythmic manner. In fact it is this lilting swing imparted by Moody's guitar that makes the record sound so very modern for the time. Equally rhythmic is Snooky's singing on *Telephone Blues* and the interplay of the voice, harmonica and guitar is particularly exciting. The reverse, *Snooky & Moody's Boogie*, is similar to John Lee Hooker's big hit *Boogie Chillun.*

James Edward 'Snooky' Pryor was born in Lambert, Mississippi, 15 September 1921, and started to play the harmonica and drums when he was 14 years old. He had to rehearse at his older brother's house, because his father was a minister, and Snooky says, 'My daddy'd hang me if he ever heard me playing the blues!' He grew up with Jimmy Rogers—they went to school together in Vance—and talking about how he got his nickname Pryor says, 'Floyd Jones he started to callin' me Snooky ... We was calling Jimmy Rogers Snooky when he was a kid. It's just a pet name.' He learned to play by surreptitiously listening to records, especially Sonny Boy Williamson's, and when at the age of 16 he moved to Arkansas he listened to Rice Miller, who was broadcasting over KFFA, and started hanging around the King Biscuit Boys. The family moved again to Missouri and then Snooky went to Chicago in 1940. Soon after, he went into the Army, and after service overseas in the Pacific he returned and was stationed at Fort Sheridan, north of Chicago. He used to come into Chicago on weekend passes and sit in with John Lee 'Sonny Boy' Williamson and Homesick James at the Purple Cat, on Madison. After his discharge from the army in 1945 Pryor moved permanently to Chicago, and started to play on Maxwell.

'The Big Bass'

Moody Jones was born in Earle, Arkansas, 8 April 1908. His mother was very religious and Moody was 'raised up in the Church'—the Holiness Church. This didn't stop him developing an interest in music, which started from the time his brother paid $3 for an old, broken guitar. After about a week and some instruction from a neighbour, Walter Harris, who taught him three chords, Moody was able to play it. At first he learned Blind Lemon's songs and then Lonnie Johnson's. When he was proficient enough he would play for country dances. For $2 and a pint of whiskey he would start playing at 8 o'clock on a Saturday night and, with the odd break in between, he would still be playing when people were getting ready to go to church the next morning. When his father died and his mother went to Chicago and remarried, Moody joined his brother in Wolf Island, Missouri. From there they moved to East St Louis and then in 1939 Moody went to Chicago.

He enrolled for a course of 12 lessons for $60 under guitar teacher

Harry Festell at a music store at 18th & Halsted, but so advanced had Moody become that after an argument over E-flat he left after only four lessons. He then quit work to practice: 'When I was playing music I'd give my whole self to it. Nothing but that, day and night I kept up on it.' His fingers had corns and callouses from the constant guitar-playing but he persevered until he could play just about everything; he played bass— 'the big bass', tenor banjo and piano. He met up with his first cousin Floyd Jones (their fathers were brothers) in the early '40s and they played together on Maxwell, Moody helping Floyd out with his guitar changes. On the street the tall, thin Moody was known mainly by his nicknames, 'Buddy' or even 'Texas Slim'. For a long time he played with Arvella Gray, whom they knew as Blind Dixon:

> Me and him used to get on the street at Maxwell and Halsted, walk up to 12th Street just playin' and walkin'. Turn around, come down the other side and we'd have 40 to 50 dollars a piece when we get back.

Moody's practice and perseverance had paid off, as Johnny Williams admits:

> Out of all the musicians of us Moody was the best. I give him credit for that. Oh no brother, that man can play you some guitar, you can believe me.

In fact he could play any type of music: hillbilly, Spanish, Irish, Mexican—whatever the customers requested. For a year he worked at 3241 W. Madison, playing hillbilly music and wearing cowboy attire on stage, with a group including a West Indian accordian player named George and James Kindle, a banjo-player from Pine Bluff, Arkansas. Moody's talents were such that he could make anything sound good and there was a hilarious episode with his home-made bass:

> I remember one time I wanted to make some money and everybody was doing everything I could do. I went and got me a wash-tub and got me a broom-handle and clothes line and made me a one-string bass and when that thing got to sounding good on the streets y'know everybody wanted to see *under* it. People gave me $3 or $4 to have a look under it and I let 'em look. Wasn't nothing under it!

Little wonder that Moody was acknowledged as the best. Even Little Walter wanted to learn guitar from him:

> I used to fool around with Little Walter. I probably taught him what he knew on the guitar. He played harmonica y'know but he used to follow me to try and play guitar. Me and him be playing together, we'd go out to make some money and he wouldn't want to play the harmonica what he could really do. He'd want to play what I was playing. So he finally learned.

```
        this is the old band boys..
 *left to right,Ed newman-left rear on bass*he's
   passed,on..(CANCER)
 **front row left John henry barbie;on guitar;he's passed,
   on... (CANCER)
 (*)center,yours truly"Moody Jones,on guitar;thank GOD
   still living....

  *James kindle on tenor banjo; he's passed on...diabetic..

     may GOD bless you,
```

Moody Jones's Maxwell Street band, and his own caption for it.

On the same day that Chester Scales recorded Johnny Young (as Man Young) with Snooky and Johnny Williams, he recorded Floyd Jones with Snooky and Moody, also at United Broadcasting's North Side studio. Both records were sold that same evening—Johnny Young's to Planet and Floyd's to Marvel. Floyd, a serious and thoughtful man, chose to sing his remarkable song about a strike at the Union Stockyards:

> Well I left home this morning, boy, y'know about half-past nine
> I passed the stockyards y'know, the boys were still on the
> > picket line
> Y'know I need to earn a dollar
> Y'know I need to earn a dollar
> The cost of living have gone so high, now then I don't know
> > what to do
>
> Well I went down to the butcher-man, y'know in his show-case
> > I gave a peep
> He said 'I gotta four cent raise man on all my meat'
> Y'know I need to earn a dollar . . . [etc.]

Floyd recalls the creation of the song:

> . . . it was early in the morning, the street-car fare was 11 cents and it went up and I forgot it. So I gave the man 11 cents and he said, 'Man, it's two cents more'. So I gave him the two cents. Then I just kept putting together, kept putting together. Then I went to the butcher. He said, 'I got a raise on my meat'—he didn't say four cent but he said 'raise'. I kept putting together. So after I start singing it on the street this fellow Big Bill Broonzy said, 'You better play with me or somebody s going to take it'. So I didn't sing it no more on the street.

Tall, with an easy-going melancholy, Floyd had been in Chicago just two years when he made *Stockyard Blues*. He was born on 21 July 1917 in Marianna, Arkansas, and his background was perfect for a bluesman. His mother Minnie played piano but died when Floyd was young; his father Robert worked in logging camps in the mid-'20s with Charley Patton. Floyd was raised with Wolf and learned to play guitar in 1933 travelling through Arkansas and Mississippi. Johnny Shines remembers him from Hughes, Arkansas:

> Floyd used to play in some of the roughest places in that area. He started playing for Richard White—I used to play for Richard White y'know. Floyd used to stand around and look, y'know he'd look, y'know he's trying to catch on to what I was doing . . . and Wolf he'd come down there and play . . . so Floyd started playing a little bit, he'd play a little more, little more and more, he got a little better and a little better . . . Floyd hung around Richard White's and Zebedee Walkers's . . . Floyd hung around all the places y'see he was trying to catch on . . . these was *frolics*! Ole Saturday night fish-fries . . . you had to be rough to survive. If you were anyways— y'know—like you were scared of something like that, somebody work you over, they work you over good.

Floyd's hard early days are reflected in his slow, sad, gold-toothed smile, which is as eloquent as his lyrics:

> Hard times, hard times here with me now
> Hard times, hard times here with me now
> If they don't get no better I believe I'll leave this town
>
> Now the company and the union men begin to meet
> Slow production—we'll give you four days a week
> Y'know it's hard times . . . [etc.]
>
> Well the men again begin to talk, for they want to raise on
>   the hours
> This is a bad time, we laying 'em off by the thousands

Hard Times was Floyd's next record but it was issued as by Sunnyland Slim and his Sunnyland Boys on the Tempo-Tone label. Floyd sang on both sides and the reverse, *School Days*, again highlighted his gifts as a sensitive songwriter:

> When I was a little boy, my mother tried to send me to school
> I didn't want to go 'cause I ain't nobody's fool
> But I got school days, school days on my mind
> Say we're too late now baby, ain't no need to be
>   standing here crying.
>
> Say I remember one evening y'know about half-past three
> I see the school kids, that's what been worrying me
> I got school days, school days on my mind
> Say I ain't got nothing for me to do now, but I'm just
>   standing here crying
>
> Well I went down to the judge, man, tried to explain
> He gave me a pencil, I couldn't even sign my name
> I got school days . . . [etc.]

There was one other issue on Tempo-Tone by the same group and this time Little Walter augmented the Sunnyland Boys and sang two mediocre numbers, one with a group vocal. Tempo-Tone was started by a tavern owner, one 'Big Earl', at 301 Sacramento, with Sunnyland Slim setting up the sessions, but in common with Ora-Nelle, Marvel and Planet it caused hardly a ripple on the surface of Chicago's record scene. Soon afterwards the Marvel and Planet sides were reissued on Old Swingmaster, a label started on 29 January 1949 by Al Benson and Egmont Sonderling of United Broadcasting. It lasted until about May 1950.

They were certainly not the first independent labels in Chicago that distinction properly belongs to Rhumboogie, which commenced operation about May 1945. It was started by Charley Glenn, probably to promote the artists he was featuring at his slick South Side club, the Rhumboogie, but again the venture was short-lived. Only three issues are known, all of them by T-Bone Walker backed by the Marl Young Orchestra, but the first *Sail on Boogie* (Rhumboogie 4000) was reputedly successful enough to sell over 50,000 copies. The Melody Lane Record Shop of 323-B E. 55th Street was next with its own label in late 1945 or early 1946 but after only two releases, both by Jo Jo Adams with the Freddie Williams Orchestra, they introduced their Hy-Tone subsidiary. The first Hy-Tone release was by the former Bluebird artist and Big Bill's ex-pianist, Memphis Slim, but with two accompanying saxes the record was very firmly cast in the city blues mould, as was most of the fare provided by Hy-Tone and indeed the rest of these early labels. There were four records by the ubiquitous Sunnyland Slim, including his minor hit *Devil Is A Busy Man,* and even one by 'Peetie Wheatstraw's Buddy', but most were in the old Bluebird style and met with the same indifference that the major companies were suffering. Sunbeam, owned by Marl Young, and Sultan were other small companies operating in 1946. The former boasted Little Miss Cornshucks on three of their seven known issues, while Sultan's three releases comprised various groupings of the Red Saunders Orchestra, including two sides by the fine city blues pianist Sonny Thompson.

These early ventures had more in common than their lack of success. The companies, all specialising in the black market, were all concerned with recording the then current city or jump blues—a style characterised by large orchestras, heavily jazz-influenced. The singers' repertoires consisted of blues-tinged ballads or highly sophisticated blues and their styles approximated closely to the popular crooners of the day. It was a completely homogeneous music which had developed in several places at once and there was no feature distinguishing the city singers or bands of Chicago, say, from those of New York, Los Angeles, Kansas City or Houston. Very much the music of the nightclubs and large dance-halls, it

Left: *Floyd Jones's* School Days *appeared on record twice, in 1948 (Tempo-Tone) and 1955 (VJ).*

appealed more to the black middle-class and accounted for most of the records made for black consumption.

Of course, there were success stories, and the not inappropriately named Miracle label was one of them. Started in 1947 by Lee Egalnick, its first big hit was Gladys Palmer's *Fool That I Am* (Miracle 104). The main artists were Miss Palmer, Memphis Slim, Sonny Thompson and the tenor-saxophonist Eddie Chamblee. Sunrise, a label owned by Leonard Evans, joined Miracle in 1947, bringing its main artist Al Hibbler. The company prospered until May 1950 when Egalnick left to form his Premium label, taking with him Memphis Slim and Eddie Chamblee. But out of over 100 releases in four years by the three labels there were only two records—by St Louis Jimmy and Johnny Temple—by artists who played in a less sophisticated style. Both had recorded since the mid-'30s and the older established singers were frequently sought out by the new independent companies entering the field. Thus when Fred Mendelssohn of Regal Records from Linden, New Jersey, slipped into town in 1949 he cut sessions by Memphis Minnie, Sunnyland Slim, Little Brother Montgomery and Roosevelt Sykes. Minnie and Slim each had one issue on Regal and Sykes had four; but had Mendelssohn seen fit to issue the Jimmy Rogers material he recorded at the same time, it's possible that he could have scooped the Chicago companies with the new style.

Bernard Dennis (guitar), Leonard 'Baby Doo' Caston (piano) and Willie Dixon formed the popular Big Three Trio.

4 / The Aristocrat of Records

The brothers Chess, Leonard and Philip, were Polish-born immigrants who arrived in the United States on Columbus Day 1928 and settled in Chicago in the Jewish section on S. Karlov. Like many immigrants before them they worked their way into the liquor business and by the '40s owned a small string of bars in Capone's territory on the black South Side. The largest was a nightclub called The Macomba at 39th and Cottage Grove, where they featured such artists as Billy Eckstine, Ella Fitzgerald, Gene Ammons and Jump Jackson. Their popularity with the black clientele was quickly appreciated by Len Chess, as was the lack of recording facilities, which confined the newer artists to a small local audience. Satisfied that the demand existed, the Chess brothers and a lady partner started Aristocrat Records to record the jazz and jump blues of the time. Lazy Bill remembers Chess from about this time: 'When I first saw Leonard Chess in 1946, he had a tape-recorder no bigger than that, going around from tavern to tavern looking for talent.'

Operations probably commenced early in 1947, for by 30 August 1947 *Billboard* was carrying details of Aristocrat's forthcoming releases, 403 and 404 by the Dozier Boys. This was not the first batch of issues, for the first known releases are Aristocrat 201 and 202 by the Five Blazes and 401 and 402 by Jump Jackson's Orchestra. Releases followed in a bewildering number of series, for Aristocrat in its numerical extravagance usually assigned a new series to each new artist! In the beginning the different series showed the chronological sequence of release and recording, as each new artist was assigned to a higher numerical series than the last. Thus after the 401 series came Lee Monti (501), Tom Archia (601), the Hollywood Tri-Tones (701), Jo Jo Adams (801), the Seven Melody Men (probably a gospel group) (901), Andrew Tibbs (1101), Prince Cooper (1201) and Sunnyland Slim (1301). The gaps in the series may represent unknown issues and it's not impossible that their first issue was an as yet untraced 101.

Most of the series were extremely short-lived although a few of the artists must have been sufficiently popular to establish their own numerical series and merit further trips to the RCA Victor or Columbia studios or, eventually, Bernie Clapper's Universal Studios at 20 N. Wacker Drive. Thus the Tom Archia All Stars had at least five releases to themselves in the 601 series and accompanied Andrew Tibbs and Jo Jo Adams on one session each. Tibbs himself enjoyed seven issues and had at least one fair success, *Married Man's Blues* and *I Feel Like Crying* (Aristocrat 1103). On two records he teamed up with the Dozier Boys and Sax Mallard's Combo. Archia, Tibbs, the Dozier Boys and possibly Lee

Monti were the most successful artists on the label initially, but their popularity was soon to be eclipsed, against all the odds it seemed, by an ex-Mississippi farmhand playing the old, crude, country blues.

Muddy Waters was born McKinley Morganfield on 4 April 1915 in Rolling Fork, Sharkey County, Mississippi. His sharecropper father Ollie Morganfield played guitar but Muddy had no chance to learn anything from him for, after his mother Berta died, he was raised by his maternal grandmother Della Jones in Clarksdale, 95 miles north of Rolling Fork on Highway 61. He seems to have got the name Muddy Waters very early—if it *did* arise from his playing and 'muddying' for fish in the Deer Creek, which lapped the edges of his father's shotgun shack—for he was three years old when he left for Clarksdale. With little schooling, the inevitable work on the plantation and church every Sunday Muddy's early days were typical

The Chess brothers, Phil (left) *and Leonard.*

of any young Mississippi black. 'I worked on the farms, I worked in the city, and I worked all around,' he said. But there was one difference.

> I always thought of myself as a musician. The jobs I had back in Clarksdale and so forth they were just temporary things. I still considered myself . . . well, if I wasn't a good musician then I felt that sooner or later I would be a good musician. I felt it in me.

His first instrument was the harmonica, which he started at the age of 13. With a friend, Scott Bohanna, on guitar, he played country suppers for '50 cents each, a fish sandwich and a pint of moonshine'. Muddy was about 17 when he first picked up a guitar but he learned quickly and within a year had outstripped Scott on the instrument. Mostly he played bottleneck style and he had very good teachers—Charley Patton, Son House and later Robert Johnson. Not that he received any active tuition from them, except a little from Son House, but learning by example he would watch

Big Bill Broonzy encourages the young Muddy Waters.

Patton and especially Son at jukes and country dances. Robert he may have seen, but he absorbed most of his style from records.

By the early '40s Muddy was playing with Big Joe Williams, guitarist Buddy Bradey and then Louis Ford, a violinist, and guitarists Son Sims and Percy Thomas for $2-$3 a night, and this is when he first got the taste for recording. In the summer of 1941 John Work and Alan Lomax, two field researchers for the Library of Congress, stopped by Clarksdale in their search for the then dead Robert Johnson and, enquiring after other singers, were directed to Muddy. He recorded two numbers, *I Be's Troubled* and *Country Blues*, at Stovall's Plantation and so impressive were they that Lomax returned the next year to record him again, alone and with the rowdy Son Sims group. Soon afterwards Muddy landed his first professional engagement, as a harmonica accompanist in the most famous of the travelling carnivals still operating, 'Silas Green from New Orleans'. But after only a short stint he was back in Clarksdale and then, his mind made up, one hot day in May 1943 he left Clarksdale at 4 o'clock in the afternoon, changing at Memphis for the Illinois Central and arriving in Chicago at 9.30 am the next morning. For the first two weeks he stayed with friends on the South Side at 3652 S. Calumet and then moved in with his cousin at 1857 W. 13th Street on the West Side. Soon after, he rented his own apartment just a few doors away at 1851 W. 13th.

Jobs were plentiful and he soon found employment in a paper factory manufacturing containers. He worked in the shipping depar.rtment loading and unloading trucks for $45 a week and earning overtime of up to $90 some weeks; Mississippi must have seemed far, far away. One thing that hadn't changed, though, was the house-parties, and after introductions by Big Bill Muddy started to play for private parties at the weekends, steadily building up a reputation. 'Finally it began to leak out y'know that they had a . . . pretty good guy from Mississippi here. They called me the "young blues singer" then y'know'. Muddy briefly returned to Clarksdale in 1945 when his grandmother died but while he was away the seeds were being sown of what was to be one of the most fruitful and exciting partnerships in the whole of the Chicago blues. Another recent arrival in Chicago from Mississippi was Jimmy Rogers. He tells how he met Muddy for the first time:

> During this time we was working at Sonora Radio and Cabinet Company—it was on the West Side—and Muddy's cousin was working there and he'd taken a liking to me and we would talk during lunchbreak or something—and he said, 'I have a cousin who'll be here'—he [Muddy] was in Clarksdale then—and he said 'He'll be in Chicago sometime this fall and I'd like you to meet him'. Anyway when he did come Zene brought him over to my house, we started talking and he said he played guitar. So one thing led to the other. We decided one weekend—we got together and started jammin' over at his house—he sounded pretty good so we decided then we'd start this house-party deal over again here in Chicago. And we'd do that weekends—we didn't have no place to go—we'd just sit around, buy a few drinks and play guitar.

Their first club date was at David and Mason's club at Polk and Ogden on the West Side; Jimmy played harmonica and the second guitarist was Blue Smitty—Claude Smith from Arkansas. Muddy was playing only bottleneck style at the time and Smitty, a tough guitarist in a more urban vein, claimed he taught Muddy to use his fingers. The group moved next to a joint at 1806 W. Roosevelt Road (possibly the Chicken Shack) and then, adding Eddie Boyd on piano, they next played the famous Flame Club. The owner wouldn't hire a harp-player though, and Rogers was left out; perhaps even the small bars were turning away from the country sound, for the most popular black artists then were Nat 'King' Cole, Billy Eckstine and Johnny Moore's Three Blazers with Charles Brown's vocals, and most artists were copying their bland, crooning styles. Muddy says of Eddie Boyd:

> He couldn't stand my playing because he wanted me to play like Johnny Moore, which I wasn't able to play the guitar like. He wanted it to be a kind of sweet blues.

However, this didn't prevent Eddie leaving to play with John Lee 'Sonny Boy' Williamson in Gary, and Sonny Boy was putting down anything but 'sweet blues'. Boyd was replaced by Sunnyland Slim and the engagement at the Flame lasted four or five weeks. All was going well until one night in the interval Smitty picked up a girl and vanished for a couple of hours leaving Muddy and Sunnyland to play the next set. The owner, incensed at paying for a trio and ending up with only two musicians, promptly fired them. Sunnyland, who was a real hustler when it came to getting a recording date or a gig, fixed up the next job at the Cotton Club on Lake Street. It lasted a week. 'Smitty pulled another trick. He came late one night and got into a fight with Sunnyland Slim and that job busted up!' The group continued in a fairly loose association with Muddy, who was determined to record, hanging around the better-known artists. When Sonny Boy had a date at the Chicken Shack or the Spot in Gary he would hire Muddy:

> Muddy had a car. Sonny Boy he didn't have a car so he'd let Muddy play the gig so he'd have transportation—and so that's what really got him hooked up with the recording as soon as he did.

Actually Muddy's first commercial session, a Melrose date for Columbia, came while he was playing with pianist Lee Brown. On 27 September 1946 Muddy participated in the combined session with 'Memphis Jimmy' Clark and Homer Harris. The sides, which remained unissued until 1971, were set very firmly in the Melrose mould and gave little hint of the sound of

Homer Harris, '40s.

things to come. It's interesting that Melrose, who had had the greatest success in recording the blues for nearly 20 years, let slip through his fingers the one man who would have kept him at the top for the next ten years too! But Melrose's knack of foreseeing trends was at last beginning to desert him and as a result the majors, RCA Victor and Columbia, started to lose interest in race recording. One significant event which further weakened their already limp grasp on blues recording was the tragic death of John Lee 'Sonny Boy' Williamson.

FEE RECEIPT NO. 66 30 3 8

STATE OF ILLINOIS — DEPARTMENT OF PUBLIC HEALTH
CERTIFIED COPY OF A DEATH RECORD

CORONER'S CERTIFICATE OF DEATH   ORIGINAL   State File No.

Permanent

1. PLACE OF DEATH: County of Cook, Illinois. City, Township, Village, Road Dist. Chicago.
Registration Dist. No. 3104   Primary Dist. No. 3104

STATE OF ILLINOIS
DEPARTMENT OF PUBLIC HEALTH
Division of Vital Statistics and Records
Registered No. 16599

NO CORONER'S FEE COLLECTED

Hospital: Michael Reese

LENGTH OF STAY: In Hospital or Institution Yrs. Mos. Days — In Community where death occured 2 Yrs. Mos. 2 Days.

2. PLACE OF RESIDENCE State Illinois, County Cook, City or Village Chicago, Township, Road Dist., Street and No. 3226 Giles Ave.

3.(a) FULL NAME John Lee Williamson   18. Hist. List Number 168 83A

3(b). If Veteran name war No   3(c). Social Security No. Unknown   6(a). SINGLE, MARRIED, WIDOWED, DIVORCED

Coroner's Certificate of Death
20. DATE OF DEATH   Month June   Day 1   Year 1948

4. Sex Male   5. Color or race Negro

6(b). Name of husband or wife Lacy B.
6(c). Age of husband or wife (if alive) 27 years

21. I HEREBY CERTIFY, that I took charge of the remains of the deceased herein described, held an INQUEST INVESTIGATION thereon, and from the evidence obtained find that said deceased came to HIS HER death on the date stated above and that death was due to ACCIDENT SUICIDE HOMICIDE NATURAL CAUSES more fully described below.

DATE OF INJURY OR ONSET OF DISEASE 6-1-47

7. BIRTHDATE OF DECEASED Month March   Day 30   Year 1914

8. AGE OF DECEASED Years 34   Months 2   Days 1   If less than one day (Hrs.) (Min.)

MANNER OF INJURY AND DEATH FROM UNDUE MEANS OR MEDICAL CAUSE OF DEATH:

9. BIRTHPLACE City or County Jackson   State or foreign country Tennessee

Skull fracture with
Cerebral laceration
Intra-Cranial hemorrhage
Assault at Street
Murder

10. USUAL OCCUPATION (Kind of job) Musician
11. INDUSTRY OR BUSINESS: Nite Club

12. Name Ray Williamson.
13. Birthplace Jackson Tennessee.
14. Maiden Name Nancy Utley
15. Birthplace Jackson Tenn.

22. Was injury or cause related to occupation of deceased? No
If so, how? None

16. INFORMANT Lacy B. Williamson (Pen and ink signature)
P. O. Address 3226 Giles Ave.

23. Place of Injury Chicago   Village, Township, City, Road Dist.

17. PLACE OF BURIAL, Cremation or Removal
(a) Cemetery
Location Jackson
County Tenn. State
(b) DATE: 6-3-19 48

Accident or injury occured AT HOME AT WORK IN PUBLIC PLACE
By Signed   Coroner
Address   Deputy Coroner
Date 7-15-19 48 Telephone

18. FUNERAL DIRECTOR'S Signature Theo Harves
Address 4445 South Parkway
License Number
Firm Name Metropolitan

24. FILED (Signed) Herman N. Bundesen
P. O. Address   JUL 19 1948   Registrar Illinois

I HEREBY CERTIFY THAT the foregoing is a true and correct copy of the record of death as made from the original certificate of death for the decedent named therein and that this certificate was established and filed with the Department of Public Health in accordance with the statutes of Illinois.

MAY 14, 1971

SPRINGFIELD

Franklin D. Yoder, M.D.
Director of Public Health
State Registrar

About 2 am on 1 June 1948 Sonny Boy left the Plantation Club on E. 31st Street with two friends. They parted at Giles Avenue and Sonny Boy walked alone towards his home at 3226 S. Giles. Just one block away from his door he was brutally attacked and his wallet, wrist-watch, hat and three harps stolen. Bleeding from wounds in his head and left eye he staggered to the steps of his house where his wife found him about 2.30 am. 'Lord have mercy,' he gasped. His clothes were dirty and his speech slurred from shock, and Lacey Belle imagined it to be no more than the result of a drunken brawl; it was only when he lapsed into a coma about 5 o'clock in the morning that she called for an ambulance. But too late; Sonny Boy was pronounced dead on arrival at Michael Reese Hospital. Inquests followed establishing the cause of death as 'skull fracture with cerebral laceration' and 'intracranial hemorrhage' but despite a thorough police investigation nobody was ever charged with his murder and the crime is unsolved. On 3 June his body was shipped back to Jackson, Tennessee, where he was buried. So died one of the greatest, most influential and best-loved blues artists of all time. He was just 34 years old. Sonny Boy's death marked the passing of an era.

RCA Victor didn't record any of their big blues names in 1948 and Columbia showed a similar lack of interest in recording the older blues styles. Neither were the new independents showing any alacrity in picking up the challenge, until Aristocrat stumbled on the new formula that was to restore the fortunes of the Chicago blues scene.

In 1948 Sunnyland Slim got a recording date for Aristocrat and wanted Muddy Waters to play guitar behind him. The story has often been told how Muddy was out on the streets delivering Venetian blinds when a friend, Antra Bolton, got the message to him that Sunnyland wanted him to record. With a flash of inspiration Muddy rang his boss, told him that his cousin had been found dead in an alley and asked for the rest of the day off. Muddy skipped off to the studio while Antra delivered the rest of his load. On the first session Sunnyland and Muddy sang two numbers each, accompanying each other's singing. Nothing much happened with these sides but the black talent scout Goldstein, who worked for Aristocrat, had heard a lot of Muddy playing in the clubs and house-parties and asked him to come down to the Union Hall and rehearse. This was when Len Chess first heard Waters and didn't think much of him. However, the second session was cut, resulting again in one record each by Sunnyland Slim and Muddy (although two other titles by Muddy with Alex Atkins on sax weren't issued). Muddy, with only Ernest 'Big' Crawford (Memphis Slim's bassist) accompanying on string bass, recorded his old Library of Congress title *I Be's Troubled* and, as *I Can't Be Satisfied*, it was an immediate success. Muddy says, 'Chess began to come close to me. Changed his tune, because I was selling so fast they couldn't press them fast enough at that particular time.' Muddy too had problems adjusting to his sudden success. He would be out at night driving his truck,

still delivering Venetian blinds, and experience the eerie sensation of hearing his voice booming out from the open windows of a hundred tenements as the record was played and played again. He confesses, 'I used to wonder if I had died!'

The immediate result was that his group was in demand at more and more clubs and they played regularly at the Boogie Woogie Inn on Roosevelt, at the Du Drop Inn, 3609 Wentworth, for Miss King and at Club Zanzibar, 13th and Ashland. Although the full group was Muddy, Jimmy Rogers on guitar and harp, and Baby Face Leroy Foster, who played both guitar and drums, Chess insisted that Muddy cut records only with Big Crawford. Presumably he didn't want to change a winning team. Muddy dug deep into his roots for his next records. *Down South Blues* used the timeless Mississippi theme of *Rolling and Tumbling* but with different lyrics, while *Kind Hearted Woman* was based on Robert Johnson's recording, Muddy even employing the falsetto vocal that Johnson used. Neither of these sides, however, was issued until recently. Those that were issued were mostly fine traditional blues sung and played in the old way, the amplified guitar being the only concession to the times. Muddy first played amplified guitar in Chicago in 1944 when his uncle, Joe Grant, bought him a Stella, but even now he says: 'I still like the plain guitar better than I do the amplified one—better sound, everything. But if

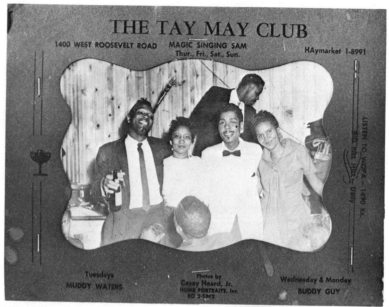

THE TAY MAY CLUB

1400 WEST ROOSEVELT ROAD   MAGIC SINGING SAM   HAymarket 1-8991
Thur., Fri., Sat., Sun.

LISTEN TO WOPA - 1490 Kc.

Tuesdays   Photos by   Wednesday & Monday
MUDDY WATERS   Casey Heard, Jr.   BUDDY GUY
                      HOME PORTRAITS, Inc.
                      RO 2-5902

Above: *Magic Sam and Little Johnnie Jones*. Right: *Robert Nighthawk, Chicago, 1964*.

everybody's using them what you gonna do?' With Leroy Foster also on guitar they cut an instrumental *Muddy Jumps One* and, under Leroy's name, *Locked Out Boogie*. These not very inspired numbers sounded more typical of the run-of-the-mill jump blues records still pouring out from the studios. But from the same session *You're Gonna Miss Me* (Aristocrat 1307) was magnificent. With the always superb Big Crawford on bass it was as exciting as *I Can't Be Satisfied*. The reverse, *Mean Red Spider*, was equally fine. Less successful were *Little Geneva* and *Canary Bird* (loosely based on *Bluebird Blues*), the thunderous amplification making the atmosphere sound stiff and strained—but for the next session the pianist Little Johnnie Jones was added and five blues of astonishing beauty resulted. With Muddy's bottleneck guitar, Leroy's second guitar and Johnnie's Maceo-inspired piano the sound was very like that which Maceo and Tampa Red created. Johnnie sang two, the original *Big Town Playboy* and the beautiful *Shelby County* (Aristocrat 405), while Muddy turned in the brilliant *Screaming And Crying* and *Where's My Woman Been* (Aristocrat 406) and *Last Time I Fool Around With You*.

Chess's eyes having been opened wide by Muddy's success, he started to look round for other country blues artists, and on Muddy's recommendation the old Bluebird singer Robert Nighthawk made the trip from Helena, Arkansas, with his pianist Ernest Lane. They recorded Tampa

Red's old number *Black Angel Blues* and *Annie Lee Blues* (Aristocrat 2301). Nighthawk played guitar in bottleneck style too but, whereas Muddy's sound was rough and exciting, Robert's was immensely smooth and restrained, much like Tampa Red, but almost totally original in sound. This was the first session supervised by Willie Dixon and from then on Dixon was to be Chess's 'right arm', as Leonard put it.

Nighthawk's real name was Robert McCollum and he was born 30 November 1909 in Helena, Arkansas. He learned guitar from a neighbour,

Houston Stackhouse, and spent the late '20s travelling the South and meeting the major singers of the Memphis and Mississippi area. After getting into trouble with the law he changed his name to McCoy, his mother's maiden name, and left the South. By the '30s he was recording as Robert Lee McCoy and accompanying other singers as a guitarist or harmonica-player. The name Nighthawk came from one of his most popular records, *Prowlin' Nighthawk.*

Robert didn't have a great voice but his bottleneck guitar style was the smoothest on record, and when he switched to electric guitar at some time in the '40s there was a unique, almost orchestral quality to the sound. He taught Earl Hooker and both Elmore James and Muddy learned a little from him too, Muddy returning the favour by getting him the Aristocrat sessions. Unhappy in Chicago, which he found too violent, Nighthawk had the rough, crumpled appearance of the itinerant Southern bluesman. Polite but taciturn, he rarely smiled. In later years he was happiest at home in Helena, making only infrequent trips to Chicago.

Aristocrat made little impression with their other country artists, who recorded mainly in the older styles. There was one session by a Sonny Boy Williamson imitator, Forest City Joe (Pugh) from Hughes, Arkansas, and his tribute to the late John Lee, *A Memory Of Sonny Boy*, appeared on Aristocrat 3101, but the session was bogged down by the unbluesy accompanying guitarist and the other titles were not issued. Also unissued was a session under the pseudonym Kid Slim by Elijah C. Jones, who had earlier made four fine sides for Bluebird. The only other real blues artist was the Texas pianist and singer Charley Bradix, who sang and played in an astonishing imitation of Leroy Carr. These sides, probably bought from Blue Bonnet Records of Dallas, and numbered 418, are the last known issues on Aristocrat.

It was obvious that Muddy Waters was playing the type of 'down-home' blues that people wanted to hear, but still Len Chess would not record Muddy's whole group. But if Chess didn't want to record them other people certainly did and, with Foster on drums, Little Walter on harp and guitar and Muddy quietly in the background, records appeared as by the Baby Face Trio on the newly-founded Parkway label. This was started in January 1950 by Monroe Passis and the Leaner brothers, George and Ernie, of Hit Record Distributors at 2320 S. Michigan. First artists signed were the Little Walter Trio and the Baby Face Trio and eight sides were cut—four vocals by Leroy and four by Little Walter, who, by then, was a permanent member of the group. It was a wild and uninhibited session, as indeed any session involving Leroy was likely to be! He was a fine singer with a warm insinuating voice which, like the late Sonny Boy's, 'got to people'. Baby Face had a curious style; high pitched, it was a mixture of Sonny Boy's and some of the eccentricities of Dr Clayton, and between verses he kept up a constant barrage of shouts of encouragement, admonitions and asides. Baby Face's natural exuberance never trivialised his performance, and he sings movingly on bouncy up-tempo songs and slow blues alike. *Boll Weevil* (Parkway 104) is interesting, as the theme must have been familiar enough to his audience, but it's unlikely they would have wished to be reminded of it. Typically Leroy treats it in a semi-humorous, off-hand way:

> Mr. Boll Weevil, don't sing them blues no more (x2)
> Because Boll Weevil here, Boll Weevil everywhere I go.
>
> Ah but the next time I seen the Boll Weevil, boy, he was sailing
> through the air
> The next time I saw the Boll Weevil he had his whole family there
>
> Mr Boll Weevil, don't sing . . . [etc.]

The up-tempo reverse, *Red Headed Woman*, contains the usual direct sexual metaphors:

> I say looka here, looka here baby, see what you done done
> Done squeezed my lemon, caused my juice to run.

Quite the wildest performance, though, was the double-sided version of *Rollin' And Tumblin'* (Parkway 501), released in March, in which everybody joins in with immense gusto, Muddy to his regret as it transpired! One side Baby Face sings anguishedly while on the other he hums as the tension and excitement of Muddy's highly rhythmic bottleneck guitar and Walter's harmonica mount to an almost unbearable climax. It was an extraordinary record and there was to be a curious sequel. Not surprisingly it came to the ears of Len Chess; Jimmy Rogers takes up the story:

> Muddy got himself in pretty big trouble with Chess [laughs]. Yeah, yeah they had a lot of fun! I laughed myself sick about it. Leonard didn't want Muddy to use that slide on any other label—but here's Muddy slipped off and cut this thing and Leonard heard it y'know. Then Muddy had to record this same number by himself on Chess.

(There is no doubt that Muddy's most distinctive feature and main selling point was his bottleneck guitar style. One night when Moody Jones sat in with the band Muddy took him aside and warned him, 'Don't fool with that slide.') So Muddy's double-sided version, which appeared on Aristocrat 412, was cut to kill the Parkway recording, and it may well have succeeded, for Parkway was soon in trouble. In March the Leaners had left to form United Record Distributors but Passis continued alone until he started a personal management agency with Mayo Williams. The Blues Rockers also signed with Parkway until 15 April 1950 but there are no known issues.

Baby Face Leroy said he was born in Mobile, Alabama, but he grew up in Coffeeville, just north of Grenada, Mississippi. About 1946 Leroy was in Chicago playing with Sonny Boy Williamson, Sunnyland Slim and Lee

Brown at house parties and was one of the crowd always at Sunnyland's house at 216 E. 31st. Biographical details of Leroy are scarce; he lived near 16th and Kristiana, he was married in Gary, Indiana, and his widow Betty still lives in Chicago making a living from running pitty-pat games.

He played unfussy drums in the tight, Chicago manner and guitar, not too well, in the sparse city style. But his main talents were drinking, singing and clowning and he was very popular. Most anecdotes recall his antics when drunk or his wild exaggerations—for instance his hospital experience with a stomach-pump:

> He told this for the truth. He say he's in the hospital and the doctor said wine and stuff was doing him so bad the doctor had to hurry up and stick a hole in his stomach and that wine just spewed out. Boy he could drink a lot of it though—wine and whisky. Baby Face Leroy get a drink of that whisky, you tell when he get drunk—he walk on one foot for a block! The other foot would never touch the ground! Y'know how they do the Mashed Potato, that's the way his foot be going, be going right on down the street. Keep up too!
>
> I'd like to see him play—his feet—never let his heel touch the floor, his feet patting the ground. Sometimes he'd have both feet goin' . . .

Baby Face left Muddy on signing with Parkway but nothing happened for him and he was later playing with Homesick James, Snooky Pryor and Lazy Bill at the Club Jamboree in South Chicago. Homesick said:

> He was all right! Good guy. I liked to work with him. Used to have a lot of fun with Baby Face. Me and Baby Face we'd always be into something. We'd be in some kind of act together.

Baby Face was young, and well nicknamed to judge from the only existing photograph, but his seriousness as a blues artist was never in doubt. The J.O.B. sides with Snooky Pryor are classic examples of the emerging small band Chicago blues. *My Head Can't Rest Anymore* (which Al Benson dedicated on his radio show to Joe Louis) and *Take A Little Walk With Me* (J.O.B. 100) are beautiful sad, slow blues with mournful vocals; the guitar has the amplification turned up so that it sounds like a bass and Snooky in a beautifully restrained accompaniment blows long, swooping phrases on the harp which round out the whole performance. The record was later sold to Chess.

Parkway and J.O.B. were new names on the Chicago scene and, although the former had to dispose of its masters to a New York independent in part-settlement of a debt, that it existed at all is a measure of the major companies' abdication from the field. 1949 was the last year RCA Victor made attempts to retain any kind of share of the blues market, by recording Washboard Sam (for the last time), Crudup, Jazz Gillum and Tampa Red, while Columbia cut their last Memphis Minnie

An anonymous enthusiast poses with the dapper Baby Face Leroy Foster.

Little Walter with (centre) *Sunnyland Slim and* (right) *Little Brother Montgomery.*

session. Columbia ended their 30000 blues series in April 1950 and in the same year RCA Victor dropped Gillum and ended the Bluebird subsidiary. For sixteen years Bluebird had established something close to a stranglehold on the whole blues scene and much fine music had been distilled from the studios according to the dictates of a fairly rigid formula. But the old formula was not delivering the goods, and, with the rewards small from blues compared with the ever expanding popular music market, the majors had neither the time nor the interest to devise new formulas. Of their former blues giants only Crudup and Tampa Red were retained and, though they were to record regularly, Tampa with two sessions a year until 1953 and Crudup one session a year until 1954, the Bluebird heyday of recording was over. From 1950 onwards blues recording everywhere was to be a grass-roots operation conducted by the people with their fingers closest to the pulse of the black communities: small, local businessmen, record shops and the new, striving independents.

They call me Muddy Waters
I'm just restless, man, as the deep blue sea.

Aristocrat started life from a small office at 71st and Phillips with James Martin of Diversey Avenue as its distributor. However, with its 180 small accounts on the South Side, which the Chess brothers knew intimately, Martin decided the brothers were better able to handle their own distribution. By 1948 they had moved to premises at 5249 S. Cottage Grove and by 1950 the Aristocrat operation had become much more professional. Curbing their numerical extravagance, they concentrated their releases in the revived 400 series; and other changes were afoot.

After February 1950 the last Aristocrat session took place. Len and Phil Chess bought out their partner Evelyn, the name of the label changed to Chess and on 3 June 1950 the handsome blue-and-white label with the chessboard motif was born. The Aristocrat label was kept until 13 January 1951 but all new releases appeared on Chess. The first issue was by Gene Ammons on Chess 1425—the number of the Chess house on S. Karlov—and most of the first dozen releases were by former Aristocrat artists. Muddy Waters' first Chess record was *Rollin' Stone/Walkin' Blues* (1426) from the same session as the Aristocrat *Rollin' And Tumblin'*. Ammons was a success and the new label's distribution was sufficiently good for Muddy to be credited with a nation-wide hit too. Both were superb country blues—*Walkin'* was the old Robert Johnson song—and Chess was off to a good start.

That Len Chess was slowly learning his blues was shown by Muddy's first Chess session proper, for which the Muddy-Big Crawford line-up was augmented by Little Walter on harmonica. The four sides recorded were all classic examples of the early poetic phase of the postwar Chicago blues,

Phone OA. 4-3641

MUDDY WATERS - G

Chess Recorder

KING OF THE BLUES

—⚜—

4339 Lake Park Ave.   **Chicago 15, Illinois**

Crawford's supple bass-playing backing Muddy's bottleneck guitar and Walter, slightly under-recorded, embellishing with harmonica phrases of great beauty. The music was exciting but still subtle and the lyrics were fine. *Sad Letter Blues* (1434), a remake of one of the unissued Columbia sides, is memorable, as Muddy sketches the complex reactions and indecision brought on by grief, with an economy of words that is all the more affecting for being understated:

> I got a letter this morning, this is the way my letter read
> I got a letter this morning, this is the way my letter read
> Says you better come home Muddy Waters, tell me your
> baby's dead
>
> I start to writing but I believe I'll go myself
> No I ain't going write honey I believe I'll go myself
> Well you know a letter's too slow, tell me a telegram may get left
>
> I said I wasn't going to my baby's burying-ground
> No I ain't going to my baby's burying-ground
> Well you know I was standing right there, child when the
> gravedigger let her down

Early Morning Blues (Chess 1490) had something of the intensity of a field-holler:

> Early in the morning before day that's when my blues come
> falling down (x2)
> Well you know that woman that I'm loving she just can't be found.

The next session had drummer Elgin (or Elgar) Evans (or Edmonds) and produced the first of Muddy's successful voodoo (or hoodoo) themes, *Louisiana Blues* (1441).

> I'm going down in Louisiana baby behind the sun
> I'm going down in Louisiana honey behind the sun
> Well you know I just found out my troubles just begun
>
> I'm going down in New Orleans get me a mojo hand,
> I'm going down in New Orleans get me a mojo hand,
> I wanna show all you good-looking women just how to treat your man.

Even the music was pure magic. Medium-slow, the voice, guitar and harmonica blend in perfect unity against hypnotic, repeated guitar figures, the whole performance lifted along by the drummer's light rim-shots. In contrast the reverse, *Evans Shuffle,* dedicated to the WGES DJ Sam Evans, was almost a country dance number. *Louisiana Blues* was Muddy's next big hit, perhaps helped by Evans's sympathetic plugging, for there was still a great resistance on the radio stations to the country blues. Only Evans and Al Benson, the other black DJ on WGES, would play Muddy's records on the air.

The Muddy Waters records of 1950 and 1951 represent the purest and

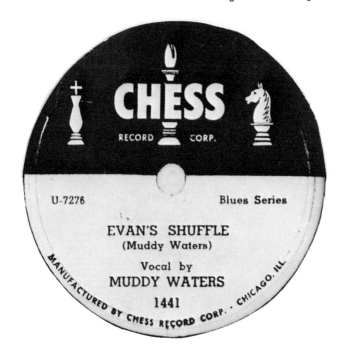

most successful strain of the new country blues. The vocal, guitar, harmonica and bass lines interwove to achieve complete artistic integration. The songs were superb too—*Long Distance Call* (1452) from February 1951 was an intensely sad and imaginative telephone blues, while *Honey Bee* (1468) with Little Walter playing second guitar was a finely drawn sexual analogy of great tenderness and beauty. This was the very springtime of Chicago blues.

Muddy had gathered about him musicians of such stature that the group was ripe to be plundered for other blues talent and on 15 August 1950 Jimmy Rogers made his first record for Chess. Curiously enough, although Jimmy had been playing second guitar on and off with the group for several years, he had not recorded with Muddy (or if he had the session remains unissued). Rogers's first issue, *That's All Right* (1435), was a big hit, its catchy tune, unusual in blues, making it instantly memorable. Rogers has said:

> I had been singing it for quite some time—in fact down through the years, my growing up with this idea—from the deep South. I would just get a word here and a word there . . . Muddy he'd say 'Well this should be a good number to put on wax' and I thought it would be too—and so he said 'The first chance we get we're going to wax it for you'—and on this session we did—I cut that number on his session—we had time left.

CHESS RECORDING ARTIST   MUDDY WATERS   Countrys Greatest Blues Artist

(Jimmy's memory is at fault here, for Muddy didn't play on it; the line-up was Jimmy, Little Walter and Big Crawford. Whether it was a Muddy Waters date we don't know, as nothing else was mastered from the session.) Jimmy has a good voice and remarkably clear diction for a Mississippi singer. He does not play bottleneck guitar, probably because his style was formed purely from records, and he never saw any of the great Delta bluesmen in action, though he was born in the Delta, at Ruleville, Mississippi, on 3 June 1924. Jimmy was one of ten children. His mother was Grozie Lane and Henry Rogers was his step-father but he was raised

JIMMY ROGERS
"Chess Recording Artist"

by his maternal grandmother Leanna Jackson and spent most of his early years in and out of Atlanta, Memphis and Ruleville. Like most of the singers his first guitar was home-made:

> I used to take wire, broom-wire y'know and stretch it up. I didn't use baling wire—it was real heavy—some of the fellas did—but I would strip a broom y'know. I would always go round and try and find me an old broom and I'd unravel the wire from the broom and put it up—it would get a much keener sound y'know—more truer sound. And that's what I started off trying to play. When you don't have anything else anything sounds good to you if you can get a sound!

This was about 1935, and, since nobody in his family played any instrument, Jimmy found his inspiration in the records of Big Bill, Memphis Minnie and later, Crudup and Louis Jordan, but in Memphis he listened to guitarists Joe Willie Wilkins and Robert Junior Lockwood. By 1940 he was playing the local house-parties.

> I was at a place called Minter City, Mississippi—we stayed there for seven, eight years I suppose—and this fella, his name was James Triblett, he used to give house-parties y'know, get-togethers—weekend get-togethers, so he said he wanted me to play this party for him. So I did—that was a big thing to me y'know to earn money for my guitar . . . he paid me $12 for the night and all the booze I could drink . . . well, that wasn't very much at that time . . . so with food and liquor he'd give me $12. Well I played for him like that, boy, maybe four, five different times and other people would hear about this and they'd come over y'know for maybe ten, fifteen miles—in fact they would gamble there too, y'know . . . and another fella called Snook Balls—he lived in Phillip, Mississippi—he had a little place there and he started talking to me about trying to get me over to his place there—another fella was teaming with me during that time—his name was Little Arthur Johnson—he played guitar too. So we went over and started playing, that was the farthest I played from home.

He met Rice Miller at Phillip with his regular group of Joe Willie Wilkins, Dudlow Taylor and Peck Curtis and sat in one night playing Joe Willie's guitar. Soon afterwards Jimmy left for West Memphis where he met Howlin' Wolf and stayed for about a year, until Sunnyland Slim took him up to St Louis with him. After a stay in St Louis of six months or so he left to live with his great-uncle in Chicago.

From 1950 until about 1956 Jimmy played, toured and recorded regularly with Muddy and shares the credit for forging the sound of the Chicago blues. While Muddy played bottleneck guitar and sang, Jimmy's second guitar added a further dimension to the group sound, carrying the rhythm with ringing, ominous bass figures. With the success of *That's All Right* Rogers recorded regularly under his own name for Chess, usually with Muddy's group. While Muddy's records had a dark and powerful urgency, Jimmy's were often more relaxed and almost polished in performance. This was particularly true of the up-tempo numbers which Jimmy favoured and it was not without reason that Chess soon labelled his records 'Jimmy Rogers and his Rocking Four'. A couple of times Jimmy formed his own band and tried to make a go of it. His pianist was Eddie Ware and in January 1951 he made a session with Ware and tenor saxophonist Ernest Cotton, which took the development of the urban blues sound a little further. The innovation here was Ware's crashing piano, the brilliant treble clusters swamping every track, while the sax played

Smitty's Corner, 35th and Indiana.

fairly unobtrusively in the background. Ware's piano-playing seemed in keeping with his personality as Rogers remembered him:

> He was a pretty wild guy—he was young and whenever you would be able to catch up with him he would play. Maybe a week or something like that—then he was gone! He was a swift guy—if you be out of work for a couple of weeks you wouldn't see Eddie—when you got a gig he's someplace else—keeps movin'.

Ware also cut some sides at Jimmy's sessions singing in an imitation of Charles Brown, and the sides are only interesting for his piano work and the accompaniment by Jimmy and, on one, by Little Walter. From this session came the superb *The World Is In A Tangle* (1453) with its cold war theme:

> Now you know this world's all in a tangle man
> Everybody begin to sing this song
> The Reds is messed up over yonder, boys
> And we ain't going to be here long
> That's why I'm gonna build myself a cave
> And move down in the ground
> You know when I go to the Army darling
> Won't be no more Reds around
>
> Now you know I got my questionnaire man
> I've got my Class Card too
> I begin to feel so worried
> I don't know what to do
> That's why . . . [etc.]
>
> Now you know they gonna march us down to the waterfront
> To cross the deep blue sea
> My baby she begins to wonder man
> What's gonna become of poor me . . .

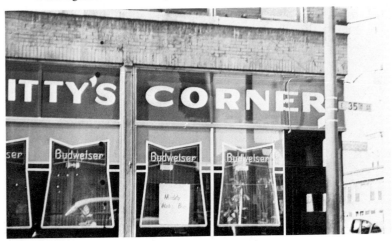

Perhaps everybody *was* beginning to sing this song, for just three months later Big Boy Crudup recorded *I'm Gonna Dig Myself A Hole,* based on Jimmy's song. The theme may have been suggested because Eddie Ware was soon to go into the army himself and was in fact on furlough when he made a later session with Jimmy.

July 1951 they recorded again. This time instead of a sax there was Little Walter on guitar and harp and the two sides released from this session, *Money Marbles And Chalk* and *Chance to Love* (1476), are, though little known, masterpieces of the genre. Both sides rippled with Eddie's piano and on *Money* Jimmy and Little Walter played guitar, switching the lead on the slow, exultant blues:

> Now I've got a little woman, she got money, marbles and chalk
> She bought me a fine Cadillac, man, that's why I don't have to walk
> But in the evening, after the sun goes down (x2)
> The womens all tell me I'm the sweetest man in town.

Little Walter - for once, playing guitar - in England, 1964.

Chance To Love was much less confident in tone as Jimmy asked the girl her address:

> Pretty, pretty baby, tell me what may be your name? (x2)
> Now the reason why I ask you I wonder if I even stand a chance?
>
> Just a few more questions I want to ask you before you go (x2)
> Name of your street and phone number, your address, what floor?

On this side Little Walter blew harp and contributed a solo of such majesty and superb control that the effect was spine-chilling. This was a period of immense creativity and there was an astonishing consistency in the records of Muddy and Jimmy. How was this achieved? Certainly some of the credit was due to Len Chess, who rehearsed them furiously down at the studios, sometimes reshaping the material. Jimmy Rogers explained:

> You were supposed to make I think it were four sessions a year . . . then as time came close—then you would start trying to work on something to be ready when the session time came up—that's the way you would do it. We'd go in at 9 o'clock [at night] and it was maybe 3 or 4 o'clock before we'd leave out. Leonard worked hard, he really would work hard—sometimes he overworked! You didn't go in there too often and made a number right away y'know—he'd be turning it around there quite a while trying to get the best you have.

An interesting example of this process can be heard on the Chess Vintage reissue LP of Jimmy Rogers (410), where the false starts to *Act Like You Love Me* (originally Chess 1543) have been preserved. Leonard even went so far as to play bass drum on Muddy's *She Moves Me* (1490) to achieve the exact sound he wanted. For someone who didn't like the blues or know much about them in the beginning Leonard was shaping up pretty well. And the results were remarkable. Jimmy had one last session with Eddie Ware which produced the classic *Back Door Friend* (1506). This was a Tony Hollins song, *Married Woman Blues,* from his 1941 OKeh session, but the new version by Rogers far outshone the original. Incidentally Hollins, who lived on Lucky's Plantation near Clarksdale (and had one postwar session for Decca when he moved to Chicago after serving in the army), must have viewed with rather mixed feelings the success other artists had with two of his songs, *Married Woman* and *Crawlin' King Snake.* Rogers also used a Memphis Minnie number to good effect, *Left Me With A Broken Heart* (1543), and the by now standard *Sloppy Drunk* (1574). Not all Jimmy's songs were his own but there is little doubt that his versions became the definitive ones.

Your Cat Will Play

Little Walter had joined the group some time around 1950 but his leaving can be pinpointed more accurately to mid-1952. Despite his youth and slight stature he had completely filled the gap left by the death of Sonny Boy Williamson, his mentor, and there were no harp-players in Chicago to touch him. Just 20 years old, Walter was at the pinnacle of his powers. At the same time as Muddy and Jimmy were developing the two-guitar accompaniments, he was dynamically extending the role of the blues harp. John Lee Williamson was credited with 'putting the harps in the Union'; Little Walter must be credited with putting them in Chicago's blues bands. Billy Boy Arnold, talking about the scene in 1951, says: 'Saxophone players were starving, piano players weren't working at all. In fact at that time you couldn't get a job without a harmonica player.'

It had been a long, hard road from Marksville, Louisiana, where Walter was born Marion Walter Jacobs, son of Adam and Beatrice Jacobs, on 1 May 1930 (or 2 May 1931, according to his sister Mrs Sylvia Williams). He was 12 years old when he left home to play club dates in New Orleans and from there he gradually made his way north. In 1943 he was still in Louisiana, holding down a regular spot at the Liberty Night Club, Monroe. After this he went to Helena, Arkansas, where he met Robert Lockwood Jr. and Houston Stackhouse and started to play guitar during his three-year stay; then on to Memphis and a meeting with Sonny Boy, who impressed him enormously. He moved again, to St Louis, and stayed eight months playing with guitarists James Dechet and Honeyboy Edwards, and then in 1947 made the final, logical move to Chicago. It was on Maxwell Street and under the wing of Big Bill and Tampa Red that he became a blues musician; up to this time he had played every style of music and took great pride in doing so. It was probably his pride too that would not allow him to admit any influences on his harp style, though he was more forthcoming about the artists who had shaped his vocal style and named Big Maceo, Ella Johnson and T-Bone Walker along with his main men, Big Bill and Tampa. After the record with Othum Brown he met Muddy Waters, when he walked into a club where the group was playing, and soon he joined Muddy's band.

The band had an untitled instrumental which they used for a signature tune and played about eight times a night. The customers asked them to record it, so at a session in 1952 when Muddy cut *Please Have Mercy* (Chess 1514) it was recorded and Walter sang a number for the reverse side. The instrumental was filed as *Your Cat Will Play* but finally issued under Len Chess's title *Juke*. It was a perfect name for such a danceable little number. Muddy and Jimmy laid down a light boogie rhythm as Walter swooped and soared above, while the admirable Elgin lightly brushed along proceedings, throwing in the odd cymbal-shot. Little Walter's record was issued on the newly formed subsidiary Checker.

After the session Muddy and his group went on a Southern tour with John Lee Hooker and when they reached Shreveport the records were on the juke-boxes. Muddy remembers that after the show they went to a club and Little Walter became excited when they noticed that everybody was playing *Juke* over and over again on the juke-box. Jimmy Rogers takes up the story with much laughter:

> We all went to get some uniforms in Shreveport, Louisiana. We went downtown to have some pants, shirts combinations—while we were gone to pick the stuff up, Walter—well he went with us that morning and got the measurement on himself. This fella said pick them up about two o'clock—we went to pick 'em up, see—and we left, he told me to bring his back. And when we left, *he* left . . . and when we got back the girl at the desk said, 'You talking about the little guy? He got a cab and left as soon as y'all left; he went to the train station'. Yeah, we left one way and he left with the other and came back to Chicago.

When the band returned to Chicago Walter wanted his money for the tour! Despite this incident he played a few more gigs with the band until one night at the Zanzibar a customer asked them to play *Juke*. He put a quarter on Muddy's knee, a quarter on Jimmy's knee and, on Walter's knee, a dime! This proved too much for Walter and he left to form his own group. Not really his own group, for he kicked Junior Wells out of his band, The Four Aces, and took over as Little Walter and his Night Cats. Muddy then hired Wells.

'We Went By The Cards . . .'

The Four Aces consisted of Junior Wells, Louis and David Myers and Freddy Below Jr. The Myers brothers (there are three but the eldest, Bob—a harp player—didn't make music his career as Louis and David did) came from Bihalia, Mississippi, just southeast of Memphis. David was born on 30 October 1926 and Louis 18 September 1929. Their father used to play guitar—mostly Blind Lemon songs—but Louis started to teach himself about the age of eight when a neighbour left his guitar at the house.

When the family moved to Chicago in 1941 they lived at 3946 S. Indiana, where Lonnie Johnson had a basement apartment. Louis kept up his guitar-playing and then Dave bought a guitar from a street musician and began to practise to records. They were still too young to get into the taverns but Louis played house-parties where he met Homesick James and Othum Brown and eventually teamed up with Big Boy Spires. About 1951, after a house-party where the Myers Brothers stole the show, David replaced Spires and added Junior Wells, who lived near them at 42nd and Prairie. They were booked into the C & T Lounge on Prairie for several months. Then, calling themselves The Three Deuces, they moved to a club on 31st Street. Louis says: 'Deuces are only good when they are wild and we went by the cards!' Later they were to be The Three Aces when they worked at the Du Drop Lounge, sharing with Big Bill, and finally The Four Aces, when Freddy Below Jr. joined the band at the Brookmont Hotel, 40th and Michigan.

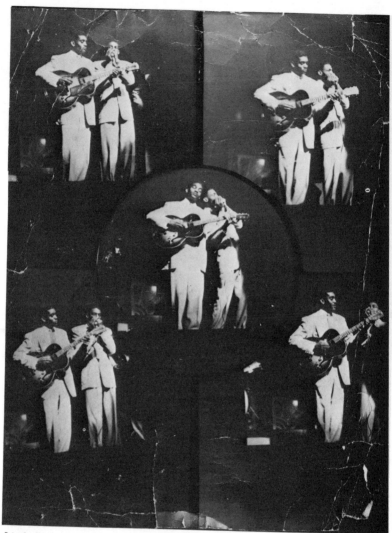

Little Walter and Louis Myers at the Apollo Theatre, 1952.

Below, a native Chicagoan, was born 6 September 1926 and always intended to be a jazz drummer. His interest was aroused after hearing Chick Webb at the old Vendome Theatre and he started learning to play at Du Sable High School in 1941. He left in 1944 to go in the army and after a tour of the Pacific returned in 1946, just too young to get work in the clubs. So he enlisted at a drummers' school where he met Elgin, Muddy's drummer, and in his spare time he played in a bebop group. Then in 1948 he went back into the army but when he came out in 1951 the blues boom was on. As he says: 'The only thing happening was the blues. Blues was the only thing in town and Elgin told me they worked 5, 6 or 7 days a week.' Elgin called up Louis Myers and Freddy bought a new drum kit and joined the band. His first night was a disaster. 'The first night I worked, I quit!' he said. Freddy had studied drums, gone to school, but he couldn't play with a solid blues band. The Myerses were mystified. How could such a good drummer not be able to play blues? However, they coached him and gradually Freddy got the hang of it and very quickly he was to prove to be the best drummer in Chicago. He says, 'We were playing the same thing that Muddy was but in a more bouncy, jazzy and swinging way.' Which made them the perfect band for Little Walter.

Mean Old World

With the same combination as Muddy's group Walter proceeded to make a different type of blues. With the Myers brothers and Below the sound was much more jazz-based, and so big was the sound of Walter's amplified harp and so revolutionary his phrasing that it seemed at times as if he was blowing a sax. He played with a control, range, fluency and imagination that was breathtaking; each solo was brilliantly constructed and pushed to its logical conclusion. His repertoire ran the gamut from slow atmospheric blues instrumentals like *Quarter To Twelve* (Checker 780), *Lights Out* (786) and *Blue Light* (799), through driving up-tempo tunes like *Juke* and especially *Thunderbird* (801) with its heavy, loping boogie figures, to mediocre semi-pop songs like *Who* (833) and *Boom Boom Out Go The Lights* (867). A poor singer with a flat voice and limited range, Walter only took up singing to give him respite from his harp-blowing; and the way he

"OH BABY" (2:40) [Vocal BMI—Jacobs, Dixon]
"ROCKER" (2:52) [Instrumental BMI—Jacobs]

LITTLE WALTER
(Checker 793)

LITTLE WALTER
● Little Walter bounces right

back into the market with what looks like one of his strongest. The latest, "Oh Baby," is a quick beat jump ditty that combines his mouth organ and vocal talents. Result is a powerful platter. Little Walter gives a bouncy reading to a romantic blues with an infectious lilt. The lower deck, "Rocker," is a quick beat instrumental that shows Little Walter's harmonica to full advantage. The man produces some terrific sounds and excitement. Another good deck, with perhaps just a shade to "Oh Baby."

poured his heart into his blowing, he needed the brief pause. On slow blues he strained to reach notes, in contrast to the contemptuous ease with which he hit them on his harp, but songs like *Mean Old World* (764), *Blues With A Feeling* (780) and *Last Night* are nonetheless moving for it. The Myers brothers' tight guitar patterns provided the perfect background to Walter's fiery harp, and they were one of the most compact and musicianly groups on the scene. Their personal relationships were less compact; Louis and Walter were never easy men to get on with, and disagreements abounded. (Louis claims *Sad Hours* (764) as his number and says that he only let it be recorded on the understanding that it would come out under his name; it didn't, of course.) Eventually the Myerses were replaced by Robert Lockwood Jr. (whose taciturn nature no doubt made a less explosive mixture than Louis's and Walter's) and Luther Tucker. Louis left in 1954, probably after losing his equipment in a fire at Club Hollywood, and Robert Lockwood replaced him. Then David left the next year and Luther Tucker joined. Then Below left later that year. From this period came Little Walter's biggest commercial success, *My Babe* (811), a Willie Dixon adaptation of the old gospel song *This Train*, which topped the R & B charts for two weeks from 23 April 1955, and in fact was in the Top Ten from 12 March until 2 July. It was just the sort of trite, catchy number to succeed at the time but as a blues record it leaves much to be desired. Walter was still having trouble keeping his band together and pulling a gun on a recalcitrant member didn't help much. He was behaving like a cowboy much of the time and would roar up to a club date in his black Cadillac with a squeal of brakes that sent everyone rushing to the door to stare. Eventually Lockwood left too and Walter was having more and more trouble keeping his band together. Jerome Arnold gives an insight into Walter's problems:

> His downfall was in his choice of friends. He sought out the worst kind of riff-raff for he seemed to feel comfortable around them. He once got into a shooting match with a winehead and ended up missing and shooting himself in the leg.

Some people are born tough, others have toughness thrust upon them. It's hard to tell which was the case with Walter. He'd had to make his own way in the world from the age of eight, and that he had survived in one of the hardest businesses in the world bore tribute to an acquired if not inherent toughness. By the mid-'50s he was drinking heavily (when Muddy first met him Walter drank nothing but milk or Pepsi-Cola), his voice had coarsened and his face was heavily scarred. He achieved greater commercial success than probably any other postwar artist and when his popularity waned he took the blow harder than anyone else. Little Walter needed the adulation of the crowds and the sympathy of friends; with it he was friendly and helpful as many will testify, and without he was lost; bitter and distrustful and lonely.

The Chess brothers were not alone in divining a market to be exploited and they were quickly followed into the recording business by other hopefuls. As early as August 1949 a nut-brown, wiry little man, Joe Brown, started the J.O.B. label with the old Bluebird artist St Louis Jimmy as a partner. Jimmy's real name is James Burke Oden and the name of the label was derived from his initials J.B.O. He claims to own the copyright but it's unlikely that he has enjoyed much financial benefit from this arrangement for Joe Brown's reputation is legendary among Chicago's bluesmen. Joe himself, born 16 June 1897, claims to be a Cherokee Indian from Oklahoma and his features and dyed-black hair certainly don't belie the possibility. But with his mischievous, self-deprecating sense of humour it's hard to tell whether he's joking or not. One thing that is certain is his nervousness over his reputation. 'Most of the boys are sore at me,' he wails. 'The records made money but I didn't.' He doesn't *look* wealthy, or even comfortable, but against his shabby appearance must be counted his proud boast that he's never had to work! There is a story that Sunnyland Slim used his own car to sell his J.O.B. records on the streets but still didn't get paid for the sessions. Eventually Slim took Joe before the union but Brown was able to prove that all contracts had been lodged with Local 208 and union scale had been paid. All this despite the union's files having been destroyed. Joe now has an affidavit, signed by one of the officials at

J.O.B.'s joint proprietor, St Louis Jimmy, and an early release.

JOB RECORDS

102-B   JB 3278 -4

SUNNYLAND SPECIAL
(Luon Drew)
Instrumental
SUNNYLAND SLIM
AND HIS TRIO

The first *J.O.B.; and one of the label's later hitmakers, J.B. Lenoir.*

the time, that everything was above board. Obviously Joe has friends at
the union but in all fairness contracts exist for some sessions at least. Later
on Joe Brown set up Lawn Music Publishers with a white partner Bud
Brandon, and Brandon, with offices on S. Michigan Avenue, seems to
handle much of Joe's business now.

Joe Brown's good nose for business was surpassed only by his good ear
for music and of all the Chicago R & B labels that achieved any degree of
permanence the greatest proportion of good blues was to be found on
J.O.B.—probably because Brown would record anybody, as long as they
put up the money! Its early days were as chaotic as any of the others',
with frequent gaps and duplications of numbers in the 100 series. The
label's first issue, by the obscure Stick Horse Hammond, was of a crudity
unusual even by blues recording standards. It was a thick shellac disc with,
instead of master numbers, the titles inscribed in the wax and the labels
hand-printed. The appearance of the record was less primitive only than
the music. Hammond was probably a Shreveport, Louisiana, singer, and
that he should crop up on a Chicago label is very curious. It may be that
this issue was an even earlier attempt by Joe Brown at launching a record
label, and the disc may only have been sold in the South; but,
characteristically, Joe remembers nothing about record or artist.

Another J.O.B. 100 was released, the previously-mentioned Baby Face
Leroy, which with the blue background and silver lettering looked more
like a record. It was later reissued by Chess. The only St Louis Jimmy issue
(J.O.B. 101) had the same number as a Snooky Pryor record, and was cut
at United Broadcasting's studio, 301 E. Erie St, on 26 August 1949. Later

Joe Brown was to use just about every studio in Chicago: RCA Victor, M.B.S., Modern (at 55 W. Wacker Drive), Webb, Sonic, Globe, Mills and Universal among them.

Releases in the 100 series had only just reached double figures by about 1951, when the 1000 series was started with Floyd Jones's celebrated *Dark Road*. The colour of the label later changed to yellow and, some time after, around 1954, a third and last series, the 1100, was started. The main artists were Sunnyland Slim, Snooky Pryor, Eddie Boyd and J. B. Lenoir. Sunnyland Slim had four records (five counting a reissue) and two others where he backed Baby Face and the drummer Alfred 'Fat Man' Wallace. Slim was the house pianist for the label, accompanying John and Grace Brim, Lenoir and Pryor.

'I Could Holler Loud And Keep A Crowd'

Slim's own J.O.B. sides are not very interesting, as they are usually instrumentals or mediocre jump blues, while his standard blues like *Down Home Child* (J.O.B. 102) generally show too little imagination or variation. He sings in a stentorian voice which is a legacy of his schooling in the roughest and loudest juke-joints of Mississippi. As he says, 'I could holler loud and keep a crowd.' Slim was born Albert Luandrew in Vance, Mississippi, on 5 September 1907 into the usual farming background, though his father, the Reverend Thomas Walter Luandrew, was a part-time preacher. His hard early years when he was raised by a stepmother made a deep impression on the huge, melancholy but kindly man. After a chance encounter with a church organ came a realisation that music afforded an escape from a life of ploughing and Slim started hanging around the local jukes of Lambert, Tutwiler and Clarksdale learning piano. Then at the age of seventeen came his first job as accompanist to the silent films at a

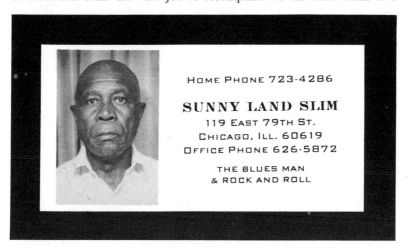

HOME PHONE 723-4286

SUNNY LAND SLIM
119 EAST 79TH ST.
CHICAGO, ILL. 60619
OFFICE PHONE 626-5872

THE BLUES MAN
& ROCK AND ROLL

cinema in Lambert for a few dollars, and soon after he moved to Memphis where he stayed for the next fifteen years. There he played on Beale Street.

> Beale Street was real tough in them days. There were some real rough joints: one at the Panama, and at the Harlem Night Club—that's at South Memphis at 1128 Florida. And then too the Goshorn Quarters was another we had. Down at 4th and Beale, Pee Wee's had one open. The Hole In The Wall, that was a rough joint. I used to make all them joints and there was no closin' at that time.

It was in Memphis that he first met Sonny Boy Williamson and Doctor Clayton and in Chicago they all hung round Sunnyland's house at 216 E. 31st. Clayton is very much a mystery man. A very distinctive singer and fine song-writer, he totally neglected himself and went to pieces after a train killed his wife and two children. Sunnyland recalls,

> So Doc wanted to muscle up with us. We didn't want Doc 'cause Doc would get drunk. They had to dress him up, put nice clothes on him; he'd get drunk and be found in his white suit lying in the snow. So finally we did get a guitar player, Baby Face Leroy, and we started cuttin' in the clubs. In 1946 we was playing the 21 Club, then we go right out there to another sporting house and we get $10 each. We start 9.30 till little before 1 or 2 . . . then we leave there go to Kenny Lester's and we go to her house, me and Sonny Boy and Leroy. We'd end up with $25-30.

This was the year that Dr Clayton died and RCA were looking around for someone who could copy his style. In December 1947 Sunnyland cut his first sessions as Doctor Clayton's Buddy. He had moved into Tampa Red's old basement at 2720 E. 31st and they used it for rehearsals. With two pianos and three large rooms there was always a session going on and Sunnyland supplemented his income by selling a little beer and whiskey on the side.

Next came the Aristocrat sessions and a host of records for independent labels. Sunnyland is one of the most recorded of all the Chicago artists and that his name appears on thirteen different labels up to the '60s shows his indefatigable energy and hustling ability even if it hasn't brought him any great success. As an accompanist he has played on countless other sessions and it's as an accompanist that he has produced his best work. On the Lenoir sessions he played superb swinging piano of a quality that, sadly, he seems to reserve for other people's records. He also provides a fine Maceo-like accompaniment to Baby Face's *Louella* (J.O.B 1002), while on the bouncy *Let's Roll* (J.O.B. 112), Lenoir's first J.O.B. record, he brilliantly complements J.B.'s rocking guitar.

Lenoir was one of the most distinctive artists—his youthful, high-pitched voice and supple swinging guitar were irresistible on up-tempo numbers. These he alternated with the slow, dragging blues on which he sang so movingly. More than any other bluesman he refutes the criticism

Red Nelson and Sunnyland Slim, 1959.

voiced by Texas singer Lightnin' Hopkins, that the Chicago men could only sing about women. Certainly one of the differences between the early singers, who were always ready to comment on current topics, and the postwar inheritors of the tradition was the dwindling range of experiences covered by the latter-day singers. Their subject matter was seriously circumscribed and almost wholly to do with women and love; the new breed of bluesmen became increasingly inward-looking and less concerned with the totality of experience. This may have been another consequence of the overwhelming move from the country to the cities, or it may have resulted from the change in structure of the record industry, in which sessions were organised casually or haphazardly (at first, anyway) with little overall direction by the record company owners. Probably the white recording directors suggested themes to the earlier singers, while the new black recording men, who often shared the backgrounds of the singers themselves, were content to let the bluesmen record what they liked or, working within a very limited budget, concentrated on what were obviously the most popular themes, unrequited love and sex. Whatever the reasons there were fewer songs of an overt social significance or topicality from the new singers, with notable exceptions. Floyd Jones is an example and so too was J. B. Lenoir and from J.B.'s very first session (recorded for J.O.B. but leased to Chess) *Korea Blues* (Chess 1449) gives an indication of

Two of the Chicago blues' foremost songwriters, J.B. Lenoir (left) *and Johnny Shines.*

the wider range of themes that he was to employ throughout his recording career:

> Lord I got my questionnaire, Uncle Sam goin' send me
> away from here (x2)
> He said J.B. you know that I need you, Lord, I need you
> in South Korea
>
> Sweetheart please don't worry, just begin to fly in the air (x2)
> Now the Chinese shoot me down, Lord I'll be in Korea somewhere.

From the same session *Deep in Debt Blues* (Chess 1463) provides further evidence of his thoughtful lyrics:

> I'm deep in debt, baby, look at the bills I got to pay (x2)
> Sweetheart if you and I were together look at the money
> we would save.

For his later J.O.B. sessions in 1953 saxophonist J. T. Brown was added and the combination put down some of the most infectious, rocking blues of the '50s. *The Mojo* (J.O.B. 1012) was outstanding, with Lenoir's boogie riffs, Sunnyland's tinkling piano and Brown's diamond-hard, distinctive sax. Early in his career J.B. developed an exciting stage act, and listening to *The Mojo* it's easy to picture him in his leopard-skin coat bobbing and weaving about the floor.

It was all a long way from the farm in Monticello, Mississippi, where he was born on 5 March 1929. His father, mother and brother played guitar and J.B. learned at a very early age. His song *The Mojo* may have been a memory of his visit to New Orleans in 1944 when he met Sonny Boy Williamson (Rice Miller) and Elmore James and sat in with them at the New York Inn on Rampart Street. He was determined to leave Mississippi and was typically forthright about it:

> The way they do's you down there in Mississippi it ain't what a man should suffer, what a man should go through. And I said, after I seen the way they treat my daddy I never was goin' to stand that no kind of way. So I just worked as hard as I could for to get that money to get away . . .

He did get away to Chicago in 1949 and worked at Swift's meat-packing factory while waiting his chance. Once again Big Bill, who was playing at Sylvio's on Lake Street, was the one to introduce him to Chicago's blues scene, and after playing with Bill for a while he met Memphis Minnie at Gatewood's and Muddy at the Du Drop Inn. Soon afterwards J.B. got his start and his friendly nature and bubbling personality quickly established his popularity.

J.B. was to go on to sing about politics, taxes and the Korean War again, as well as comment on the situation of his people—there was even one song about the hair-straightening process—but his blues were interesting for their themes rather than for any poetic imagery in his lyrics. And this was generally true of most of the singers in this early creative phase—the poetry was to be found in the music. But occasionally singers did appear who could rivet the listener's attention with a well-turned phrase of more than usual imaginativeness. One such artist was Johnny Shines, who in a brilliant record for Joe Brown, *Brutal Hearted Woman* (J.O.B. 1010), sang the memorable verse:

> I remember when we first met one Friday in the afternoon (x2)
> You said if I wanted your love darling, I'd have to wring the
> silver out of the moon.

Shines was accompanied by his longtime Memphis associate Big Walter Horton, who blew such superb harmonica as to establish his position in the front rank of Chicago's harp players. The reverse, *Evening Sun*, is virtually a showcase for Big Walter's harp, which he blows in long, swooping phrases of a flawless beauty. Shines's first record for J.O.B. is perhaps the most remarkable of all. With Big Moody Jones on bass, *Ramblin'* (J.O.B. 116) is the definitive recreation of Robert Johnson's *Walkin' Blues*, the searing bottleneck guitar and impassioned vocal making it one of the masterpieces of Chicago blues. Johnson's influence on Shines's guitar style was profound and a direct result of their association in the late '30s. Shines first met Robert in Helena, Arkansas, and they eventually teamed up in 1936 or '37, playing through Tennessee, Missouri and Arkansas. Johnny stayed close to Robert to learn his style, just as he had hung round Howlin' Wolf a few years earlier. Born into a family with some musical tradition in Frazier, Tennessee (a suburb of Memphis), on 25 April 1915, Johnny was 17 years old before he took up the guitar. His influences were at first the records of Blind Lemon Jefferson, Lonnie Johnson, Scrapper Blackwell and Charley Patton, but mainly he followed Wolf, trying to learn his style. By 1933-4 he had mastered enough guitar to play semi-professionally round Memphis, meeting such singers as Little Buddy Doyle, Allen Shaw and Willie Tango. But his association with Robert Johnson was to be the most fruitful.

Johnny moved to Chicago on 25 September 1941 and soon entered the club scene, playing his first date at Frost's Corner that same year. He was never really a professional for he was working at a day job and playing music only in the evenings and weekends. Occasionally he would get a band together and work the out-of-town clubs like the Apex Chateau at Robbins, Illinois, and in the Wisconsin border towns; he held one five-piece band together from about 1943 to 1945. Lester Melrose recorded him for Columbia in 1946 but the session remained unissued until 1971. The sides have an engaging Delta roughness, but feature no bottleneck guitar, and lack the brilliance of his later records. His next record came when Jimmy Rogers took him along to Chess and, as Shoe Shine Johnny, he recorded on the spot on 23 October 1950, with the alumni of Muddy's group. These are very powerful sides. Again he surprises in his choice of lyrics, *So Glad I Found You* contains the line

Baby you have been to college, now holding three degrees

but he completes the verse typically:

Come with me out to my cabin and teach them things to me.

Lonnie Johnson was the major influence on Shines's vocal style and there are echoes of Johnson in Johnny's incredibly loud, fruity singing and the overlong holding of the last note of each line. Jimmy Rogers played guitar, since Johnny's talents in anything but bottleneck style are limited, but the record was not issued, as Chess explained to Johnny: 'I've got one out on Muddy [i.e. *Louisiana Blues*] and it would kill the sales on it'. If this was the reason (which is doubtful, as Chess was keen to record other artists to compete with Muddy) then it's strange that it wasn't released a few months later. It's even more strange that Len Chess, recognising Muddy's slide-guitar as being his main selling point, didn't promote Shines as a bottleneck stylist. Had he done so, Johnny's recording career might have taken a turn for the better. As it was the two J.O.B. records appeared, Johnny accompanied Snooky Pryor, Homesick James and Arbee Stidham on some sides, and then his brief recording career was terminated through a disagreement with the powerful Al Benson. Johnny played music occasionally, after his daytime construction job, until 1958, when, thoroughly disenchanted with the music business, he retired.

Shines is a huge man with a natural dignity, and his serious, almost philosophical nature commands respect. One of the most articulate and intelligent of bluesmen, he has built up a reputation as a gifted composer and he claims he has recorded an as yet untraced *Eisenhower Blues* which is a bitter parody of the 23rd Psalm:

> Ike is my shepherd, I am in want.
> He makes me to lie down on park benches
> I used to ride in a Cadillac but now I don't.

Other fine artists whom J.O.B. was to introduce to a Chicago audience were the Kentucky singer John Brim and his wife Grace. John played guitar, Grace played drums and harmonica, and they both sang. Sunnyland Slim was the pianist on the J.O.B. sides and they are nice examples of Brim's earlier Broonzyish style, *Drinkin' Woman* (J.O.B. 1011) especially.

The three early Snooky Pryor records for Joe Brown were excellent, with *Crying Shame* and *Eighty Nine Ten* (J.O.B. 1014) from early 1953 outstanding. Both are classic blues based on traditional material:

> Eighty Nine Ten runs right by my baby's door (x2)
> Yes, I aint goin' down, down Eighty Nine Ten no more

and

> It's a pity, baby, I declare it's a crying shame (x2)
> Yes, you know I killed my woman 'cause she was loving another man

> Yes, I got a burden, I really can't hardly bear (x2)
> Yes, I'm goin' to the county jail, I may get the electric chair.

Once again there is an almost perfect unity of Pryor's voice and harmonica and Eddie Taylor's guitar. *Going Back On The Road* (J.O.B. 115) is interesting for its use of the *Dust My Broom* theme with Moody Jones imitating the traditional slide patterns but picking with only his fingers. Another of Pryor's close friends, Floyd Jones, also appeared on J.O.B., with the first version of his classic *Dark Road* (J.O.B. 1001). The first verse is derived from Tommy Johnson's *Big Road Blues* but Floyd turns it into a chilling masterpiece all his own; the piano and guitars create a dark, brooding atmosphere accentuated by Floyd's falsetto whoops and moans at the beginning and end of each line, the whole performance evoking the eldritch loneliness of being stranded at night on a Mississippi highway.

> Well I can't go down
> This dark road by myself, dark road by myself
> Gonna be early in the morning, it's gonna be early in the morning
> Goin' carry somebody else.

> Well my mother died and left me
> Oh when I was quite young, when I was quite young
> Said Lord have mercy, said Lord have mercy
> On my wicked son

> Well stop the train conductor
> Conductor let me ride, let the poor boy ride
> Say you have to buy your ticket, say you have to buy your ticket
> Son the train ain't none of mine
>
> Well I started walking
> Down this lonesome road
> Now don't you hear me crying
> I started walking down the long old lonesome road
> Gonna be early in the morning
> Boy you'll see me go.

Transcription cannot do justice to this, one of the great experiences of the Chicago blues.

Rough Treatment

When asked about Joe Brown, Floyd recalls:

> Every stuff I made I didn't get any results, I can tell you that. I said, 'Look, man, what about the copyright?' He said, 'Well, I'll copyright it and it'll come back to you.'

Dark Road was popular enough for Chess to record it when Floyd fell out with Joe Brown. This time Floyd did get some results:

> Let me tell you truly I got a dollar and 27 cents from Arc Music out of all those years and it stayed in Jew Town on the juke-box all around there for six years. I know this number sold and I never did get anything for it.

Still trying, in 1953, back with J.O.B. he recorded the sequel, *On The Road Again* (J.O.B. 1013), which took up where he'd left off:

> Well, kinda worried and crying, boys, I'm out on the road again.

Moody was still playing the big bass on Floyd's records. They had been

together regularly since about 1944—with Snooky Pryor at Club Jamboree in South Chicago, and at a bowling alley in East Chicago, Indiana, where they held the gig long enough to get a paid vacation. Other clubs were the Millgate by the railroad tracks near 112th Street and on the West Side at 1601 W. Lake with Johnny Young, Johnny Williams and drummer Jimmy Robinson.

Moody rarely sang but he did write one song which he cut for Joe Brown on 28 April 1952. Brown didn't seem interested and Moody forgot all about it, until guitarist Hudson Showers recorded it for Joe Brown around August 1953. *Rough Treatment* (J.O.B. 1014) was a superb song and Hudson's young-sounding voice made the not uncommon theme of a mean stepfather all the more affecting.

> My stepfather treat me so mean, he made my mother get on her knees
> She said if you hit my son again, I'm goin' have to call the police
> I had rough treatment from a baby up until this ole very day
> I had to do the things I didn't wanna, just to have a place to stay.

The one significant thing that Joe Brown's artists had in common was their lack of commercial success. This is in fact the story of all the singers recording for the small independents. Their shoestring budgets meant that the only artists available were the new ones or others who had been dropped by the bigger companies. (United Records began in 1951 with Roosevelt Sykes and Robert Nighthawk.) So, working with new or rejected talent, a small record company would persist in the hope of the elusive big hit. If it came, the company would establish itself or, more likely, the big selling artist would be snapped up by one of the bigger companies. Big fish eat little fish! Joe Brown's moment of glory came with Eddie Boyd's *Five Long Years* (J.O.B. 1007) which was a tremendous hit and reached the top of the national R & B Charts in 1952.

> Well if you've ever been mistreated
> You know just what I'm talking about
> I worked five long years for one woman
> She had the nerve to put me out.
>
> I got a job in a steel mill
> Truckin' steel like a slave
> For five long years every Friday
> I went straight home with all my pay
> Well if you've ever been mistreated . . . [etc.]

Eddie Boyd had worked in a steel-mill since the end of his RCA Victor recordings in 1949 and he tells a confused story of how he recorded *Five Long Years:*

Left: *mural advertisement for the Club Flamingo.* Over page: *a West Side panorama, 1960. The view is along West Lake, looking towards Desplaines and Halsted.*

I rented a studio, paid for my own time and I went in there and cut this session and Joe Brown asked me to let him have it. I didn't want to fool with him. So I said, 'Look if you're not gonna exploit the record I done leased this master to you under these conditions. If you don't have it rollin' within three weeks I take it back from you'. So he said he'd do it but he didn't! So I went to him and said, 'Man, you ain't getting no action, I want my master.' He says, 'Well, Art Sheridan wants the master, all right?' I said it's not all right, 'cause this is my material and it belongs to me and I owns the copyright. So we went to see Art. See I knew Art needed a record 'cause the last thing he had was the Five Chances [Eddie is in error if he's referring here to the Five Chances record on Chance 1139, for this wasn't issued until August 1954, two years later] and that thing was dying; he appreciated this and he pushed the record.

Joe's version of events differs, naturally, but his recollections of the session are vivid enough. Boyd was playing a gig at the Harmonia Hotel at 30th and Indiana when he called Joe up wanting to record, and they cut *Five Long Years* that same night, 19 June 1952. Incidentally, Joe wasn't satisfied with the sound, and had it mastered three times.

Considering the way Sheridan seems to have taken over, it appears that Joe Brown, far from losing his chief artist, never had him in the first place!

After a disagreement with Sheridan Boyd signed a contract with Al Benson, who sold it to Chess. The result was thus the same: Chess acquired another top-selling artist. Joe Brown reissued an earlier Boyd recording, from June 1951, to cash in on *Five Long Years*, but neither J.O.B. nor Boyd was ever to repeat the success.

Joe Brown continued to release records on J.O.B. at irregular intervals through the '50s and '60s, and even now is negotiating the release of his unissued material. The tapes are mostly in bad condition, unfortunately, because Joe continues to play them on his home recorder, but much of the music is beautiful. Included are Otis Spann's first session, with J. T. Brown: *T-99, I'm Just A Lonely Man, The Bible's Right* and an instrumental, *L.A. Midnight Groove*; Baby Face Leroy's last session, *Late Hours At Midnight* and the prophetic *Blues Is Killin' Me;* Memphis Minnie's last session, *In Love Again* and *What A Night;* the unknown artists Harry Brooks and Percy Parham in *Black Mare;* and many fine titles by Floyd Jones, John Brim, Snooky Pryor and Johnny Shines.

Boyd's explanation of the wheeling and dealing behind the scenes is particularly illuminating about the problems of the small independent record producer and also about the tangled nature of the alliances between the record men. Joe Brown had what was potentially a very big record but none of the resources to exploit it. Sheridan, owner of a plastics pressing plant and his own label, Chance Records, was also a distributor. His factory probably pressed the disc but it was his function as a distributor and thus his ability to promote the record that was crucial. In this he was helped by Bill Simmonds, a DJ with WDIA in Memphis, and latterly of Sun Records, who broke the record in the South. Small wonder then that Eddie refers to it almost as if it was Sheridan's record. Probably to all intents and purposes it was, in everything but the label name, and this, coupled with the freelance nature of Boyd's recording, explains why Joe Brown was never able to establish his J.O.B. label.

One label that did establish itself quickly was United Records of 5052 S. Cottage Grove, which was started on 25 August 1951 by Lewis 'Lou' Simpkins and his partner Leonard Allen. Robert Nighthawk had two releases but success came early from their city artists, with hits by the Four Blazers and especially Jimmy Forrest. When his *Night Train* (United 110) topped the National R & B charts in 1952, United quickly forgot Nighthawk and took no further interest in the downhome styles until their States subsidiary was started.

But what of Art Sheridan? He was probably better placed than anyone to set up as an independent record producer. Operator of Armour Plastics and American Record Distributing and with a franchise to record, Sheridan was to tie up his twin interests through his own label.

'He Took A Chance And . . .'

The formation of Chance Records with an address at 2011 S. Michigan Avenue was announced in December 1950 and the first sessions were cut, with Sheridan's blessing, by a local real-estate man, Steve Chandler. The first issued sides, by John 'Schoolboy' Porter, caused a lot of trouble for Sheridan with the Musicians Union, which claimed that the sidemen were not union members, and his recording licence was revoked. The problems must have been sorted out, for Chance Records pushed ahead slowly with about 30 releases in their first two years. Of these five were gospel, six were downhome blues and the remainder R & B or jazz. Oddly enough the first of the new country blues artists to appear on Chance was the Detroit-based John Lee Hooker, who had three astonishingly crude issues, but the first Chicago bluesmen on Chance were the mysterious Delta Joe (probably Sunnyland Slim) (1115) and Little Walter (1116). The Little Walter was a reissue of the Ora-Nelle record and was obviously released in an attempt to cash in on the huge success that Walter was enjoying with Checker. This would date it fairly firmly to 1952. As the Delta Joe may have been bought from the obscure Opera label (which had another issue by Delta Joe from the same session and a St Louis Jimmy record) it seems probable that Chance's first Chicago blues session was by Homesick James.

'I Was Always A Drifter'

Homesick was born not James Williamson but John William Henderson, son of Mary Cordelia Henderson and Pluz Williamson, on 30 April 1910 in Somerville, Tennessee. Pluz played drums but it was his mother's guitar—and in particular her playing of *John Henry* with a pocket-knife across the strings—that inspired the young boy. Not that she gave him any encouragement, quite the reverse; when he first started to learn the instrument at about nine or ten years old it was to a neighbour, Tommy Johnson, that Homesick turned. This was not the great Mississippi Tommy Johnson but a farmer whose 'real name' was Red Howell. (In Homesick's story everyone seems to enjoy the advantage of more than one name—he has a brother, 'real name' Robert MacNeil, a distant cousin Elmore James was really Elmore Brooks and Elmore's father, Joe Willie James, was known as Frost James!) At the age of 12 Homesick ran away from home, successfully avoiding the attentions of his parents for the next eight or nine years. He moved throughout Tennessee, meeting Sleepy John Estes in Brownsville and playing with Yank Rachell and Sonny Boy, with whom he had grown up. Sonny Boy was reputedly a cousin and considering Homesick's tangled family tree it's quite possible.

In North Carolina for a brief spell he met Blind Boy Fuller and in Mississippi he met Howlin' Wolf, Floyd Jones and Johnny Shines. Homesick explained his wanderings:

> I was just playing and singing then. I didn't work, no sir! With that hot sun out there in them fields I wasn't going to stay out there and get baked. That's the reason I left home. That's why I played the guitar!

Centre: *Sue, co-proprietor of Andrew and Sue's Lounge, W. Van Buren.*
Right: *Homesick James.*

In Memphis he teamed up with another guitarist, Little Buddy Doyle, and
harmonica-player Walter Horton:

> They used to have a lot of difficulty with me . . . every week I'd be
> pawning my guitar and they'd have to get it out—Big Walter had to
> get it out, if he didn't Buddy Doyle had to get it out. I used to play
> picnics up at Oakland, Tennessee, that's where we used to work at
> all the time. Y'know the big days work would be at the picnics.
> Walter, Buddy, Frank Stokes, Jack Kelly, all us used to work right in
> the same area for many years.

Little Buddy Doyle made two fine sessions for Vocalion in 1939 and
Homesick claimed he accompanied him, with Big Walter Horton. He
remembered cutting two songs at one of the sessions, *Whiskey Headed
Woman* and *Bad Luck Blues*, which were never released. They were
probably recorded while Homesick had returned to see his mother for he
had been living in Chicago for a couple of years, moving there with Sonny
Boy. He frequently played with Sonny Boy, who didn't have a regular
group, and in 1945 or '46 they played at the Purple Cat, 2113 W. Madison,
with Big Bill and Lazy Bill Lucas. With friends like Bill Broonzy, Sonny
Boy and Lonnie Johnson, Homesick might have expected to see his name
on a record label earlier than he did. But he had to wait until 1951 when
Joe Brown took him along to Art Sheridan. At the first session two
numbers were recorded at the old RCA Victor studio, 230 S. Michigan,

Lonesome Ole Train (Chance 1121), a song he'd learnt from his old neighbour Tommy Johnson, and *Farmers Blues.* Lazy Bill played piano and Alfred Elkins played bass but the record hardly did Homesick justice, showing all too clearly his problems with his timing; on *Farmers Blues* his stunning bottleneck guitar solo is cut off dead as he comes in too early with the last verse. Homesick was working regularly at the clubs at this time with Lazy Bill and Porkchop (Eddie Hines), an old associate from medicine shows down in Brownsville, Tennessee, in the '30s. He played at the 1015 Club on Madison, and at Abraham Ross's Club Jamboree, 3328 E. 90th at Mackinaw, he worked in groups that included Baby Face Leroy, Snooky Pryor, Floyd Jones, Lazy Bill, Alfred Elkins and Little Willie Foster. There was another unissued session, with Snooky Pryor, for Chance and then from his third session came the record that gave him his name, *Homesick* (1131): 'Lazy Bill called me Homesick—I wasn't though!' But the record sold and the name stuck. It was a much better record than his first—although his singing was high and strained in the manner of his later records, his bottleneck guitar had that compound of mellifluous grace and power that characterises his work. The reverse, *The Woman I Love*, used the *Little School Girl* melody and had Johnny Shines playing second guitar.

'Cover Up The Devil'

Lazy Bill, who played pounding piano on these sides, also had a record for Chance. There was nothing fancy about Bill's playing; he was just a good solid piano man who deserves to be better known. He came from Wynne or Caldwell, Arkansas, where he was born on 29 May 1918 into a poor farming family. His first instrument was a guitar, obtained by his father:

> I remember so well just like it was yesterday, he traded a pig for it. Money was scarce down there, we didn't have no money. The boy wanted seven dollars for it—we didn't have no money but we had plenty of pigs.

This was in 1930 and then two years later:

> He got me a piano in 1932 for a Christmas present. That was the happiest Christmas I ever had.

The piano was left behind when the family moved to Cape Girardeau, Missouri, and Bill didn't play piano again until he came to Chicago. Unlike Homesick, and all the other itinerant musicians, whose wanderings have earned them a permanent niche in blues legend, Bill was isolated from the living blues tradition and it wasn't until he met Big Joe Williams in St Louis that he had any contact with other musicians. Bill had been playing hillbilly music on the streets of Cape Girardeau and Big Joe was the first bluesman he ever met. It's from this meeting that Bill's blues career dates. He came to Chicago in 1941 and quickly established himself with the

Above: *Lazy Bill Lucas, Willie Nix.*

famous artists of the day. He played guitar with Sonny Boy Williamson on gigs at places like Battle Creek and South Bend, Indiana, and met Big Bill, Curtis Jones, Roosevelt Sykes and Lonnie Johnson. Little Walter had a room in Bill's father's house and Bill and Walter played together on Maxwell Street. Talking about the '40s in Chicago Bill hints at the gradual change as the new generation of bluesmen got a toe-hold on the Chicago blues scene:

> All the big clubs was folding up—all the old-timers left. I don't know why they [the clubs] wasn't making money then; it was wartime, long about 1945 or 1946 they was closing up, but yeah, money was kinda plentiful in 1945 I thought.

This is the first hint we have of a depression in the Chicago club scene of the time and it closely parallels the decline in blues recording activity of the major companies. Clearly the older blues singers were being squeezed out as the newer jump blues took over the big clubs and the smaller clubs found a wealth of semi-professional blues talent on their doorsteps ready and willing to play for $12 a night. Lazy Bill's first job, as a guitarist, was for such a club:

> We all joined the union together, me and Willie Mabon and Earl Dranes too, two guitars and a piano, no drums, no nothing. We took our first job in 1946 on December 20th. That was in the Tuxedo Lounge, 3119 Indiana . . . it was a real nice club, no dancing. You just sit down and drink. Those after hours clubs always had good crowds 'cause after two o'clock everybody would come to the Tuxedo Lounge.

Bill switched to piano and as a result didn't play with one group all the time because of the greater demand for piano players. Mabon and Dranes formed the Blues Rockers (and recorded the Aristocrat and Chess sides) and in 1948 Bill played with Little Hudson's Red Devils. Bill had met Hudson earlier and encouraged him to sit in with him and Sonny Boy or Willie Mabon. The Red Devils played at the Plantation with Hudson Showers on guitar, Bill on piano and James Bannister on drums.

> The drummer had a red devil on the head of his drum, with pitchforks. He did play in church too. Would you believe they had to cover the devil up with newspapers . . . he cover up the devil when he go to church!

Perhaps remembering his stint with the Red Devils, on his Chance record Bill sang Sylvester Weaver's *Devil Blues* as *I Had a Dream* (Chance 1148):

> I had a dream I was sleeping, found myself way down below (x2)
> I couldn't get to Heaven, you know the place I had to go.

Most dream songs are modelled on Broonzy's and are delivered in a self-mocking, sardonic way, but this turns into an outrageous piece of slapstick:

> The devil had me cornered, stuck me with his old pitch-fork (x2)
> He put me in an oven, he had me for roast pork.

Even on the reverse, *She Got Me Walking*, Bill couldn't resist in a puckish moment introducing his friends into the song:

> I don't want to see Snook, not even Homesick James
> The way my baby left me, I really believe he's to blame.

Snooky and Homesick were not on the session, though; Bill's backing musicians, the Blue Rhythms, were Muddy's drummer Elgin and guitarist Louis Myers, hastily recruited after Len Chess had prevented Muddy himself from making the session. The record wasn't very successful and Bill found difficulty in getting work like other bluesmen. He suffers from a nervous affliction and as a result is nearly blind; because of this, Homesick has said, people didn't want to hire him. Today this sincere and kindly man lives in Minneapolis on a Government disability grant, eking out his meagre pension playing a few nights a month.

Other Chances

Chance's companion label, Sabre, started about August 1953 but releases were only sporadic. The first (100) was a pseudonymous Tampa Red (as the Jimmy Eager Trio) but the best blues issue was by Willie Nix (104) *Just Can't Stay* was a semi-talking blues which used the old Mississippi *Catfish* theme, but the lyrics were pure Chicago:

> Here I is again
> Standing on the corner 47th South Parkway
> I walked up to the little girl
> Said 'Can I have a word?'
> She said 'You can't do the things that you used to do
> Because I have a job making much money as you do'
> I said 'I'm so sorry dear
> Getting up seven o'clock going them job
> Will wear your little fine self out . . .'

Between the sung verses the jive continues:

> You know man I was walking on the corner 31st and Giles
> I walked into a tavern, guess who I see
> Same little girl
> I said 'Can I talk a little trash?'
> She said, 'Talk a little trash at me if you have to spend
>   some cash'
> I said 'What you mean?'
> She said, 'This is one thing that's for sure
> Put something on the bar 'scusing your elbows . . .'

The insistent guitar was played by Eddie Taylor, probably Willie Foster played harp, Sunnyland played piano and the whole record was pushed along by the tightest drummer in the business, Nix himself. The record was a brilliant updating of a traditional theme of unrequited love to the urban setting with its images of hustlers, whores and easy money. Nix was 30 years old and hadn't long arrived in Chicago from his native Memphis. Tall and thin, with an astonishing facial resemblance to his fellow Memphian Walter Horton, Nix sang in a warm, insinuating voice. Sam Phillips had recorded him for his Sun label (billing him 'The Memphis Blues Boy') and he had had records released on Modern and Checker, but this lone Chicago session was probably his best. The other coupling was issued on Chance 1163. The sound was very much like the Muddy Waters group and Nix was actually filling in for Muddy at Smitty's Corner, 35th and Indiana, one night a week when Muddy was playing in Gary, Indiana. Willie's big chance came in 1958 when Muddy and Otis Spann toured England:

> I had Smitty's to myself then, and I really packed 'em in! But it's been a bit tough of late. You know I lost that job, played a few clubs on Wentworth and Rush and Lake—did the rounds.

In 1960 he was seen in Monroe, Louisiana hoping to hop a freight to Bakersfield, California, in time for the pea crops, but he now lives in Memphis.

Sheridan seemed to take longer to learn about the blues than the Chess brothers; the earlier items on the label were crude in comparison with the Chess material of the same time. A case in point is Big Boy Spires, whose contract Sheridan had picked up after Spires had been dropped by Chess. His one record for Checker, *Murmur Low* (752), was a beautiful, classic performance with rippling guitars, whereas the Chance record was clumsy and pedestrian. Perhaps Chance Records was for Sheridan a part-time interest, for there is little evidence that Art or his general manager Ewart Abner took anything like the·pains that Len Chess did with his blues artists. Or maybe Sheridan was more interested in the vocal groups that were beginning to make a big impact on the R & B scene, for releases by groups like The Flamingos or The Moonglows outnumbered their blues issues.

The years 1953 and 1954 were good years for the blues in Chicago. By then the 'classic' style pioneered by Muddy Waters and others was well established and the Chess artists were making an impression in the National record charts whereas before their success had been mainly locally. Fired by the success of Muddy and Little Walter the other record producers in the city began to look around for bluesmen to record, and this bandwagon effect is well illustrated by the sudden representation of the new country blues in their catalogues for these years. Even United was inspired to record Robert Nighthawk again for its States subsidiary (which began on 24 May 1952). This change of policy was probably instituted by Leonard Allen after the death of Lou Simpkins in May 1953 at the age of 35; within a period of 18 months from mid-1953 to the end of 1954 States had recorded Nighthawk and the new names Junior Wells, James Bannister and Big Walter Horton.

New companies entered the field too, Al Benson started Parrot Records in 1953 while in the summer of 1953 Chance released a session cut for the newly formed VJ company. One record was by the vocal group The Spaniels and it entered the National Top Ten; the other historic release was Jimmy Reed's first record.

The Hawk's Biting

By the mid '50s almost a new generation of bluesmen was in action—artists whose musical background spanned only a few years and whose entire musical upbringing had been in the clubs of Chicago, their mentors such musicians as Muddy Waters and Elmore James. Such an artist was Joseph
● Benjamin Hutto, born in Blackville, South Carolina, 26 April 1926, the fifth of seven children born to Calvin and Susie Hutto. They were a farming family with a strong religious background—Calvin was a preacher—and the children, four boys and three girls, formed a gospel group, The Golden Crowns. When the family moved to Augusta, Georgia, they sang in the local Galilee Baptist and Holy Trinity Churches.

After his father died in 1949 J.B.'s mother took the family to Chicago on receiving glowing reports from her eldest son, who was working as a chef on the Milwaukee Railroad. They settled on the West Side, on Lake Street, and J.B. quickly got a job as a painter and plumber and in the evenings hung around the clubs. First he tried drums and played with Johnny Ferguson and his Twisters at Red's Lounge, Damen and Madison, and then he tried the piano. Finally settling for guitar, he met Porkchop in Jew Town and they played together on the streets.

Adding another guitarist, Joe Custom, they landed their first gig at the 1015 Club where George Maywether sat in on harp one night and then joined the band. The job lasted about seven or eight months but the manager Blake 'was a drinkin' man and he didn't keep the club going,' and they moved to the Globetrotter Lounge on the corner of Damen and Madison, just a few doors from where the Twisters had played. It was at the Globetrotter that Art Sheridan's talent scout (possibly Ewart Abner) had sounded him out about recording. J.B. signed a two-year contract and one night they went down to the Chess studios on Cottage Grove and cut his first session.

The label on the record proclaimed 'J.B. and his Hawks'.

> The Hawk's the wind in Chicago and when it blows it's cool! You say to somebody, 'You coming out?' and they say, 'No man, the Hawk's biting tonight.'

And J.B. blew upon the Chicago scene with one of the noisiest and toughest bands ever. Singing in the fierce, declamatory style of his idol, Elmore, and backed by the heavily amplified guitar of Joe Custom, the crude harp of George Maywether and the elemental percussion of Maxwell Street's Porkchop, they sounded ready to devour anything in sight! J.B. is modest enough to admit his limitations as a guitarist and the brunt was borne by Custom while Porkchop played drums with a foot-pedal and thrashed away on washboard and cow-bell. Hutto's singing was superb and his lyrics were carefully put together. On *Now She's Gone* (Chance 1155), a slow blues in stop-time, he sings:

> I would have cried baby—what good would it do?
> You couldn't have heard me cry the doggone blues
> So I'm sitting here lonely, my head hanging low
> I'm thinking about the little girl that won't be back no more
> Because she's gone, everybody know she's gone
> Yeah then they all try to tell me, hey J.B. you treat her wrong.

Another slow blues was the exultantly sexual *Pet Cream Man* (Chance 1160), which was based on a Walter Davis song, *If You'll Only Understand*, though the lyrics go right back to Texas Alexander:

> Get your butter from a farmer, get your milk from
> a Jersey cow (x2)
> You can get your pet cream from me gal, if you only know how.

An amusing but unfortunate postscript was Sam Evans's refusal to play the record on his DJ show, which was sponsored by Pet Milk!

The other two songs from the same session were fast and furious and it was noticeable that the tempo of the blues was increasing.

Left: J.B. Hutto is still a popular performer in clubs and at blues festivals. Here he is accompanied by Herman Hassell (guitar) and Frank Kirkland (drums): Turner's, 39th and Indiana, 1966.

United/States

Robert Nighthawk's *Maggie Campbell* (States 131) was an accelerated version of the Tommy Johnson number, almost as fast as his earlier *Kansas City Blues* for United. The reverse, *The Moon is Rising*, was a beautiful slow blues with Robert's smooth bottleneck guitar well to the fore. Apart from the occasional employment of faster tempos his music hadn't changed from the Aristocrat days. There was always a distinctive 'Southern' feel to it, as his band provided a looser, more sophisticated blues backing. With no boogie piano, no wailing harp and no socking drums Robert's music by the '50s was already an almost aloof echo of different times and different places.

Not so Junior Wells! If Nighthawk had been recorded by States to compete with his erstwhile 'pupil' Muddy Waters, then clearly Junior Wells was recorded to compete with Little Walter. And as if to press the point Wells recorded with his one-time group, the Myers brothers and Freddy Below, who were at that time accompanying Walter on all his records. The States session resulted from a chance meeting with one of United's executives when Junior was sitting in with Memphis Slim's band one night. It's difficult not to compare Wells with Walter; they were both young (Walter made his first record when he was about seventeen, Wells when he was eighteen) and rather wild, they both played with Muddy's group and they both blew harp as if their very lives depended on it. As singers they were about on a par, and as harmonica-blowers they were very close. Walter scored as a composer, for he had always played and sung his own songs whereas Wells drew heavily upon John Lee Williamson for his inspiration and of his eight issued States sides three were Sonny Boy's songs. *Hoodoo Man* (States 134), with verses from two of Sonny Boy's numbers, was brilliant; the group, augmented by Henry Gray on piano for this number only, achieved an easy relaxed swing as Junior blew beautifully controlled harp and the versatile Louis Myers switched to slide guitar. The momentum spilled over on to the other side, *Junior's Wail*, an interesting instrumental with a strong melody and almost hillbilly guitar and harp phrasing. Junior blew alternately in long, swooping and short, stabbing phrases and at times his melodic invention equalled Little Walter's, as on *Lawdy, Lawdy* (States 139) from the second session. An unknown pianist was added for this date (and if the credits to Clark are to be believed it was possibly Memphis Jimmy), which produced the fine prison blues *So All Alone* (States 143). Probably this second session was cut while Junior was AWOL from the army, which would fit his image of a wild and rebellious youth.

His parents farmed near Marion, about three miles from West Memphis, Arkansas, and Amos Wells Jr. was born in the John Gaston Hospital, Memphis, 9 December 1932 (or 1934). A gospel-singing grandmother wanted Junior to follow in her footsteps but by the age of nine he was

singing and playing harp on the streets of West Memphis, learning from his childhood friend Junior Parker and watching Howling Wolf and Rice Miller in action. When his mother left for Chicago in 1946 Wells followed her and in 1948 he had a little brush with either the law or blues legend there:

> I went to this pawnshop downtown and the man had a harmonica priced at $2.00. I got a job on a soda truck . . . played hookey from school . . . worked all week and on Saturday the man gave me a dollar-and-a-half. A dollar-and-a-half! For a whole week of work. I went to the pawnshop and the man said the price was $2.00. I told him I *had* to have that harp. He walked away from the counter—left the harp there. So I laid my dollar-and-a-half on the counter and picked up the harp. When my trial came up the judge asked me why I did it. I told him I *had* to have that harp. The judge asked me to play it and when I did he gave the man the 50 cents and hollered, 'Case Dismissed'.

Not long afterwards Junior, well under age, sneaked into the C & T Lounge at 22nd and Prairie where Tampa Red and Johnnie Jones were playing. Tampa fussed because Junior was so young, but Johnnie, no great respector of convention, persuaded Tampa to let the boy play. Junior tells the rest of the story:

> The owner put me out so I played in front of the place with my amplifier. The cop on the beat said I better get in *inside* the tavern and play!

About 1949 Junior and the Myers brothers formed the Three Deuces (later raised to the Four Aces) and the group stayed together until Little Walter took it over and Junior was hired to replace Walter in Muddy's band. (He had previously met Muddy at Sam Evans's Ebony Lounge.) One Muddy record was cut with Wells, *Standing Around Crying* (Chess 1526), but the association was prematurely terminated when Junior was drafted into the army. This interruption in Wells's blues career was unfortunate for by any standards his States records were a very impressive debut.

Junior Wells.

Much cruder was the James Bannister record (States 141), which was a surprising issue considering the general professionalism of the other States artists. The obscure Bannister, who came up to Chicago with Dennis 'Long Man' Binder from Rosedale, Mississippi, was a drummer with Little Hudson's Red Devil Trio and had been recorded for Sun Records in Memphis but *Gold Digger* was his only issued disc. Very probably with Little Hudson on guitar, both sides were painfully slow 12-bar blues which

Bannister sang in a high, bitter voice. The lyrics were interesting, but there was nothing ingratiating about the music, which was sour and down and out. The slight echo added to the voice and the dangerously amplified guitar created a tension which the lyrics about policy and court room trials did nothing to dispel. The record would have been more at home on the J.O.B. label—in the States catalogue it obtruded.

Mumbles, 'Little Walter', Tangle Eye, Shakey and Big Walter

The United label concentrated on city blues and typical of the shouters was Tommy Brown but on his one record (United 183) as well as the inevitable riffing saxes, there was a sparkling harmonica accompaniment by Big Walter Horton. The session was produced by Willie Dixon and the musicians had been up all the night before, rehearsing in Dixon's basement. *Southern Women*, credited to one Allen, was obviously a Willie Dixon song and 'Allen' again took credit for the Big Walter release, *Hard Hearted Woman* (States 145). Walter sang feelingly in his none too strong voice and blew fine harmonica. The lyrics were good—

> You's just a hard hearted woman, you studies evil all
>   the time (x2)
> Well you must have been mistreated to have evil on your mind

—but it was the 'big' production that was interesting. There were two saxes riffing quietly in the background and Dixon even took several breaks on bass. Lee Cooper's guitar was not very prominent and it seemed as if Dixon was trying to break out of the classic harmonica-guitar drums format. The last of States's blues releases, it was issued in early 1955 and in the space of just one year States had dabbled in every subordinate style of Chicago's blues—from Nighthawk through Wells to Bannister and Horton.

Walter's background had all the elements of the new Chicago bluesman. He was born on a farm in Horn Lake, Mississippi, on 6 April 1918; moved to Memphis when his father, Albert, got a job with the city; played on the streets in his early teens to help support his mother and sisters after his father died; and led the scuffling life of the bluesman, playing music when the jobs were there and taking casual labour when they weren't. Hanging around Handy's Park, 3rd and Beale, the young Horton met all the local and itinerant musicians of the time—legend credits him with a recording with the Memphis Jug Band, *Kansas City Blues*, at the age of 13 and, some years later, the mysterious records with Little Buddy Doyle. It's impossible at this late stage to unravel fact from fiction but other artists who were there at the time vouch for his presence on the Doyle session at least. Certainly Horton played with Doyle in the late '30s, as he did with other major Memphis artists like Jack Kelly and Dan Sane. Frank Stokes, however, was his particular favourite and Eddie Taylor even volunteers that Stokes was Walter's stepfather.

Like the others Walter would travel the countryside, sometimes with Big Joe Williams, sometimes with David 'Honeyboy' Edwards (he claims to have been blowing amplified harp as early as 1940 in Jackson, Mississippi, with Honeyboy when they were working for H. C. Speir), and with Floyd Jones. It was as a result of a trip with Floyd that Walter first came to Chicago in the '40s. But late in 1950 he was back in Memphis and recording for Sam Phillips. The first sides were leased to the Biharis of Modern Records and issued under the pseudonym Mumbles, much to Walter's disgust. In February 1952 he was recorded with Jack Kelly, the duo being billed as Jackie Boy and Little Walter, and finally on 25 February 1953 with Jimmy DeBerry he cut the brilliant instrumental *Easy* (Sun 180). Walter got $3 for this number; indeed, his payments for the record sessions add an interesting footnote to the Sun operation: in all he received from Phillips $59, of which two sums of $3 and $2 were personal loans and $1 was the cost of a harp. Though Walter signed a contract, this was to be his last session for Phillips, for not long afterwards Eddie Taylor came to fetch Walter to play in his band, in Chicago.

He played only two weeks with Eddie, joining Muddy when Junior Wells was drafted. This association didn't last long either, because Muddy fired him for unreliability, which may have been a bit hard on Walter, who claims he was sick with pneumonia and did send Henry Strong in his place. Next he was with Shines, Johnny Young and drummer Kansas City Red for a short time at the Purple Cat, from which time his record with Shines for J.O.B. dates. Nothing happened for Walter from his States record— 1954-5 saw him playing regularly at the Cosy Inn, 43rd and State, with guitarists Johnny Temple and Joe Clark and drummer Robert Whitehead, and then came a succession of jobs at the small neighbourhood bars of Turners, 4012 Indiana, and the Hollywood Rendezvous, close to his home.

Never strong, Walter has been dogged by sickness through his career. He is tall and thin, and the hard times show through his face. While sometimes he's childishly enthusiastic, more often he's morose and uncommunicative—until he plays, and then this gaunt, shambling figure of a man, harp cupped in his hands, eyes rolling, comes alive and blows with an undreamed-of eloquence.

Tough Times

Once the 1949 recession was over the US economy boomed again, helped by the Korean War, and from 1951 to 1953 black America enjoyed a certain amount of prosperity. The demand for labour was such that the non white unemployment rate dropped successively to 4.1% in 1953, the lowest ever recorded. In all 1953 must have seemed a propitious year to start a new record label, or so it seemed to Al Benson, DJ, booking agent and one of the most powerful entrepreneurs on Chicago's music scene. His Bronzeville Record Manufacturing Company launched the Parrot label

Walter 'Shakey' Horton, a '50s publicity shot.

from 32 N. State Street (later moving to 4307 S. Parkway), but ironically by the time the first issues appeared the United States were already in the grip of the next serious recession. By January 1954 the slow-down was assuming the magnitude of that of 1949 and by March unemployment had risen to 5.8% of the total labour force. For non-whites, of course, the figure was much higher and the average for 1954 was 8.9% or more than double the 1953 figure; and worse was to come.

Al Benson's blues enterprise, 1953-56.

The blues for once responded immediately. That there was a new mood abroad and no shortage of singers ready to point out their economic difficulties is clear from the '54 releases and it was especially appropriate that Parrot recorded two of them. From late 1954 came John Brim's *Tough Times* (Parrot 799):

> Me and my babe were talking, and what she said was true
> She said, 'It seems like times is getting tough, like they
>   was in '32
> You don't have no job, our bills are past due
> So now tell me baby, what we gonna do?'
> Tough times, tough times is here once more
> Now if you don't have no money, people, you can't live
>   happy no more.

J. B. Lenoir wasn't one to let the situation pass without comment and, typically, his *Eisenhower Blues* (Parrot 802) turned into a direct political attack as he pointed an accusing finger:

> Taking all my money, to pay the tax
> I'm only giving you people the natural facts
> I'm only telling you people my belief
> Because I am heading straight for relief
> I've got them Eisenhower Blues
> Thinking about me and you, what on earth are we gonna do?

This may have been rather strong meat even in the new mood of militancy, for the record was soon replaced by *Tax Paying Blues*, an identical song except that all references to Eisenhower were removed. J.B went even further the next year (by which time the non-white unemployment rate had soared to 10.1%) in another version of the song, not then released but now available (Chess 410), foolishly titled *Everybody Wants To Know* instead of the more appropriate *Laid Off*. His lyrics have become positively revolutionary:

> You rich people listen, you better listen real deep
> If we poor people get so hungry we gonna take some food to eat
> Uh, uh, uh, I got them laid off [blues]
> Thinking about me and you, what the President gonna do?

Other singers were making the same kind of noises: at Chess Detroit bluesman Bobo Jenkins recorded his *Democrat Blues* (Chess 1565) while at Chance J.B. Hutto's *Things Are So Slow* (Chance 1165), though less political, gained a piquancy from being the last issue on the label. J.B.'s exit was as impressive as his entrance:

> I went to work this morning, was all set to start
> My boss walked up and told me, 'Son raised my hours
> Things are so slow, don't think we need you anymore'
> He told me, 'Things are so slow, don't think we need you anymore'.

The last two verses were grimly prophetic:

> I had a dream last night, I was standing in a great long line
> A line like they had, boys, in 1929
> Things are so slow . . . [etc.]
>
> In 1944 everything was going along strong
> I say it's ten years later boy, and everything's going wrong.

J.B. had been given the song by a man and his wife who came into the Globetrotter Lounge one night; both had lost their jobs.

These were certainly good years to have the blues and it's significant that the peak years of popularity of the Chicago blues should coincide with the hard times of 1953-4. It's significant, too, that the popularity of the blues at such a time could be predicted by the traditional interpretation of the blues function, that of release from sorrows. That may have been a reason why people were buying blues records, but not the major cause, for the experience is not parallelled by the '60s, a period during which the non-white unemployment rate was never less than 10% and which was also the leanest for the blues. It seems likely that the upsurge in popularity of the less sophisticated blues style was due to structural reasons like the existence of highly gifted interpreters of the idiom and the much better distribution of the independent labels' product to tap a market that had always been there.

Blue Lake

Sunnyland Slim, for Al Benson's Blue Lake subsidiary, had a brief moment of glory in July 1954 when Sam Evans, who also had a couple of record shops, reported that he 'just couldn't stock enough of *Goin' Back To Memphis* (Blue Lake 105). With Snooky, Floyd and Moody Jones

Above, left: *the original trade-paper caption ran: 'Valaida Snow introduces her first release on the Chess label to disk jockey Al Benson on radio station WGES in Chicago. The sides are "I Ain't Gonna Tell" and "If You Don't Mean It." '* Right: *Jody 'Guitar' Williams, of Benson's Blue Lake label.* Opposite: *Dusty Brown, who recorded for Benson's Parrot label and later for Bandera.*

accompanying, it was a noisy reworking of the old *Minglewood* theme, much beloved of the Memphis artists. There were other fine blues on the label too. Jody Williams, as Little Papa Joe (116), had a nice city blues, while in the classic Chicago idiom there were brilliant releases by Detroit bluesman Baby Boy Warren (106) and Little Willie Foster.

Foster was probably from Belzoni and Johnny Williams remembers giving him his first job when, with Willie and his cousin Robert, he played the 520 Club, 520 E. 63rd Street. Foster ran with the same group of musicians much of the time, playing at the Jamboree with Homesick and Lazy Bill or with Floyd and the others, and for his record, *Falling Rain Blues* (Blue Lake 113, Parrot 813), he had Floyd on guitar and Lazy Bill on piano. Once again the lyrics were worthwhile:

> Got up this morning, looking through my window pane (x2)
> Thought I could see my baby walking out in the showers of rain.
>
> Lawd, my baby's gone, she's gone down in old Shady Grove (x2)
> That's where they carried my baby, carried her down to
>   her burying ground.

Another harp player Benson recorded soon after was Dusty Brown, who was born in Tralake, Mississippi, in 1929. He'd been in Chicago since 1946,

working as a cab-driver before taking up music in 1953. His first club date was at Lover's Lounge, Madison and Paulina, and then for the next three years he was resident at the Casbah Lounge, Kedzie and Lake, and then for four years at Charlie's Lounge at 1811 W. Roosevelt Road. His first and only record for Parrot, *He Don't Love You* (Parrot 820), was cut in 1955. It was a nice blues with heavy piano backing from Henry Gray but Parrot was soon in trouble for using non-union musicians and eventually Benson was blacklisted and in 1956 the label ended.

7 / The Chess Set

The Chess brothers threw themselves into the record business with an enthusiasm and energy unequalled by the other independents. While Phil stayed in Chicago taking care of business Len made innumerable trips down South, at first selling records from the back of his car but all the time making contacts. On one occasion he recorded Arthur Crudup in Jackson, Mississippi (with a ruthlessness that caused the normally placid Crudup to swear 'I'm never going to record for that man again!'), but the bulk of the Southern material that Chess issued came from the important tie-up with Sam Phillips, at the time an independent producer. Phillips recorded many of the new names in the Chess catalogue: Dr Ross (Chess 1504), Walter Horton (Chess 1529), Willie Nix (Checker 756), Woodrow Adams (Checker 757) and Joe Hill Louis (Checker 763), as well as the more city-styled Jackie Brenston, Rufus Thomas Jr. and Billy 'Red' Love. Chess also leased masters from other small producers or companies—and sometimes took over their artists. From J.O.B. came the Baby Face Leroy and two J. B. Lenoirs and then on 29 December 1951 Floyd Jones recut his beautiful *Dark Road* and *Big World* for Chess, this time with Little Walter and Jimmy Rogers accompanying. Again these were flawless performances and Floyd returned to the studio the following September to record *You Can't Live Long* and *Early Morning* (Chess 1527).

Until 1950 nearly one-third of the Aristocrat and Chess releases had been downhome blues—a remarkable proportion for a major independent label—and this high average was to be maintained until 1955. But one year in particular, 1952, was exceptional, for very nearly half the releases were of the new country blues, achieved mainly through the Phillips deal and the introduction of the Checker subsidiary on 17 May.These years saw the last fling of the Melrose singers; there was a session by Memphis Minnie and a combined one by Big Bill and Washboard Sam. But the results were generally very sad. Minnie recorded with her husband Little Son Joe and even had Little Walter on harp in a futile attempt to bring them up to date while Bill and Sam's session was even more disastrous and Sam retired from the business. Bill, however, had found favour with the folk audiences in Europe and his prolific recording career continued unabated in his new role.

At the same time in Chicago the new bluesmen were still being sought out and Muddy's old partner Blue Smitty finally got his chance on 11 July. Claude Smith came from Marianna, Arkansas, where he was born on 6 November 1924, and he apparently learned to play the piano at the age of six and guitar while in his teens. Moving to Chicago in 1945 he soon teamed up with Muddy; he remembers that Muddy was playing only bottleneck guitar at the time and that he taught him to pick with his fingers. Smitty's own influences he lists as Crudup, Yank Rachell and Charley Christian, and there are very modern if eccentric touches to his playing. *Sad Story* (Chess 1522) was remarkable, like *Rough Treatment* a moving and intensely personal narrative which sounded as if it had been wrung out of the singer's own experience. But, again like *Rough Treatment*, it was somebody else's song; Walter Davis had recorded it 11 years earlier as *The Only Woman*. Davis's graphic description of the death of his mother is faithfully copied by Smitty even down to the very day, 26 May, although he changes the year from 1935 to 1951. The sound, though rather chaotic, is a few years ahead of its time. Like Davis's it's in a minor key, which accentuates the mood of despair, but Smitty's guitar, erratically alternating a solid bass rather like Jimmy Rogers's with fleet-fingered treble, suggests that he might have held his own with the blues stars of the '60s. Equally doomy was the superb but unissued *Elgin Movements* while, in complete contrast, *Date Bait* was a swinging boogie with fine piano possibly from Eddie Ware, the side marred only by Smitty's awkward guitar solo. This was to be his only session and Smitty dropped out of sight, eventually leaving Chicago.

Morris Pejoe (actually Pejas) from Palmetto, Louisiana, had a pleasant record for Checker in the more commercial Fats Domino manner. He wasn't strictly a bluesman like the Mississippi singers and had started out playing hillbilly music on the violin when he moved to Beaumont, Texas. But on hearing the Texas men, Hopkins, T-Bone Walker and especially

Louisiana-born bluesmen Morris Pejoe (left) and Henry Gray. The two are heard together on Pejoe's Checker record.

Gatemouth Brown, he switched to guitar and the blues. In 1951 in Chicago he met fellow Louisiana artist Henry Gray at the Upstairs Lounge, 258 W. Washburne, and they teamed up for the next four years.

After some persistence on Pejoe's part Chess recorded him and *Tired Of Crying Over You* (Checker 766) was a rocking 'uptown' blues made memorable by Gray's piano work. Gray himself recorded, as Little Henry, a couple of numbers at a further Pejoe session on 11 May 1953. *Matchbox Blues* and *I Declare That Aint Right* were both fine but like other examples of mid-'50s Chicago piano blues they went unissued.

Henry Gray was born in Kenner, just north of New Orleans, in 1925, but was brought up in Alsen, Louisiana. He'd been in Chicago since 1946, learned much of his piano from Big Maceo and before meeting Pejoe he had played with Little Hudson's Red Devil Trio. Pejoe had a disagreement with Chess and switched labels soon after but Gray stayed with him until he joined Howling Wolf's band in 1956.

A very different kind of bluesman was Big Boy Spires, who was recorded a year earlier. Arthur Spires was born in Yazoo City, Mississippi, in 1912 and in his youth heard the local musicians, guitarists Adam Slater and Henry Stuckey and Henry's pianist brother Nemiah (or did he mean Nemiah 'Skip' James?). An uncle, Robert Spires, played guitar for the usual round of country suppers and house-parties but Arthur didn't start to learn the instrument until the late '30s. The main place for music in Yazoo City was the Beer Garden, run by a Mr Crowder, and Big Boy remembers Lightnin' Hopkins, who was making regular trips to the area, playing there in 1939 or 1940, when Spires was good enough to play second guitar behind him. In 1943 Spires moved to Chicago and met guitarist Eddie Ell, who had just finished a course of guitar lessons with teacher George Burns at the Lyon & Healey music store, and Spires too signed on with Burns. He played briefly with Louis Myers and Junior Wells and later, with Ell and Little Earl Dranes, he worked clubs like the H & T on State Street. The Checker session followed from a promotional disc the group cut with each of them taking turns singing. Spires got the contract and the others backed him on the resulting session. Spires was, and still is, a limited guitarist but by confining himself to the upper three strings of the instrument he creates an idiosyncratic sound. His timing was bad, too, but the other guitarists covered skilfully, weaving an intricate and complex rhythm and making a virtue out of necessity. There were very strong echoes of the Tommy Johnson and Ishman Bracey guitar duets with Charlie McCoy in Big Boy's music, and *Murmur Low* (Checker 752) was a version of Johnson's *Big Fat Mama Blues*. Spires always referred to the song as *Fat Mama Rumble* but Len Chess opted for the less picturesque *Murmur Low*. Spires sang well without any marked similarity to Crudup (from whom he is supposed to have taken his sobriquet) but his Checker record, fine though it was, brought him no commercial success. Soon after, with his own group the Rocket Four, he was working the clubs such as the

L.T. Smith (drums), Johnny Williams (guitar), Little Willie Smith (harmonica), Arthur 'Big Boy' Spires (guitar).

Be Bop Inn, the Castle Rock at 50th and Princeton, the Cotton Club and Stormy's Inn, Root and Princeton. The Rocket Four comprised, variously, guitarists Ell, Dranes, Otis Smothers and Johnny Williams, harmonica-players Little Willie Smith, John Lee Henley (who had one record on J.O.B.) and P. T. Hayes, drummers L. T. Smith (Little Willie's brother), Ted Porter, Dave 'Dizzy' Pitts and pianist Willie Smith (no relation to the other Smiths). In 1953 Al Benson introduced Big Boy to Art Sheridan and the session for Chance resulted.

There is much confusion about the personnel on the Chance record, probably because the session was made twice with different groups. Johnny Williams identified 'a boy we called Duke on drums and P. T. Hayes was on harmonica.' Williams remembers it particularly well because he himself cut two songs at the same session which were never released. The Spires record still sounds a very slipshod affair, though *About To Lose My Mind* (Chance 1137) did contribute one memorable verse:

> That woman got ways like a Ford out on a farm (x2)
> Every time I raise the hood, man, I find something wrong.

The case of Big Boy Spires serves well to illustrate the professionalism and flair of the Chess operation. Len Chess by some means got the very best out of an artist who was not the most accomplished in his field. Beautifully sung, beautifully played and beautifully recorded too, the Checker release is a gem of Chicago's postwar blues. At the other end of the scale was the Chance issue, made for Art Sheridan in a cheap studio, badly recorded and under-rehearsed; even after a remake Spires turns in just a routine performance.

Another singer whom Chess recorded to advantage was John Brim. John was born on a farm about ten miles from Hopkinsville, Kentucky, on 10 April 1922. From a child he was interested in the guitar, and he and his friend Homer Wilson used to practise listening to records of Big Bill and Tampa Red. There were local jukes but nothing like the live music scene of his Mississippi contemporaries, and Brim was largely self-taught. In 1941 he followed the traditional migration route to Indianapolis and then in 1945 moved again to Chicago, where he met Tampa, Big Maceo, Big Bill and Sonny Boy. He played with Sonny Boy for about a year and a half from 1946 as well as odd dates with Muddy, L. C. McKinley, Eddie Boyd and Willie Mabon. In 1947 he met a woman drummer, singer and harmonica player and they were soon married. The next year John was leading his own group with his wife Grace on drums, Homer Wilson on guitar and Jimmy Reed, whom he had met at the Club Jamboree in South Chicago, on harp. Then John and Grace joined Big Maceo and went to Detroit. When Maceo recorded for Fortune in Detroit he took the Brims along and John cut his first record at the session with Grace taking the vocals. Maceo was playing only right-handed since his stroke, and then came his last and fatal stroke and he died on 26 February 1953 in Chicago. A month later, in Chicago, came Brim's first session for Chess, and with Little Walter, the Myers brothers and Freddy Below, *Rattlesnake* (Checker 769) was recorded. The song had started life as *Hound Dog* by Willie Mae Thornton for Peacock Records of Houston and a cover version, *Bear Cat* by Rufus Thomas Jr for Sun, followed. Don Robey of Peacock slapped an injunction on Sam Phillips and Chess withdrew Brim's record before release. Now available on a Chess Vintage reissue (1537), Brim's version turns out to be one of the great moments of Chicago's blues, with instrumental passages of a rare beauty and one glorious singing moment as the guitars and harp blend in a remarkable unity. Brim was unlucky again with his next session, on 4 May; he and Eddie Taylor recorded *Lifetime Baby* and *Ice Cream Man*, but neither was issued. Again, both are available on recent albums; *Lifetime* is a very moving prison blues, while the up-tempo *Ice Cream Man* employs the *Pet Cream* sexual metaphors as Brim recites a list of ice cream confections, Popsicle and Dixie Cup. Soon afterwards he moved to Gary and formed his Gary Kings with pianist Willie Smith and the Dalton brothers, W.C. on guitar and James on harmonica. But his next record, *Tough Times* for Parrot, was made with his old friends Reed and Taylor, after Albert King had introduced him to

Al Benson, and it wasn't until January 1955 that his first Chess record appeared: *That Ain't Right* and *Go Away* (1588), with Grace and the Dalton brothers. Brim's own band was rougher than the impeccable Little Walter-Myers-Below group: noisy but very exciting. *That Ain't Right* was an excellent slow blues with fine lyrics while on the up-tempo reverse Brim is singing *to* the blues when he orders:

> Go away, go away and leave me alone
> You just come to worry me 'cause my baby's gone.

His lyrics were always interesting:

> My brother told me, my sister said the same
> 'The way you're acting lately you're going insane
> Get a hold of yourself and mighty soon
> If you don't we'll be coming to your funeral'
> Go away . . . [etc.]

Despite the introspective nature of the songs he shouts the lyrics in a dark, dangerous voice, and it was noticeable how his music had become much more aggressive. By his last session, with Little Walter's group in April 1956, the words had become as threatening as the music:

> Tell me, tell me baby, what is this I hear
> About you putting me down for someone new ,
> I just want to warn you, before you make a move
> Now be careful, baby, what you say and do
> You know I hate mighty bad
> To have to do away with you.

and further:

> Come here, baby, look me dead in the eye
> You know if you attempt to quit me, that's when you gonna die
> Now be careful . . .

John Brim suffered the fate of most of his contemporaries and achieved little success with his music. He was an average guitarist, a fine singer and an excellent song-writer, and that his talents were not distinctive enough to set him apart from the other artists of his day is a commentary on the abundance of blues talent in Chicago in the '50s. More than anything, this restless new audience was seeking something different in their blues heroes (which certainly wasn't the case in the heyday of the Bluebird Beat) and this fact was well appreciated by Chess. These second-rank artists were frequently exploited by the companies, who would record them not with the intention of releasing anything by them but merely as a source of material for the company's established singers. Sometimes plans came a little unstuck, though, as Eddie Boyd relates:

> Before I made *Five Long Years* I cut a session for Chess. Now he told me, he says, 'I record you to get some songs for my boy. You don't have no talent, you can't sing, you can't play. I'll record this

John Brim 1953

Chess artists John Brim (left) *and Eddie Boyd.*

stuff and I'll pay you for it, then give it to my boy.' He was talking
about Muddy Waters. After he'd recorded this, I say 'Well, there's
one thing about it, you can't do me like Lester Melrose did, you can't
record a tune and don't release them on me, I own the copyright on
them.' And his eyes come up 'cause at that time there was most of
the bluesmen who didn't know what the word copyright meant! So
he didn't borrow the tunes. I know how he thinks 'cause I know Len
Chess when he didn't have fifty dollars.

The final irony came when Boyd split with Art Sheridan and signed a
contract with Al Benson. Benson promptly sold it to Chess, who must
have revised his original opinion! Boyd's records sold well for Chess and
the association continued for the next four years although he never
repeated the phenomenal success of *Five Long Years*. Chess was probably
right at first in finding little that was distinctive in Boyd's music, but he
was more a city-styled blues artist anyway, and there was always a market
for the more sophisticated blues. In fact Eddie had 14 releases on Chess,
five more than his nearest 'competitor', Willie Mabon.

Mabon wasn't strictly a bluesman and always preferred to be an
entertainer. This shows in his singing and choice of material but his
piano-playing was the blues, solid, relaxed and easy-rolling. He came from
Memphis, where he was born on 24 October 1925, and was influenced by
the many fine boogie and blues pianists in the town. In 1942 he came to
Chicago and took music lessons in order to play jazz. At the same time he
met all the name artists of the day, but the rather quiet and refined young
man didn't like the clubs and, in fact, didn't like Chicago. He recalls that it
took him three days to get unpacked!

ROCK & ROLL SHOW OF 1957

★ **FEATURING** ★

WILLIE

("I DON'T KNOW")

MABON

★ **PLUS** ★

GUITAR GUS FAMOUS BLUES GUITARIST

ANN BUTLER

Sensational Baton Dancer

CURTIS JONES RECORD STAR OF "HIGHWAY 51"

PLUS THE SENSATIONAL

JUMP JACKSON

AND HIS ORCHESTRA

"Not Now Baby" - "Red Light"

RHYTHM & BLUES AGENCY 5727 SOUTH LASALLE PH. NORMAL 7-4161 or 4152 **CHICAGO, ILL.**

Willie also signed a contract with Al Benson and ended on Chess. His first release, with Ernest Cotton on tenor sax, was *I Don't Know* (Chess 1531) a dressed-up novelty version of Cripple Clarence Lofton's great barrelhouse number, ideally suited to Willie's entertaining talents. Mabon wasn't a good singer but his insinuating voice made the most of the lyrics

Johnnie and Letha Jones and Willie Mabon, Scotty's, Wood and Ogden, 1963.

and the record was immediately successful, reaching the top of the National R & B Charts in 1952. Handsome and personable, Willie enjoyed further successes with similar material: *Poison Ivy* (1580), which reached number 9 in January 1955, *I'm Mad* (1538), another number 1, *The Seventh Son* (1608) and *Would You Baby* (1564) were all big sellers over the next four years.

'I Am The Wolf!'

Chess was looking for distinctive blues artists and from Sam Phillips came one of the label's unique talents, Howling Wolf—a giant of a man with a voice to match his powerful 270lb frame and ferocious demeanour. That Wolf ever appeared on the label is an example of either the luck enjoyed by the Chess brothers or their ruthlessness in winkling out their competitors' discoveries. In 1950 Sam Phillips was recording blues artists for the Bihari brothers of Modern Records, Hollywood, and at a B. B. King session Ike Turner, the Clarksdale pianist, caught the eye of Jules Bihari, who insisted that he play piano on the date, although Turner was one of Phillips's artists. Bihari further upset Phillips by offering Ike a job as talent scout for Modern Records and it was Turner who discovered the Wolf. Bihari sent money and a contract and a session was arranged at Phillips's studios but Phillips got his own back on Bihari by calmly sending the acetates and masters to Chess! These first sides, *How Many More Years* and *Moanin' At Midnight* (Chess 1479), were released on 15 August 1951 and were an immediate success.

Wolf was over 40 when his first record appeared and if he had felt neglected by the record companies up to that time he was soon to find himself in the middle of a bewildering tug-of-war between Chess and Modern Records. The Biharis quickly retaliated with a session in West Memphis and Wolf even recorded one of the same songs, thinly disguised as *Morning At Midnight* (RPM 333). Rival sessions followed thick and fast as Wolf was recorded under the aegis of Ike Turner for Modern or Sam Phillips for Chess. Thus October 1951 saw Wolf recording for Modern, January 1952 for Chess, February for Modern and April for Chess again. It must have been about this time that Chess rushed down from Chicago and had Wolf sign an exclusive contract. Wolf, not exactly overawed by the proceedings, summed up the situation in a typically phlegmatic way:

> I was a farmer and I didn't know what was happening. I was glad to get a sound out, you know.

Financially Wolf had fared much better than most of the other bluesmen; from Chess alone he had received session fees and advances of $1,000 and probably something like that from the Biharis.

Wolf was born Chester Arthur Burnett on 10 June 1910 in eastern Mississippi, probably between West Point in Clay County and Aberdeen in Monroe County (he has given both locations for his birth-place), but his interest in music wasn't awakened until the family moved to Young and Morrow's plantation near Ruleville in the Delta in 1923. He was nearly 18 when his father bought him a guitar and he first met Charley Patton. Patton lived on Will Dockery's plantation near Ruleville but at cotton harvest time in the fall he made the rounds of the various plantations entertaining. After cotton-picking was over for the day Wolf hung around and Patton, who had taken a liking to the boy, taught him the rudiments of his guitar style.

At some time or other he came into contact with almost every major Mississippi artist; in particular he remembers the Mississippi Sheiks, and Dick Bankston and Jim Holloway from Drew, as well as Son House and Willie Brown. On record he was especially fond of Blind Lemon Jefferson. In 1933 the family crossed to the other side of the Mississippi by way of Memphis to the Phillips plantation, about 16 miles north of Parkin, Arkansas. Wolf was a slow learner, and music usually took second place to his farming life except when the travelling urge took him. His travels took him through Greenwood, Winona, back to his old home at West Point, then down to Columbus, across to Indianola and Greenville. He'd cross over to Arkansas, up to West Memphis, to Parkin, Pine Bluff and Brinkley. Then back home to help his father again on the farm.

He first became interested in the harmonica when Rice Miller (Sonny

Boy Williamson No. 2) courted and married his step-sister Mary. Sonny Boy would show him how to blow the harp and Wolf would go away and practise into the night. He next met Robert Johnson in Robinsonville and the three of them went on the road for a while, playing around Itta Bena, Greenwood and Moorhead, until Wolf, dissatisfied with the money he was making and Sonny Boy was keeping, returned again to his father's farm. In 1941 the demands of the army interrupted this life of farming and sporadic musical activity and Wolf was drafted, spending most of his tour of duty in Seattle, Washington. Four years later he returned to his father on the Phillips plantation but soon left to farm for himself at Penton, Mississippi. There he raised two crops and his musical interest was revived by playing in nearby Robinsonville and Tunica with veteran singer Fiddling Joe Martin and Woodrow Adams. With music beginning to occupy his mind more and more he decided to leave for West Memphis. By then he was playing electric guitar and harmonica but, wishing to concentrate more on his singing, he formed a band in 1948 with guitarists Pat Hare, who came from Parkin, and M. T. 'Matt' Murphy, who came from Sunflower via Memphis, and local boy Junior Parker on harmonica. A drummer, Willie Steele, and a pianist, 'Destruction', made up the rest of the group. When Matt Murphy left with Junior Parker to form the Blue Flames another guitarist, Willie Johnson, joined the band. With them Wolf toured Arkansas and Mississippi but the big break came when they landed a spot on radio station KWEM in West Memphis. So successful were the broadcasts that Wolf was given a regular programme as a DJ advertising corn, grain and agricultural implements. Wolf sold the advertising himself,

getting local small store owners to sponsor the programme, and he held the job up to the time he left for Chicago. He was living at 314 South 11th Street in West Memphis at the time when Chess and Modern were competing for his recording favours and he had been using the name 'Howling Wolf' for some years previously. The sobriquet was so apt for his style of singing that it's difficult to give much credence to Wolf's various and confusing explanations of how he came by the name. Around Dockery's plantation he was known as Bull Cow and Foot:

> They say I had big feet! But I just stuck to the Wolf. I got that from my grandfather. He used to tell me stories about the wolves in that part of the country . . . and I would get frightened.

And then if he misbehaved,

> They told me they was going to put the wolf on me. So everybody else went to calling me the Wolf.

Alas, it's a fairy tale. He'd first used the name professionally when he started broadcasting over KWEM; up to that time he had delighted audiences by leaping on the stage and announcing himself as 'Big Foot Chester'. 'Howling Wolf' came from Funny Papa Smith's famous record but it was peculiarly appropriate to his fierce singing style, punctuated with falsetto whoops and howls. Wolf's singing was his most obvious debt to the heavy-voiced Charley Patton (though he also copied his clowning on stage) and it was probably the most exciting voice on record for a long time. His harmonica-playing was a very rough approximation of Rice Miller's and the whole sound of the band reflected the disparate influences of Memphis.

One fascinating aspect of the postwar blues is that while Chicago's blues reached back to the very roots of Mississippi, a lot of the music from the South, and Memphis in particular, at that time seemed relatively sophisticated. Wolf, for instance, always recorded with more than the basic harmonica-guitar-drums trio which typified Chicago and from the beginning his bands were of five pieces at least, always including a pianist and a drummer. But, more than the size of the groups, it was the musical tension within them that gave a free-ranging, almost jazzy flavour to the music. On the one hand there was Wolf's own direct and basic harp-blowing and Albert Williams's or Ike Turners' tight boogie piano; on the other, the slashing solid-bodied electric guitars of Willie Johnson or Pat Hare; and this uneasy musical alliance, which was crudely effective on up-tempo jump numbers, frequently ruptured on the slowest of slow blues. The music was rough and raucous but if the band seemed in danger at times of splitting apart Wolf's overpowering voice held it together.

Wolf's lyrics were fragmentary in the Mississippi tradition but his songs were usually original or his own interpretation of earlier themes, which suited the record companies very well. Once the new independent record producers had understood the copyright situation and realised the bonuses to be earned from music-publishing royalties, there was an almost complete reversal of attitude. Soon the publishing royalties were to be highly important, and, as each record company set up its own publishing firm, the recording emphasis was on original compositions which could be published by a subsidiary. At one session Wolf recorded two of John Lee Williamson's songs, *Bluebird* and *Decoration Day*, which were never released, possibly because the copyright was held by Melrose's firm. Few of the songs were ever copyrighted in the artist's name anyway, despite the legend on the record label, and the royalties accruing were shared by the record company owners or executives, often under assumed names; indeed, this was considered a legitimate 'perk' of the business.

Chess were late in utilising the publishing situation and it wasn't until 1 August 1953 that Leonard Chess and Gene Goodman set up Arc Music to publish all the Chess material. Previously Chess songs had been published by John 'Lawyer' Burton—a shadowy figure on the Chicago music scene—or not at all. None of the Aristocrat material was copyrighted at the time.

Most Promising Newcomer

Wolf moved North to Chicago in the fall of 1952, probably of his own accord rather than at any insistence from Chess, for the white DJs at KWEM were jealous of Wolf's popularity and Wolf too was probably jealous of the success of the younger men who had gone North. Despite his remarks to the contrary it seems likely that Wolf found it tough in Chicago at first. He did no recording for a year and little is remembered of his first year there. There were the odd gigs, at the Rock Bottom at Hoyne and Washburne, for which he had to borrow Floyd Jones's amplifier, and at the Club Zanzibar, a date that Muddy had engineered for him. Since his first record Wolf hadn't had a national hit, though his records were always big sellers in the South and especially in Memphis. His first Chicago recording with the Chess house musicians, *I Love My Baby* and *All Night Boogie* (Chess 1557), was advertised in *Cash Box* on 2 January 1954 and soon afterwards he returned South to bring his band back. Willie Steele had gone into the Army but Willie Johnson and Hubert Sumlin made the trip. It was his next record, *No Place To Go* (1566), that started to sell. Hypnotic, restrained and superbly sung, it was listed in *Cash Box's* 'Coming Up In R & B' feature on 1 and 8 May as 'breaking out' in Chicago and it was described in an advert in the next issue as 'an overnight hit'. By 5 June it was listed number 2 in Memphis and it stayed in the Memphis and Shreveport charts for over a month. Chicago had quickly made its mark on Wolf's music—on record at least. As the Chicago rhythm men took over, the band sounded much tighter and more disciplined; only the guitars of Johnson, Sumlin and sometimes Jody Williams were reminiscent of Memphis. Not that they tamed the Wolf; quite the reverse in fact, for as the rhythm section of Otis Spann, Willie Dixon and Earl Phillips laid down a thunderous beat, it allowed Wolf to explore further dimensions of violence and aggression.

His greatest success came with his next record, *Evil Is Going On* (1575), although once again sales were confined mainly to the South. For example, *Cash Box* for 9 October lists it at number 2 in Shreveport, 5 in Atlanta, 7 in Memphis and 10 in Nashville, and it was still in the Nashville and Shreveport charts on 27 November. It was deservedly popular, a great big shouting song on one of Wolf's favourite themes, the back-door man:

Yes if you make it to your house .
Knock on the front door
Run around to the back
You'll catch him just before he go
That's evil, evil is going on
I am warning you brother
You better watch your happy home.

The menace was continued in his next coupling, the grimly threatening *I'll Be Around* and *Forty Four* (1584), a brilliant band version of the famous piano theme with lyrics hardly more comforting: 'I wore my forty-four so long, done made my shoulder sore.' But while Muddy and especially Little Walter could break into the St Louis, Los Angeles, San Francisco and even Newark charts, Wolf's popularity was down South. However, Wolf ended the year secure in the knowledge that he had been voted 22nd in the *Cash Box* poll for Most Promising New R & B Artist of 1954.

'I Had It Tough, You Know, In Them Days . . .'

All the main features of Howling Wolf's story—of scuffling through the South building up a purely local reputation; then a chance to broadcast, which brought him to a wider audience and the chance to record; and finally a contract with Chess and the subsequent move north—have exact parallels in the story of the last major bluesman that Chess was to record persistently—Sonny Boy Williamson No. 2.

Since 1951 Sonny Boy had recorded for the Trumpet label of Jackson, Mississippi, but rarely did the studio groups of mainly jazz and night-club musicians do him justice, and these Southern recordings, like Wolf's, were often a none too happy mixture of differing styles. They were however, virtuoso performances from Sonny Boy himself, who towered over the groups like some country Colossus with his unique mastery of harp and voice. Sonny Boy was by nature a loner with a completely self-contained creative genius which set him apart from his fellow musicians. Difficult, suspicious, reticent when not being boastful, he cut a mysterious figure which none of his public utterances did anything to dispel. Willie Williams, Willie Williamson, Rice Miller or Willie Miller—what was his real name? Born in Glendora in 1897 (as he has sung on record)—or was it in Tallahatchie on 9 April 1909 (as his passport proclaimed), or 1894 or 1899 (other dates he has variously given)? How old was he really and where did he come from? Indeed, *who* was he? Nearly everybody who

Robert Jr Lockwood and Sonny Boy Williamson No. 2.

remembered him from the Mississippi days knew him as 'Rice' Miller, but the latest evidence suggests his real name was Alex Miller (there was a brother called Willie) and that he was born in Glendora, Mississippi, probably around 1897. Sonny Boy would tell nothing of his early years—'I had it tough, you know, in them days' was all he would ever say, and any glimpses of his life in Mississippi are caught only through the reminiscences of others. Thus there was his teaching Wolf to play the harp and a brief marriage to Wolf's step-sister. From Eddie Burns and Johnny Shines comes a picture of Sonny Boy, coat open, with the sun glinting on his belt in which he carried his many harmonicas, wearing cut-up rubber boots, ever ready to oblige with a song for some small change. From Burns also, a story of Sonny Boy firing his whole band one night and playing the rest of the dance entirely unaccompanied. And from other singers, hints of his 'evil' reputation. These are the only fragments left of a life of 30-odd years playing the blues in the small towns and jukes of Mississippi and Arkansas.

His first big break came in November 1941, when, with a band including Joe Willie Wilkins on guitar, Dudlow Taylor on piano and Peck Curtis on drums, he was hired to broadcast on King Biscuit Time over KFFA in Helena, Arkansas. The programme, sponsored by Max Moore, The Interstate Grocer of Helena, ran every Monday to Friday at 12.15 to 12.30 pm, advertising King Biscuit Flour. This must have been the time when Miller first started to live the lie of being Sonny Boy Williamson, a lie he almost certainly lived to regret but one he was stuck with, and felt forced to buttress at every opportunity, weaving more and more incredible strands into his story. Thus, 'I'm *the* Sonny Boy, there ain't no other one but me,' he persisted, and he maintained that *his* name had been copied by the younger John Lee Williamson when he first recorded. Max Moore was perfectly well aware that he was not *the* Sonny Boy who was making records in Chicago for he gave him the name to cash in on John Lee's reputation and enormous popularity. The impersonation was further complicated when at the end of each programme Herb Langston, the announcer, would tell the listeners that they could get all of Sonny Boy's records at their local store! The deception was only possible because John Lee stayed in Chicago and never toured, but he did in fact make one unsuccessful trip to Helena in an attempt to stop them using his name. Interstate's tongue-in-cheek reply that their artist was Sonny Boy Williams was in full knowledge that most blacks pronounced Williamson as Williams anyway!

The KFFA broadcasts could be heard within a range of 100 miles, which took in the Delta and the 'heavy' blues country of Arkansas, and Sonny Boy reached ever larger audiences. As his popularity increased, Interstate even named a new product after him, and soon he was advertising Sonny Boy Corn Meal (which had a caricature of him on the sack) along with that 'fine, white, dainty . . . and light King Biscuit Flour.' Sonny Boy stayed around Helena for a couple of years and then seems to have taken to the road again. Other local musicians would do the King Biscuit Show when Sonny was away but whenever he was in town he would do the programme himself. In 1945 he married Mattie Jones, his second wife, and returned to Helena. Then in 1949 he moved to West Memphis and with Willie Love and Joe Willie Wilkins broadcast over KWEM, advertising the Broadway Furniture Company. In 1951 Lillian McMurry, who owned a record and furniture store in Jackson and had just started Trumpet Records, went in search of Sonny Boy with her brother and a friend to record him and remembers the trouble they had finding him. No one would tell the two men anything and they searched from Belzoni to Flora and past Greenville until finally they came to a shack with a jukebox in the front and living quarters at the back. Once again the people inside shook their heads; no, they'd never heard of Sonny Boy Williamson. Mrs McMurry by then realised that two white men weren't going to get anywhere so she went in and introduced herself as a record company owner, 'and this lady grinned and said, "Why, come right in, Mrs McMurry, he's right in the back room".'

Sonny Boy went to Jackson and signed the contract and he recorded until Trumpet, unable to collect from many of their distributors, went out of business some five years later. The association was generally a happy one, for Mrs McMurry was fond of Sonny in the maternal way of the white segregationist, and also she had a reputation for scrupulous fairness and honesty in dealing with her artists. (Sonny Boy received all his royalties and even now, 15 years after the demise of the label, at the McMurrys' furniture store there is a batch of envelopes containing royalty cheques awaiting artists who never showed up again.) His early Trumpet records were mainly fine blues sung to a jump band accompaniment. What Sonny's rather plaintive voice lacked in force was made up for in expression and delicacy; his harp-playing was less vigorous than his contemporaries' but had enormous subtlety and shading. Some of the songs were classics and the lyrics were brilliant. Thus, *Eyesight To The Blind* (Trumpet 129):

> You're talking about your woman, I wish to God man that you
> could see mine (x2)
> Every time the little girl starts to loving she bring eyesight
> to the blind.

Sometimes the lyrics were intensely personal, as in *West Memphis Blues* (144):

> I bought a home in West Memphis back in nineteen and forty-nine (x2)
> I came home one Sunday mornin', my home was burning down.
>
> Lord Miss Alice Brown she treated me so nice and kind (x2)
> She says 'Sonny Boy, your credit is always good, I don't care
> when you come around'

—and 'Yes, you'll find me at the Streamline Cafe every day of my life'.

Trumpet's best seller, according to Mrs McMurry, was Sonny Boy's *Mighty Long Time* (166) which sold 60,748 copies. (It's typical of Mrs McMurry that she can sit down with a desk calculator and produce the exact figure in a matter of minutes; it's typical, too, that she should ignore Elmore James's *Dust My Broom*, which was probably a bigger hit.) *Mighty Long Time* was a beautiful slow blues with an unusual vocal bass accompaniment by Cliff Givens. Equally effective was another atmospheric blues. *No Nights By Myself*, which was leased to Johnny Vincent's Ace label (511). Less impressive were his last sessions from late 1953 and 1954; mostly with sax accompaniment, they were an attempt to break into the shouters' jump blues market. The songs were mediocre too, although *Getting Out Of Town* (215), a remarkable Latin-styled number with a shuffle beat, had a relaxed charm all its own and was sufficiently popular in New Orleans to get into the *Cash Box* Hot Ten for a couple of weeks in November 1954. However, these bizarre experiments were soon to cease, for Trumpet sounded its last notes in 1955 and Sonny's contract was sold to Buster Williams in Memphis, who in turn sold it to Chess.

When Sonny Boy joined Chess in 1955 the company had just enjoyed its most successful year ever, thanks to Muddy and Little Walter. Muddy's music had changed slightly from late 1952, when yet another major bluesman joined the band. It was claimed that pianist Otis Spann was Muddy's half-brother but he was introduced to Waters by Len Chess while Spann was playing with Morris Pejoe. Whether Muddy and Otis were related or not their personal and musical relationship couldn't have been closer and it was hard to think of one without the other. Otis was born in Belzoni, Mississippi, on 21 March 1930. His mother, Josephine, was supposed to have played guitar and his father Frank Houston Spann to have played piano, but the local Jackson pianists Coot Davis and, particularly, Friday Ford were Otis's inspiration. Ford took the young Otis on his knee and held him up to the keyboard before the child's fingers were properly formed but Otis claimed that he never forgot Ford's music, and when his father encouraged him by buying him a piano, against the objections of his church-going mother, it was Ford's style that he tried to

Johnnie Jones (standing) entertains Otis Spann (in sombrero) at his home, 1963. Also present, Otis's then wife, Marie (for whom he named a 1965 Vanguard recording).

recreate. There are stories that he won first prize of $25 in a Jackson talent contest when he was eight and he was playing regularly for local bands from the age of 14. They are more likely than the outrageous tales the chubby and immensely good natured Spann would often invent to keep his listeners happy! After his mother died in 1947 he either joined his father in Chicago or was sent by him to stay with relatives there, and in the late '40s, working as a plasterer by day, he was playing in a group by night at the Tick Tock Lounge at 37th and State.

Spann was the natural successor to Big Maceo and both he and Johnnie Jones learned from Maceo. Otis played piano in Maceo's solid, hard-hitting manner and, when he was to record, even sang like him in a smoky, sad voice. In the band Otis was a tower of strength. Never obtrusive (in fact Spann believed the harmonica to be the most important instrument), he was the perfect accompanist and ensemble player and every note he played seemed just right. By this time the piano's role had dwindled to that of a percussion instrument and Spann's contribution was a magnificently rolling bass or, in the band passages, crashing treble work which perfectly fitted the new sound of the city.

Ork-ing Is Torrid

By 1954 Muddy's music had stepped firmly away from the traditional Mississippi background—away from the intimate two-guitar and harmonica patterns and away from the introspective 12-bar themes towards a more raucous, rocking sound that quickened with the tempo of life in Chicago. Gone was Muddy's bottleneck guitar, and, as he concentrated more on singing and fronting the band, his voice took on the shouting urgency of the complete urban bluesman. He had started the year with *Mad Love* (Chess 1550) still in the charts (with Little Walter's *Blues With A Feeling* (Checker 780)) but his first release of 1954 was to be his biggest record ever—*Hoochie Coochie Man* (Chess 1560), a colourful song which was virtually an incantation of magical-sexual images. In the first week it sold 4,000 copies and quickly entered the charts all over the country. *Cash Box* made it the 'Sleeper Of The Week', reviewing it thus:

> Muddy Waters crashes through with his strongest sales gatherer in many, many releases. Waters, always a solid salesman, waxes a strong piece of material, *I'm Your Hoochie Coochie Man*, that should push its way close to the top if not all the way. The chanter throws every one of his tricks into his job and he receives ork backing that is certainly not the least important part of the disc's success.

It stayed in the National Top Ten from March to the summer and in Memphis it topped the charts for a whole month from February. Little Walter was also having great success with *You're So Fine* (Checker 786), which in January immediately replaced *Blues With A Feeling* in the best-sellers and remained there until April.

Above: *Muddy Waters, unknown (maraccas), Otis Spann, Henry Strong, Elgin Evans, Jimmy Rogers. The picture (presumably from the early '50s) is from Chess files, but applies to no known recording session.*

That month, though, Walter had mixed luck; the Jukes lost their equipment and he narrowly escaped with his life in a fire at the Club Hollywood in Chicago, and then on the way home that night he was involved in a car crash. But consolation came in the shape of an award from *Cash Box* for his next record, *Oh Baby* (Checker 793), which was to take over from *You're So Fine* and occupy the *Cash Box* charts for the next four months, while Walter was away touring Texas. With all this activity Chess moved in May from 750 E. 49th Street to larger offices and its own studio at 4750-2 Cottage Grove. Unfortunately the Chess engineers lacked the brilliance of the recording men at Universal (who had cut all the Chess material up till then) and the recording quality suffered accordingly, although it certainly didn't affect their sales. In June Muddy's new one, *I Want To Love You* (Chess 1571), went into the charts and Chess had another hit on its hands.

'Last Night I Lost The Best Friend I Ever Had'

And then came tragedy. In the early hours of 3 June, at his home at 4554 S. Greenwood, Henry Strong, Muddy's harp-player, was stabbed, the knife penetrating a lung. Big Walter had sent him to Muddy at the Club Zanzibar as a replacement one night and he had been with the group for two years. Strong came from West Memphis and had been in Chicago since 1947.

FEE RECEIPT NO.

STATE OF ILLINOIS – DEPARTMENT OF PUBLIC HEALTH
CERTIFIED COPY OF A DEATH RECORD

720254

ORIGINAL 14 June 54   **CORONER'S CERTIFICATE OF DEATH**   STATE FILE NO. C 40259

DECEDENT'S BIRTH NO.   STATE OF ILLINOIS 32 894   DIST NO. 3104   REG. NO.

1. PLACE OF DEATH a. COUNTY Cook ILLINOIS	2. USUAL RESIDENCE (Where deceased lived. If institution; residence before admission). a. STATE Illinois b. COUNTY Cook

b. CITY (If outside corporate limits, write RURAL and give township) OR TOWN Chicago   c. LENGTH OF STAY (in this place) 7 yrs.   c. CITY (If outside corporate limits, write RURAL and give township) OR TOWN Chicago

d. FULL NAME OF HOSPITAL OR INSTITUTION (If not in hospital or institution, give street address or location) 4554 S. Greenwood   d. STREET ADDRESS (If rural, give location) 4554 S. Greenwood

3. NAME OF DECEASED (Type or Print) a. (First) Henry b. (Middle) c. (Last) Strong
4. DATE OF DEATH (Month) 6 (Day) 3 (Year) 54

5. SEX Male 6. COLOR OR RACE Negro 7. MARRIED, NEVER MARRIED, WIDOWED, DIVORCED (Specify) Never Married 8. DATE OF BIRTH Sept. 1, 1928 9. AGE (In years last birthday) 25 If Under 1 Year Months Days If Under 24 Hrs. Hours Min.

11a. USUAL OCCUPATION (Give kind of work done during most of working life, even if retired) Musician 10b. KIND OF BUSINESS OR INDUSTRY Entertainment 11. BIRTHPLACE (State or foreign country) Arkansas 12. CITIZEN OF WHAT COUNTRY? U.S.A.

13. FATHER'S NAME J. Q. Strong 14. MOTHER'S MAIDEN NAME Ada Whittaker

15. WAS DECEASED EVER IN U.S. ARMED FORCES? (Yes, no, or unknown) (If yes, give war or dates of service) No 16. SOCIAL SECURITY NO. Unknown 17. INFORMANT a. Signature Ada Neal
b. Address 3328 Indiana c. Relationship to the deceased mother

18. CAUSE OF DEATH
I. DISEASE OR CONDITION DIRECTLY LEADING TO DEATH*
*This does not mean the mode of dying, such as heart failure, asthenia, etc. It means the disease, injury or complication which caused death. ENTER ONLY ONE CAUSE PER LINE FOR (a), (b), and (c).   INTERVAL BETWEEN ONSET AND DEATH

Direct cause (a) STAB WOUND OF THE CHEST (LUNG)

Morbid conditions, if any, giving rise to the above cause (a), stating the underlying cause last. due to (b) STABBED WITH KNIFE

due to (c) DURING ARGUEMENT

II. OTHER SIGNIFICANT CONDITIONS Conditions contributing to the death, but not related to the disease or condition causing death

19a. DATE OF OPERATION 19b. MAJOR FINDINGS OF OPERATION 20. AUTOPSY? YES [X] NO [ ]

21a. ACCIDENT SUICIDE HOMICIDE (specify) MURDER 21b. PLACE OF INJURY (e.g., in or about home, farm, factory, street, office bldg., etc.) IN HOME 21c. (CITY, TOWN, OR TOWNSHIP) CHICAGO (COUNTY) COOK (STATE) ILL.

21d. TIME OF INJURY (Month) JUN (Day) 3, (Year) 1954 (Hour) 3:30 a.m. While at work [ ] Not While at Work [X] 21f. HOW DID INJURY OCCUR? STABBED WITH KNIFE

22. I hereby certify that I made inquiry into the cause and manner of this death, and that I find the deceased herein described died from the causes and on the date as stated above.

23a. SIGNATURE Walter E. McCarron CORONER 23b. DEPUTY CORONER Louis Maddern 23c. DATE SIGNED Jun 25, 1954

RECEIVED FOR FILING ON: JUL 1 1954

BURIAL-REMOVAL-CREMATION (date) JUNE 9 Signed: SUB REGISTRAR DEPUTY REGISTRAR
Cemetery LOCAL Location MEMPHIS TENN.
Firm Name W. HARRIS FUNERAL HOME LOCAL REGISTRAR: Vernon N. Lundeen ILLINOIS
Firm Address 4857 S. STATE ST. Address Reserved For State Office
Signature W. HARRIS License Number 453 Jc

V&R 202 DEPARTMENT OF PUBLIC HEALTH — Division of Vital Statistics and Records

I HEREBY CERTIFY THAT the foregoing is a true and correct copy of the record of death as made from the original certificate of death for the decedent named therein and that this certificate was established and filed with the Department of Public Health in accordance with the statutes of Illinois.

MAY 30, 1972

SPRINGFIELD

Franklin D. Yoder, M.D.
Director of Public Health
State Registrar

Little Walter said:

He was the best harp-blower in Chicago next to me because I taught him all I knew. He was only in his 'teens—very small and we used to call him 'Pot' but he got messed up with a woman. She got angry with him, and just meaning to cut him she went and killed him. He died in the back seat of Muddy's car, on the way to the hospital.

Actually Strong was 25 when he died. Muddy had much difficulty replacing him; eventually 'Little' George Smith joined but stayed only to the end of the year. Neither Henry Strong nor George Smith recorded with Muddy; at Len Chess's insistence, the harp-player used was always Little Walter, whose popularity was probably even greater than Muddy's. There was plenty of work on the road and the band went on tour: first to Birmingham and then, in July, Arkansas; back North for a date in Detroit, and then a four-month nationwide tour ending in Los Angeles. Little Walter had another hit with his next record, *You Better Watch Yourself* (Checker 799), released in August, and then in October Muddy won yet another *Cash Box* award with *I'm Ready* (Chess 1579):

> A middle tempo bounce item that showcases the talented blues chanter's vocal salesmanship. Muddy swings out. Lyrics are pretty potent and Waters delivery is Grade A. Beat is solid and ork-ing is torrid. A great bet to make it.

Cash Box was right—with its train-like rhythm and a superb chromatic harp solo from Walter it proved irresistible and quickly made the Top Ten. It was noticeable, though, how the songs had changed as well as the music. *I'm Ready* was a Willie Dixon song with lyrics tailor-made for the country boy trying to make it in the city. With the accoutrements of 'a high travellin' pistol on a graveyard frame, that shoots tombstone bullets wearing balls and chains', a 'square' could impress a 'chick' and moreover take care of himself. It was an up-to-the-minute distillation of the hopes of life in the city, of respect and sexual success, but despite the humorous exaggeration the overall impression is of a glib invitation to violence.

In a muted reply Little Walter expressed the other side of the blues with his next record and last hit of the year, *Last Night* (Checker 805), a moving tribute to his best friend Henry Strong, cut down by just that kind of easy violence. But not many of his listeners would have seen the connection, for so impersonal and ambiguous were the lyrics that Walter might just as well have been singing about a girlfriend leaving him. This was in fact Walter's second version; there had been an unissued session, possibly on 3 June, at which he recorded both *Last Night* and *My Babe* for the first time. It's interesting to speculate that the unissued version of *Last Night* may have been much more personal, and was held back for that very reason.

When the votes were counted in the annual *Cash Box* Best R & B Artist poll, Walter, who had been in the charts every week of the year with five consecutive hits, was in 6th position with 39,767 votes, just ahead of Muddy, at number 7 with 38,206—a remarkable showing, when Joe Turner topped the poll with 54,016 votes. In all it was a wonderful year for Muddy and Little Walter and especially for Chess Records, which was now established on a very sound financial foundation. This staggering success was achieved through the dedication and tireless efforts of the Chess brothers, in making friends and influencing people like DJs Alan Freed in Cleveland and Dewey Phillips in Memphis and record distributors like Stan

Lewis in Shreveport. While Phil stayed at home looking after the shop, Len was touring the country—in January they were both in Cleveland at Freed's DJ party and then Len was off to the South until late February. In May Len was in Memphis arranging a big dance at the Hippodrome Ballroom with Dewey Phillips of WHBQ (the stars were Muddy, Little Walter and Howling Wolf) before moving on to Louisiana and then back to Detroit looking for new talent. In September Len was again in Memphis and in November in Nashville while Phil was in Detroit. But it all paid dividends.

Chess really promoted their major artists, as can be seen from the numerous tours of Muddy and Little Walter—their bands seemed to be continually on the road in 1954. Chess also seemed to get rather more exposure in the music magazines than most of the independents and the backing of *Cash Box* was immensely valuable in persuading reluctant distributors or jukebox operators to take their product. Most important of all were the long associations with the record men of the South. If a Chess record 'broke' it was more often in Shreveport than Chicago and a glance at the *Cash Box* Top Ten in Shreveport would suggest that it was the heaviest blues town in the whole of the United States. But it was due to constant plugging of the Chess material on Stan Lewis's sponsored radio programmes. Other important radio programmes were sponsored by Ernie's Record Mart, from Nashville, and Randy's from Gallatin, Tennessee.

'It's What's In The Cash Box That Counts'

If the *Cash Box* charts are to be believed, and ignoring the practice of payola, it's clear that there were regional differences in taste—that while the sleek R & B of shouters, balladeers and vocal groups sold well in black areas throughout the United States, there were still some pockets of resistance where the blues were obstinately strong. The main blues areas were the South, of course, and especially Memphis, Shreveport and Nashville; the mid-West, Chicago and St Louis, and to a lesser extent the West Coast. Significantly the blues could make little or no impression in the Northeast. At a time when Muddy Waters and Little Walter were high

in the charts only one each of their records ever penetrated, for instance, the New York or Philadelphia Hot Ten and only Newark, N.J., ever listed their records with any kind of regularity among those netting heaviest play'. Distribution obviously influenced the situation in each area and New York-based Atlantic, with its uptown R & B artists like Joe Turner, Ruth Brown and The Drifters, had the Northeast sewn up, while Chess, with Muddy, Little Walter and Howling Wolf, was similarly very strong in the bible-belt South. But distributors' prejudices as well as franchises were

factors influencing the success of the various styles in the black areas, and that the blues had to overcome initial reluctance on the part of distributors to stock the material is evidenced by *Cash Box's* review of *Hoochie Coochie Man*, which urged: 'Don't be afraid to go on this one. It's in.' But though the distributors may not have been very adventurous they were the best judges of what would sell in their domains, and the plain fact was that the blues sold far better in some places than in others.

This can be seen by examining the companies' product in the same area where distribution facilities are assumed to be equal (which may not be strictly true). The East Coast labels Atlantic, Herald and Savoy did issue blues with their R & B fare but while none of them appeared in the Northeastern charts they would occasionally break out in the South. (For example, Baby Face's *Red Headed Woman* on Savoy was number 10 in Memphis for a couple of weeks.) Conversely, the first real success that Chess/Checker scored in New York and Philadelphia was with the vocal group The Moonglows—exactly the kind of fare with which Atlantic was regaling the northeastern buyers.

While the evidence is not conclusive, and payola obviously had a large effect, it does suggest that differences in taste did exist and that distribution was only a secondary factor tending at times to distort the picture and create anomalies. That San Francisco seemed a better market for Muddy and Little Walter than Los Angeles, and that St Louis seemed to be the only out-of-town area that was a good and regular market for Parrot and United records—and Memphis Slim in particular—must have been owing to the relative strength of distribution of the labels—or their payola arrangements!

But 1954 was a funny year anyway and this apparent new appetite for the Chicago blues so expertly distilled by Chess must be seen against the economic backdrop of mass black unemployment and shrinking sales in the R & B record industry. Perhaps the new country blues had captured a larger share of a declining market only by maintaining their sales, but there was probably more to it than that, for this emergence of the blues, while not uniform across the country, was frequently noted by the hard-headed jukebox operators. For instance, *Cash Box* even deemed the market right for Baby Face's *Red Headed Woman*, cut four years previously for Parkway and reissued in April 1954 on Savoy. Rated B+ (excellent), it was 'a rocker infectiously sold' and the 'disc should catch sales and spins.' Also, in a review of *Louise* by J. B. Lenore (sic) on J.O.B. *Cash Box* said: 'A good deck that is performed in *the style that the market is buying*', and the message was duly noted by the new companies entering the field.

In fact *Cash Box*, in an excess of enthusiasm, even listed J.O.B., five years old at the time, as one of the new companies of 1954! Even RCA Victor had got back into the Groove with an R & B subsidiary on 13 February, but again it was to be an independent company, and this time a black one, that would challengé Chess for supremacy over the next decade.

VJ Records—the V stands for Vivian and the J for Jimmy—was started in mid-1953 by Vivian Carter and Jimmy Bracken at 1155 E. 47th Street. They had been partners in a record shop in Gary since 1948 (although Bracken is remembered by the Detroit singers as the parking attendant at the Harlem Inn) and Vivian was at the time a well-known DJ on WGRY, Gary. The first two releases by Jimmy Reed and The Spaniels had appeared on the Chance label and the connection with Chance is rather confusing. It's probable that they took the records to Sheridan to issue before the VJ venture was under way. The given recording date of 29 December 1953 is certainly wrong; this is probably when VJ reissued them, for Reed himself talks about an audition for Miss Carter on 6 June 1953. The Chance issues must have been soon after for The Spaniels were in the charts in September. Another partnership was started on 16 December that year when Vivian and Jimmy Bracken were married in a spur-of-the-moment ceremony (surely the kind of heaven-sent Christmas story the music trade press dreams about) in the Chicago offices of United Distributors. Vivian was still on the radio and the following February moved from WGRY to another Gary station, WWCA, after Sam Evans (and his five-hour show The Chickadee Hour) moved to WGES in Chicago.

Back in Chicago VJ issued its second disc by The Spaniels and moved offices to 412 E. 47th Street. At the end of March came The Spaniels' third disc, *Goodnight Sweetheart* (VJ 107), which was to prove an enormous success. Reed meanwhile had started much more slowly though his second disc, *I Found My Baby* (VJ 105), was showing promise by May. But most promising of all was Floyd Jones's *Ain't Times Hard* (VJ 111), which, released in July 1954, must have struck a responsive chord in the black audience. Floyd had first recorded the song six years earlier for Tempo-Tone and, while the lyrics were equally pertinent to 1954, the new version, accompanied by Snooky Pryor, Eddie Taylor, Sunnyland Slim and Alfred Wallace, was musically right in the mainstream of the classic Chicago style. *Cash Box* for 7 and 14 August carried excited reports of the disc's progress by VJ's sales representative Leo Kolheim:

> Orders really starting to roll in on Vee Jay's latest *Ain't Times Hard* by Floyd (Dark Road) Jones. In fact Leo claims he's been working nights to handle the output of discs ... Happiest man round our town is Leo Kolheim because of his latest Vee Jay clickeroo *Ain't Times Hard*. Many here call this diskery one of the peppiest in the biz.

Eddie Taylor and (below) *Jimmy Reed.*

The record, though, was destined to be only a minor hit, but it shares with Lenoir's ill-fated *Eisenhower Blues* and Bobo Jenkins's *Democrat Blues* the distinction of being the last of the successful blues records with any social comment. Floyd's music was serious and thoughtful rather than brash and danceable and he was to have only one more commercial release before VJ dropped him in 1955.

In November of 1954 Jimmy Reed's latest was as usual showing plenty of promise and *Cash Box* reviewed *You Don't Have To Go* (VJ 119):

> Jimmy Reed is really in there pitching as he handles the slow bouncy blues with feeling and gusto. Effective wax.

The reverse, *Boogie In The Dark*, was described thus:

> Flip is an instrumental boogie of moderate tempo. The trio makes infectious music that is good juke-box.

Jimmy Reed was indeed 'good juke-box'—the lazy, compelling singing, the fierce upper-register harp playing, the powerful, rolling bass-guitar and heavily accented drumming all added up to a sound that was immediately recognisable and, as relaxed as it was rhythmic, eminently danceable. These early records show more of Reed's Mississippi background than his later ones—he even plays some slide guitar on *Boogie In The Dark* and *Rocking With Reed*—but there is little emotional force in his rather nasal, whining vocals.

The VJ management: James Bracken, Ewart Abner (seated), Vivian Carter, Calvin Carter.

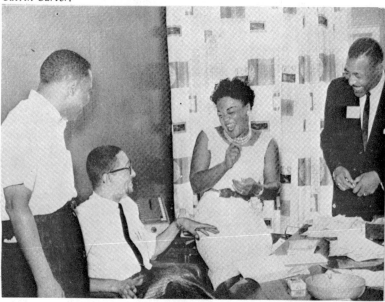

Jimmy was born James Mathis Reed on 6 September 1925 in Leland, Mississippi, the youngest of ten children born to sharecroppers Joseph and Virginia Reed. His mother was a great churchgoer and Jimmy sometimes sang in church but it was his father, who played harmonica, who encouraged him and by the time he was seven Jimmy could pick out tunes on the guitar. It was about this time that he first met Eddie Taylor but their paths diverged until meeting again in Chicago some 20 years later. After very little schooling, at the age of 16 Jimmy left to better himself in Chicago where he had a succession of casual labouring jobs until he was drafted into the Navy in 1943, to spend the entire five years in Coronado, California. On his discharge he returned to Chicago and for the next two years he worked at the Valley Mould Iron Foundry in South Chicago, spending all his spare time practising guitar and learning to play the harmonica. Most evenings he would be in the Club Jamboree waiting to play Homesick's or Baby Face's guitar. This was where he met John Brim and where he and Eddie Taylor resumed their childhood friendship. Eddie remembers:

I was playing a little way from where Jimmy was living. He came over there one night and saw me—that's why we teamed back up together. At that time he wasn't going nowhere. Wasn't hitting no nothing. Just rapping on the guitar and blowing on harmonica. So I just told him lighten up off his guitar and blow his harmonica and I put the beat to it.

Eddie was a much better guitarist and his blues background runs far deeper than that of Reed, who was a comparative newcomer to the music scene. Almost every element of Eddie's upbringing conspired to turn him into a bluesman. He was born in Benoit in the Mississippi Delta, on 29 January 1923. He recalls that

Memphis Minnie and my mother went to school together. She used to nurse me when I was a baby . . . and I used to listen to her play guitar . . . I was two years nine months old when they [his parents] separated. I had a younger brother and an older sister—in other words I had to be the man of the house . . . I do my housework, fields, cut wood, milk cows—I pick cotton—I'd pick two-three hundred pounds cotton y'know a day.

A boyfriend of his mother was a singer and guitarist called Bull Cow; another was Morrison Johnson, Robert Johnson's harp-playing brother. Little wonder then that at seven or eight years old the boy had the music running through his brain:

I didn't stay home when I was little. I had a bike y'know with no fenders on it—I go everywhere. Everywhere in Mississippi, rambling. Out everywhere they play guitars. I'd go off and come back, stay three or four months.

Then he'd be off again. They had moved to Stringtown and this was where

Eddie Taylor accompanies his wife Lee Vera.

Charley Patton used to play. He also heard Patton at Benoit, Leland and Shaw and Son House at Robinsonville and Tunica. The other guitar-players he hung around were less well known—people like Nedhouse, Popcorn Jesse, Bull Cow, Little Quick and Boots. Most of them played at house-dances which Eddie describes:

> At that time down in Mississippi the towns close up something like 12 o'clock or 1 o'clock and you say, 'We going out such and such house, he giving a party tonight.' Well, they play cards, shoot dice and one part of the house, maybe the kitchen and the front part, they have guitar-playing and dancing—all the beds taken down, maybe two or three chairs sitting round the edge of the wall and they have the rest of the floor for dancing.

But he had problems being so young and so small:

> See some places, oh, they wouldn't let me go in because I was so little. When I got there and they wouldn't let me inside I'd go under the house. You see down in Mississippi the porches is raised up from the ground. I go up round the back and crawl through the front porch, sit right under. But I could hear the music y'see. And I sit until the day, until the sunrise. Listen, I go to sleep under the house—wonder a snake didn't bite me y'know! But I'd get the sound of that music in my head.

The sound of the music was to stay in his head:

> A guitar in the country don't sound good until late at night. It has a good ring to it at night. I just sit around those guys and I used to see and when you get something in your head ringing it's got to get out, see. And them sounds used to get in my head and I used to tap a broom—take my mamma's broom and tear the wire off it . . . the first guitar I got was in 1936—my mamma ordered it from Sears Roebuck, 12 dollars. I couldn't tune a guitar. You see the first guy that tuned a guitar for me was a guy called Popcorn but his name was Jesse something. This is at Stringtown.

Once Eddie had mastered the tuning he began to play on the streets:

> I used to go to town on a Saturday—when you out in the country and work all week and you go to town Saturday evening you don't get there till about 6 o'clock when the sun go down and I used to be standing up playing, I'd have a crowd around me and up the street a little further another guy called Honey [David Edwards] he have a crowd right over there. But he was a better guitar-player than I was but I could beat him singing. I could play Arthur Big Boy Crudup's stuff and I could go back and get some of Charley Patton's and get some of Peetie Wheatstraw's stuff. When white people be standing around I play some of Roy Acuff's y'know hillbilly stuff—I mix it up. That's how I got more money than he got, he never did get but over maybe six or seven dollars. Mine be 25-30 dollars in my guitar. But people drop dollars in mine—they put nickels and pennies in his. But he could beat me playing but see this stuff it's not so much your playing, it's the expression you put into your playing.

Eddie met just about everybody in his travels; Wolf in 1932 or '33, Floyd Jones, Muddy Waters when he was running around with Big Joe Williams, Homesick James in Mason, Tennessee. Ike Turner he went to school with in Clarksdale and then when he moved to Memphis in the mid-'40s he met Johnny Shines, Robert Lockwood, B. B. King, who was just starting out then, Buddy Doyle and Walter Horton and Joe Hill Louis and his brother Lockhart. In fact he played with Joe Hill and Lockhart with Eddie's brother, Milton (now dead) playing drums, and also in Memphis he played with Jack Kelly and his brother, Garfield. It was in Memphis that Eddie bought his first electric guitar:

> Me and Willie B [Borum] only somebodies had a electric guitar 'cause that time I had a good job y'know. I didn't go into the army because I was driving a truck for a company had a contract with the army. So it kept me out.

Again the guitar came from Sears Roebuck:

> Let's see, 60 dollars for the guitar and maybe 50 dollars for the amplifier, 100 — about 120-125 dollars you get the whole thing. But that was too hard to get then y'know.

Then in 1949 came the letter from his policeman father and Eddie joined him in Chicago. While working in the packing department of a radio and TV firm he played on Maxwell Street at week-ends, teaming up with Jimmy Lee Robinson. Jimmy's memory is better than Eddie's at this point and he remembers how tough it was:

> Eddie used to come over to see me play and I started to teach him what little I knew about music. 'Cause he knew mostly blues and I showed him how to play hillbilly and all that stuff. And then we'd play the white clubs, just me and him. We had a harp player for a little while, we called him Cooder. He's still in Jew Town, trying to play drums now. So we worked together for quite a while when we got a job on Kedzie, in the 13th block, place called Jake's Tavern. We played there for three dollars a night, from 7 pm till 4 or 5 in the morning. I only had one suit; Eddie had no soles in his shoes. We walked everywhere to these jobs, carrying the amplifiers, and play for five, eight, ten dollars a night. Yeah, we did that for a few years.

Another gig that Eddie and Jimmy Lee played was at the Club Alibi, 3726 Wentworth, with Milton Taylor on drums while Muddy and his group were one block up working for Miss King at the Du Drop Inn, 3609 Wentworth. Then Eddie was at the Congo Lounge with James Scott Jr. for a long time. Then he went down to Memphis to get Walter Horton to join a band he was forming to play the Club Jamboree. Horton came back with Eddie but left after two weeks to replace Junior Wells in Muddy's group. About this time came the meeting with Reed that was to prove so fruitful and Jimmy joined the band, with drummer Kansas City Red. But it was Jimmy's unique vocalising that attracted attention and a recording contract with VJ, and with his more forceful personality Reed took over the band.

Once Jimmy had hit in March 1955 with the appropriately titled (for VJ were planning to drop him) *You Don't Have To Go* there seemed no stopping him, and, although his next record didn't do so well, he was back in the national R & B charts in January 1956 with *I Don't Go For That* (VJ 153) and became the most consistently successful bluesman for the next two years, in which every one of his records made the charts. At the end of 1954 VJ had moved offices again, to 4747 S. Cottage Grove, where they were very near the Chess organisation. With Reed they were poised to challenge Chess's supremacy in the Chicago blues stakes.

Jimmy's big year was 1956 with five consecutive hit records (Muddy had two that year and Little Walter only one); his essentially simple brand of Chicago blues had taken over from the Chess sound. Built on the two-guitar boogie bass it was a new sound, very much of the city. Of course the simple guitar boogie had been used by all the Chicago men but in Reed's music it was incessant; sometimes gently rolling, other times ponderous and slow; the effect was hypnotic. But this rigid instrumentation (until the '60s there had been only one session with a pianist) lent little variety and the tunes were all very similar. One atmospheric

instrumental, *Odds And Ends* (VJ 298), did have a weird violinist added, successfully as it happens, and there is some pretty guitar on the pop song *Honest I Do* (VJ 253) by, allegedly, Remo Biondi, but these trick effects were probably attempts to relieve the tedium of much of Reed's sound. His style, though a degeneration of the Chicago blues, was a paradox— musically limited, emotionally shallow, barren of any poetry, it was still immensely appealing in an era when the blues were for dancing. And Jimmy's real talent lay in his ability to put over the most trite and sentimental songs and still make them sound like the blues; *Caress Me Baby* (VJ 333) and *A String To Your Heart* (VJ 270), for instance, are utterly successful.

Jimmy had problems with his timing and at the recording sessions would usually start singing too early or too late. The prop he was to lean on was Eddie Taylor, and they would sit facing each other when recording so that he could watch Eddie's guitar changes. Much of the success of Reed's records is due to Taylor, who provided the solid bass figures, and indeed Eddie is better recognised as an accompanist than as a solo artist. His first recording under his own name was a version of Sonny Boy's *38 Pistol* which was not issued, and it wasn't until 1955 that *Bad Boy* (VJ 149), his first record, appeared. Cut at a Reed session, it makes interesting comparison with Reed's work. The heavy bass is still there but Taylor's individual guitar style of shimmering bass notes and straight-picked treble clusters makes for a much more complex sound. The song was superb and Eddie's high, clear voice made the most of it. One more session at the end of the year produced his classic coupling, *Big Town Playboy* and *Ride 'Em On Down* (VJ 185), which sold 37,000 copies. *Playboy* was Johnnie Jones's great song, while the reverse was the traditional Mississippi theme associated with Booker White and Big Joe Williams. The next year, with a completely different group—including George Maywether on harp and the excellent Jimmy Lee Robinson on electric bass—Eddie recorded the very exciting *You'll Always Have A Home* (VJ 206), a tour-de-force of electric Chicago blues. Less successful was *Looking For Trouble* (VJ 267), which seemed to need a harmonica and stronger accompaniment; but this was in 1957, by which time the companies were beginning to lose interest in the blues.

Eddie's association with Jimmy Reed is one of the great partnerships in blues, although it's not been without its ups and downs. Reed's health problems—he started suffering from epileptic attacks about 1957—led to heavy drinking and Taylor split with Reed on two occasions at least. The first time he replaced Jimmy Rogers in Muddy's band and the second time he went with Elmore James. There were also problems with Jimmy's new manager, Al Smith, but as Jimmy is nobody without Eddie and Eddie doesn't seem to be able to make it on his own they usually end up together again.

After VJ's success with Reed, 1955 and 1956 saw the company looking round for other blues artists, and there were sessions by Big Joe Williams, Snooky Pryor and young Chicagoan Billy Boy Arnold. Big Joe—or Po' Joe Williams, to revert as the label did to his pseudonym of the '30s—came up from St Louis, bringing harp-player Sam Fowler with him, and cut four sides of great power. Joe was the last of a fast dwindling breed, the journeyman blues singer, and his songs were peppered with memories of 40 years of travelling; of Mobile's Davis Avenue and St Louis's Kings Highway:

> If your woman want to go street-car riding
> Don't take her down on Jefferson and Franklin Street (x2)
> If you do you'll be worried and bothered
> By every jitterbugging cat in the world you meet.

The songs were old-fashioned and Joe was getting on but he didn't sound at all out of place in the electronic atmosphere of the VJ session; in fact he seemed to enjoy himself hugely. Sam Fowler was a Sonny Boy disciple (one of the songs, *My Baby Left Town* (VJ 227), was Sonny Boy's *Shotgun Blues*) and his shrill, wavering harp, matching Joe's brilliant and heavily amplified guitar, testified to many years of working together. In all it was probably VJ's most exciting session. The public, though, was less than excited and only two of the sides were issued—the time for Big Joe's raw, country blues was past and from now on the accent was on youth.

Johnny Hi-Fi (guitar) and Billy Boy Arnold, '50s.

One of the youngest of VJ's new singers was William 'Billy Boy' Arnold, who was born in Chicago on 16 September 1935, just a few months after his parents had left Georgia. His introduction to the blues came from records and he and his mother would listen over and over again to his idol, John Lee Williamson. Billy's imagination was further fed when his father casually mentioned that Sonny Boy used to frequent the Club Georgia, which was run by Big White, Billy's second cousin. But in 1947 Billy was far too young to go in and hear him. The family lived at S. 132nd Street and on Fridays Billy sold the *Defender* on street corners, spending all his five or six dollars earnings at a 63rd Street record shop buying Sonny Boy's records. Then when he got home he would put the records on, get out his Sears Roebuck harp and practise until he learned the songs. He was working at his uncle's butcher shop at 31st and Giles when he discovered to his great excitement that Sonny Boy lived nearby. The next thing was to find out his address, which he managed by chasing after a man with a guitar (it was Lazy Bill) who walked past the shop one day. The first time he called he was too nervous to knock on the door but the next week with his cousin he plucked up courage. Lacey Belle answered, Sonny Boy wasn't home. Then the following week Sonny Boy himself answered the door and invited him in. Surrounded by a group of friends including Johnnie Jones, the good-natured Sonny Boy showed his twelve-year old admirer how to 'choke' the harp. He then invited Johnnie Jones to blow some harmonica but Billy only had ears for Sonny Boy. Billy was only to

A Billy Boy Arnold band of the '50s: Arnold holds mike, the guitarist at right is Jody Williams, and seated at bottom is Henry Gray.

see Sonny Boy once more when, two weeks later, he spent another afternoon talking and practising with him. His last memory of him was later that afternoon, getting into a cab with his amplifier. The next time he called Sonny Boy was dead.

Billy continued to practise and his next influences were Little Walter and then Junior Wells, whom he met about 1951 at a pawnshop where Junior was buying some harps. That same year he teamed up casually with Bo Diddley, who was playing on the streets with a washboard-player and a maraccas-player, and then through Blind John Davis he had a chance to make his first record. This was for the Co-Ben company for its Cool label, but, accompanied by a totally unsuitable group, Bob Carter's Orchestra, the record was very disappointing. Cool gave him the name 'Billy Boy' because he was only 17 years old.

Soon after came his first professional job, playing one-nighters with Johnny Temple, and after that a series of short stints with Johnny Shines and a one-nighter with Otis Rush. By October 1954 Bo Diddley had formed a group to work places like the Sawdust Trail and Castle Rock and Billy Boy joined him again. Next Bo and Billy Boy made a dub of *Dirty Mother Fucker* (which they wisely retitled *Bo Diddley*) and *I'm A Man* and took it in turn to United, VJ and finally Chess. Leonard liked the numbers and in February 1955, with Otis Spann on piano, they cut them for Checker. Leonard didn't like Billy's harp playing, which he felt was too much like Sonny Boys', and when Bo told him that, Billy Boy, thinking Chess had turned him down, recorded his first session for VJ. Turning up at Chess the next day with Diddley he found that Leonard did want to record him and he had to explain that he'd just cut for someone else. The song in question, *I Wish You Would* (VJ 146), was made with Henry Gray (piano), Jody Williams (guitar), Earl Phillips (drums) and Milton Rector (electric bass); this was reputedly the first session from Chicago to feature electric bass. With its novel 'Diddleyish' beat it was quite catchy and began to sell until Len Chess, who saw it as competition to *Bo Diddley*, pulled a few strings—or in this case pulled out a few plugs—and had it taken off the air. However, it was the other side, *I Was Fooled*, with storming piano from the excellent Henry Gray, that was the more impressive blues side. Billy Boy's was only an average talent but with a tight group and good material he turned out some nice sides like *Don't Stay Out All Night* (VJ 171) and *You Got Me Wrong* (VJ 192). His later records were poor and Billy Boy is sincere and honest enough to admit their shortcomings. Much of the blame he laid at VJ's door—the casualness of its operation and its lack of interest in its artists. Billy Boy would turn up at the studios and with the sidemen VJ furnished and little rehearsal have to record tunes selected by the company. Calvin Carter had joined VJ as A & R man while Ewart Abner, who had previously been with Chance, became general manager. Also from Chance came Al Smith who, with Calvin, produced most of the sessions. Smith was born in Greenville, Mississippi, in 1924 but after the 1927 floods his family moved to Pace, Mississippi, where his mother opened a roadhouse. There Al heard his first bluesmen and was inspired to learn the bass, which he played in the school band. At the age of 16 he left for Mobile where he joined the Merchant Marines. After a two-year stint he was in Milwaukee working as a cook and then the next year, 1943, he moved to Chicago to work in a munitions factory. His musical career began properly in 1945 as a bandleader. With eight pieces and a singer, Tiny Topsy, he described it as a 'be-bop' band but when the group broke up in 1952 he formed an R & B band and signed with Chance to provide a house band. After Chance folded in late 1954 he joined VJ as A & R man, bandleader and songwriter and eventually became Jimmy Reed's manager.

But at VJ there was little of the spirit of the Chess organisation, where Leonard worked closely with his artists and just about everybody in the studio cooperated with ideas and assistance to produce the best possible result. Other singers have voiced criticisms similar to Billy Boy's; some blame Abner for the company's attitude, others Bracken. (Billy Boy once overheard Jimmy Bracken say, with pride, that he wouldn't pay any artist two cents in royalties but Eddie Taylor did rather better with his $43 for *Big Town Playboy*!) But whatever the singers' individual grievances it's probable that VJ's treatment of its relatively unsuccessful bluesmen was more or less the same as any other record company's.

Jimmy Reed and (below) *his sometime bass-player Jimmie Lee Robinson.*

Snooky Pryor had a fine session in 1956, the last year in which VJ was to seek 'new' bluesmen. *Judgement Day* (VJ 215) had great lyrics and an easy rolling guitar accompaniment from Floyd Jones and Johnny Young while *Someone To Love Me,* in contrast, was unusual for its stomping guitar riffs. But VJ by then had grown big enough and successful enough to have lost interest in all but its big-selling blues artists, Reed and John Lee Hooker, who had started with VJ the previous year. Hooker's raw Mississippi-style blues, powerful and dramatic, were successfully assimilated into the small-group Chicago sound and once again the chore of curbing erratic timing fell to Eddie Taylor. As well as Taylor and Reed, VJ's house musicians included guitarist Joe Leon (Jody) Williams, pianist Henry Gray, bass players Quinn Wilson and George Washington and drummers Earl Phillips, Al Duncan and Tom Whitehead. Jimmie Lee Robinson and Milton Rector played electric bass on some sessions and the overall VJ sound, heavily electric, was caught brilliantly, as usual, by the Universal Studios engineers.

9 / Decline and Fall

By the late '50s the Chicago blues scene had contracted as both VJ and Chess shifted their emphasis to the popular music market. Only Reed and Hooker at VJ were recording blues while Chess had dropped all but its major singers; only Muddy, Little Walter, Wolf, Sonny Boy Williamson and J. B. Lenoir were left. Ironically the seeds of the destruction of the Chicago blues had been sown back in 1954, the year of their greatest commercial success.

An item in *Cash Box* for 6 March of that year reported that Chicago's South Side record sales were 25% down and by August the men whose livelihoods depended on their ability to spot the trends were in a huddle over the situation. Some of the more optimistic juke-box men put it down to the normal summer recession but the shrewdest among them proclaimed, 'A new music must simply come into being', and, a real *cri de coeur*, 'A hit-maker must come along—and soon too.' The problem was the rise of TV, which challenged the radio shows, the main stimulus for record sales, and the generally depressed economic circumstances which prevented people from buying the discs anyway. Younger people seemed less affected and, with the growing sales to teenagers of the group records by The Spaniels and The Moonglows, for instance, it was felt that these same kids would buy other R & B stars if the records could get promotion again on the top record shows. But with the evening DJs Sam Evans, Al Benson, McKie Fitzhugh and others fighting the televiewers, very little R & B was being broadcast and this new and rising market of teenagers was not being reached.

In the very same issue of *Cash Box*, 14 August 1954, that gave space to all this heart-searching, in fascinating juxtaposition, was a review of Elvis Presley's first record and another news item headlined, 'Sun's unusual Country and R & B pairing creates excitement':

> *That's All Right* is an R & B tune and *Blue Moon Of Kentucky* is out and out Country . . . reports from key cities indicate it will be a big seller. Music Sales Company, Memphis, distributor for Sun, reportedly sold over 4000 copies in the first week.

As if in answer to the record men's prayer a new hit-maker had come along.

With the advent of rock 'n 'roll the independent companies which had been restricted to meeting the needs of the black public realised their opportunity to break into the white popular market with its far greater financial rewards. Rock 'n' roll triggered off a new recording boom, again under odd conditions, for this was the era when one-man companies could have a nationwide hit with a first release and new companies mushroomed

BO DIDDLEY

Chuck and Bo - from the publicists' angle.

in an attempt to crash the market. Chess wasn't going to be left behind, though, and by the time the explosion really came it had already enjoyed three Top Ten hits by artists who sang more rhythm than blues.

Charles Edward Berry was introduced to Chess Records supposedly by Muddy Waters and brought with him a tape of a C & W-styled *Ida Red*. Capitol and Mercury had turned it down but as usual the Chess brothers saw something that the others didn't, its possibilities as an R & B disc. They recut it as *Maybelline* (Chess 1604), gave a dub to Alan Freed at WINS in New York and Chuck Berry was off to a tremendous start. It entered the charts in August 1955, made number 1 and won *Billboard's* Triple Award. Already in the Top Ten was Bo Diddley with his song of the same name and the famous Diddley beat was born. Berry and Diddley were intriguing singers whose highly mutated form of blues were aimed at the teenage market with its preoccupations of cars, young love, drive-ins, jukeboxes and soda fountains. Chuck especially extolled the American Way of Life (and a white one at that) with his brilliant teen-dream fantasies while Bo, more sceptical, concentrated his devastating sense of humour nearer to the roots in songs like *Cops And Robbers* (Checker 850) and *Say Man* (Checker 931).

The effect on the blues, though not immediate, was nonetheless ultimately disastrous. Jimmy Rogers's records of 1956 showed the decline; *Walking By Myself* (Chess 1643) was a catchy pop-song saved only by Walter Horton's inspired harp solo. Even this might not have been, for Charles Edwards was the harp-player originally planned for the session and Horton only stood in when Edwards suffered stage-fright. But the change in style was made all the more pointed, coming after his earlier release of the year, when Chess issued a title made two years previously, the beautiful *Blues All Day Long* (Chess 1616). But worse was to follow. Chess probably felt that Jimmy's light voice could adapt to the pop material that Willie Dixon offered him, but with more modern lead guitarists, Jody Williams and Reggie Boyd, on the sessions, three poor records followed and in 1959 Jimmy's recording career ended. Rogers had left Muddy finally about 1958 to form his own band with Mighty Joe Young on guitar, Henry Gray or Phil Jenkins on piano and S. P. Leary or A. J. Gladney on drums. When this group broke up Jimmy joined Wolf for a while but a family tragedy (one of Jimmy's children died) caused him to lose interest in a life involving long periods on the road away from his wife Dorothy and family.

Muddy and Little Walter were the main sufferers from the demand for a more pop-orientated, rocking music. The sensitivity and rapport of the early days of Walter, Muddy and Jimmy vanished under a welter of powerhouse sound—beauty had lost out to the beat. The imaginative blues songs had gone by the board and there was a depressing similarity to the new songs which, more and more, were being provided by other writers. St Louis Jimmy produced new sets of lyrics to be churned out against the familiar tunes while Willie Dixon wrote his interminable stop-time songs. Everything was belted out at the same high level, as Muddy indulged a propensity for exaggerated vocal gymnastics that the songs seemed to require. *She's Nineteen Years Old* (Chess 1704) was probably the most successful from this period and *Walking Thru The Park* (1718) generated at least a vicarious excitement but *Come Home Baby* and *Good News* (1667), on which Muddy sounds like any run-of-the-mill city singer, were the low-spots of an undistinguished period. The personnel of the band at the time was James Cotton (harmonica), whom Muddy had brought back from West Memphis to replace George Smith, Spann (piano), Pat Hare (guitar) and Francey Clay or Willie Smith (drums).

Cotton was born in Tunica, Mississippi, on 1 July 1935 and was taught harp by Sonny Boy after he left home and came to West Memphis in 1945. He first recorded with Wolf and then with Willie Nix and he had a good record for Sun before joining Muddy. But he was hardly a match for his illustrious predecessors, while Hare, a tough young man (which is only to be expected from anyone christened Auburn Hare), played guitar in the Memphis 'city' style. Sometimes Andrew Stephens played electric bass, which merely enforced the rigidity of the rhythm section.

Little Walter, after a very bad patch through 1956 and 1957, produced a few notable sides like *Ah'w Baby* (Checker 945) and the similar *Everything Gonna Be Alright* (930), *Key To The Highway* (904) and *Blue And Lonesome* (1117), on which he blew a chromatic harp solo that almost equalled his best work of six years before. But with Walter as with Muddy such moments were by now the exception rather than the rule. It

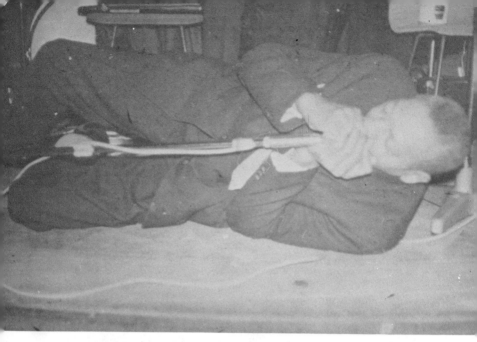

may be significant that by this time Leonard Chess was losing interest in his bluesmen and concentrating on the more obviously commercial artists who were scoring the spectacular successes. Ralph Bass joined the company from Federal, where he had recorded Kid Thomas (Lou Watts), and took over production of many of the Chess sessions.

Some artists were less affected by the trends. J. B. Lenoir, for example, had joined Chess after the collapse of Parrot in 1956 (according to a report in *Cash Box*, 24 March 1956, which stated that 'John Burton buys Parrot and Blue Lake'—the masters were later sold to Chess in 1959). J.B. had always had a bright, rocking band and as to be expected there was little effect on the quality of his music. Lyrically he was as interesting as ever with another version of *Eisenhower Blues* (unissued) and one fascinating song about the hair process, *Don't Touch My Head* (Checker 856):

> I got shined shoes and a nail manicure
> A diamond ring, man, I got everything
> So don't you touch my head (x3)
> 'Cause I just got a [braid?] process.

Above: *Sonny Boy Williamson No. 2, as many audiences will remember him. From one of his British tours of the '60s, when he would sing: 'I'm goin' to make London my home, because the people back in my country just don't know what in the world is goin' on.'* Right: *Howlin' Wolf and his band at the Ash Grove, Los Angeles, 1968.*

There was a fine slow blues, *I've Been Down So Long*, on the reverse but with his regular and immensely swinging band of two saxes, Alex Atkins and Ernest Cotton, pianist Joe Montgomery (brother of Little Brother Montgomery) and Al Galvin on drums, J.B. did more rocking and rolling than anyone. But after a last session with an organ and vocal group, Chess dropped him.

In contrast Sonny Boy and Wolf continued recording right through the '60s and, if they seemed relatively unaffected by the trends, it could be explained by a certain obstinacy in their natures. Or by the fact that their music had never shown the solid characteristics of the mature Chicago style anyway—or at least not until they got to Chicago. Sonny Boy's first Checker recordings were a great improvement on his last Trumpet sessions, as he settled easily into the Chicago mould. He probably needed a tight Chicago band to discipline him and *Don't Start Me To Talking* (Checker 824), a marvellous signifying blues, with Muddy's group, showed him to far better advantage than any of his earlier recordings. His records were to show a remarkable consistency until well into the '60s, which was a very sad period for virtually every other bluesman.

Sonny Boy was the last of the great blues poets and his songs were a riot of colour and imagination. There was an almost surreal quality to some of his lyrics and *Unseeing Eye* (927) contains one of the most bizarre verses in the recorded history of the blues:

> That unseen eye reminds me of a midnight dream (x2)
> It reminds me of someone, someone I have never seen.

Sonny Boy would have earned Lightning Hopkins' approval for his songs were not solely concerned with women. There were tender love songs like *Cross My Heart* (910), with its unconscious humour as Sonny, one of the most accomplished of liars, sings, 'It's a sin to tell a lie', but women were just part of the whole blues experience that he voiced for his people. Rather, loneliness and frustration were his main discontents as in the beautiful *It's Sad To Be Alone* (943), *Lonesome Cabin* (956), the wry *Fattening Frogs For Snakes* (864) and *All My Love In Vain* (824). The menacing *Your Funeral And My Trial* (894) was almost straightforward in comparison, an up-tempo rocking blues. But Sonny's material provided constant surprises. There was even an astonishing, albeit unsuccessful, adaptation of a mediaeval English folk song (probably via many hillbilly versions) in *Wake Up Baby* (894), a sly personification of the black man (or was it Sonny Boy himself?) in *The Goat* (943) and a riotously funny recreation of a Southern 'coon chase in *The Hunt* (975). This duet with Willie Dixon must have been very close to the 'Two Black Crows' comedy routine that Sonny and Willie Love used to enact on the train to New Orleans. More than anything his songs had wit and style, an elegance and an imagination that emerged unscathed from the debris of the rock 'n' roll explosion.

While Sonny Boy went his own way Wolf succeeded against the odds in adapting his style to the new demands. He was still using traditional sources in 1956, whence dates one of his greatest performances, the eerie and spellbinding *Smokestack Lightning* (Chess 1618). With its falsetto howls and moans it owes much to the Delta tradition and the debt is equally clear too on other tracks like *I Asked For Water* (1632), *Poor Boy* (1679) and *I'm Sitting On Top Of The World* (1679). But on the later records the more obviously rural traits were dropped and the band, with Spann, Henry Gray or Johnnie Jones replacing jazzman Hosea Lee Kennard on piano, achieved a bright, raucous and rocking sound.

Back Door Man and *Wang Dang Doodle* (1777), *Shake For Me* (1804) and *Just Like I Treat You* (1823) are clearly more urban in derivation and have a massive, jangling and exciting beat. *Down In The Bottom* (1793) still used Mississippi's *Rolling And Tumbling* theme and slide guitar but *Spoonful* (1762) could hardly be traced back to Charley Patton. These were Willie Dixon songs and much better than the tired cliché-ridden material he was churning out for Muddy and Little Walter. Some idea of how tightly Dixon had the Chess blues recording operations in his grasp

Key figures in Chess management: left, *Ralph Bass, producer, outside the present GRT-owned Chess studios;* right, *producer-composer-performer Willie Dixon.*

can be seen from Wolf's records from the early '60s, when, out of ten single releases, three-quarters at least were songs by Big Dixon.

'I Am The Blues'

Willie Dixon came from Vicksburg, Mississippi, where he was born on 1 April 1915. As a boy he sang in spiritual groups and learned to play the string bass. The family moved to Chicago in 1935 and Willie took up professional boxing for a few years as a heavyweight. After the fight game he turned to music as a career and in 1940 first acquired a taste for the recording business when, playing bass in The Five Breezes (with Gene Gilmore and Leonard 'Baby Doo' Caston), he recorded for Bluebird. More records followed with groups like The Four Jumps Of Jive, with Gilmore, for Mercury in 1945 and The Big Three Trio, with Caston, for Bullet and then Columbia in 1946. The Big Three were very successful and their sophisticated jump blues proved popular enough for them to have 13 records issued by Columbia through 1947. Then in 1951 came Dixon's introduction to Chess when he produced Nighthawk's *Black Angel* Aristocrat session.

His songwriting activities seem to have started about 1954 with some good blues for Muddy, *Just Make Love To Me* and *I'm Ready,* and from then on Muddy and Little Walter recorded many of his songs. Willie claims he has written over 250 songs and often the quantity is more evident than the quality. Sometimes the lyrics were clever as in *Close To You*, recorded by both Muddy (Chess 1704) and Sonny Boy Williamson (Checker 1080). Sonny Boy sang: 'I want to get close to you baby as the spots on a dice.' But more often they were puerile as in Walter's *Crazy For My Baby* (Checker 986) and *Crazy Mixed Up World* (919). His best songs seemed reserved for Wolf and while there were still the trivial *Hidden Charms* (Chess 1890) and *300 Pounds Of Joy* (1870) there was also the marvellous *Wang Dang Doodle*, which was further proof of Dixon's skill in adapting traditional material. As *My Babe* was an adaptation of the gospel song *This Train, Wang Dang Doodle* was based on the old lesbian song, *The Bull Daggers Ball,* and although 'Fast Talkin' Fannie' replaces 'Fast Fuckin' Fannie' Dixon's version with its catalogue of low-life characters is only marginally less colourful than the original.

> Tell Double Crossing Ed
> Tell Abyssinia Ned
> Tell ole Pistol Pete
> Everybody gonna meet
> Tonight we need no rest
> We really gonna throw a mess
> We gonna break out all the windows
> We gonna kick down all the doors
> We gonna pitch a wang dang doodle all night long, all
>   night long
> Tell Fats and Washboard Sam
> That me 'n' everybody gonna jam
> Tell Shakin' Box Car Joe
> We got sawdust on the floor
> Tell Jennie Mae till I die
> We going to have a time
> When the fish scent fill the air
> There's snuff juice everywhere . . .

Violent pleasure forms one of the main strands of Dixon s songs; the other ingredients are superstition and magic as in *Hoochie Coochie Man* or Wolf's *I Ain't Superstitious* (Chess 1823), and sexual prowess, as in Muddy's *I'm A Natural Born Lover* (Chess 1585) and *Young Fashion Ways* (1602), with its concomitant theme of back-door seduction as in Wolf's *Back Door Man* and *Tail Dragger* (Chess 1890).

Dixon was working with Memphis Slim at the Gate of Horn in 1959 when they landed an overseas tour. Playing for white audiences Willie learned a vast quantity of folk material and included in his act little homespun homilies calculated to please such an audience. While extremely tedious in person, one such piece on record, Wolf's *Going Down Slow*

Howlin' Wolf (right) *and his long-time guitarist Hubert Sumlin.*

(Chess 1813), was very successful, the spoken passages enriching an already fine record (although an alternative take without Dixon's comments sounds tame and lethargic in comparison).

Playing to the audience was only one example of Willie's astuteness: despite his birthdate he was certainly no fool and from the mid-'50s onwards his gargantuan figure looms ever larger over the Chicago scene as a musician, songwriter, agent, A & R man, record producer and music publisher. That his rise to fame should parallel exactly the decline of Chicago's blues was more than coincidence, for it was the Bluebird story all over again, reading Dixon for Melrose and Chess for Bluebird. Once again one man was responsible for nearly all the blues recording in the city and, more than that, was also responsible for writing most of the material. However talented that one man, the result had to be monotony and tedium in much of the output. Wolf and Sonny Boy suffered less from this musical incest, probably because they wouldn't (in Sonny Boy's case) or couldn't (in Wolf's) learn the new songs. Muddy, on the other hand, eager to change with the market, was a willing pupil and hence was subjected to various experiments. However, among the insipid 'Tribute to Big Bill' and 'Folk Singer' sessions there was one totally convincing recording with Earl Hooker's band. *You Shook Me* (Chess 1827) and *Little Brown Bird* (1839) were ultra-modern blues with organ and saxes but far more convincing than the contrived nostalgia of the other sessions. Willie Dixon's influence has been for good and for bad and he stands astride the scene as a kind of Mayor Daley of the Chicago blues. One of the stagey homilies that so delighted European audiences was titled *I Am The Blues*—certainly in Dixon's case it was no idle boast.

10/The West Side

In 1940 the two main areas of black residence were the traditional Black Belt on the South Side, which stretched along State Street from Roosevelt Road to 71st Street, and on the Near West Side, the area between Lake Street and Roosevelt Road. There were also scattered blocks on the Near North Side between North and Chicago Avenues and, on the far South Side, a few blocks around 95th and State (the Lilydale community). Further east there was a small enclave between 87th and 95th Streets by the steel mills of South Chicago, and to the west the Morgan Park area centred on 111th Street. But between 1940 and 1950 Chicago's black population was swollen by about 220,000 (a 77% increase on the 1940 figure), with the most rapid growth occurring in the immediate postwar years of 1946-9. Migration accounted for the bulk of the increase, with the migrants spread fairly evenly throughout the older established black areas but with more and more moving to the West Side. The South and West Sides were already badly congested and in response to this increased pressure on accommodation there was a fairly rapid expansion of the residential areas from 1948 onwards as, usually, the older black inhabitants led the move into previously all-white districts.

In this movement they were abetted by the market forces, as the real estate men became increasingly aware of the higher profits to be realised from letting to blacks who were able and willing to pay the inflated property prices demanded. The expansion was almost entirely a block-by-block movement into the districts bordering the Black Belt, often accompanied by violent opposition from the white residents, for by 1950 there was only one new area of black settlement, the Altgeld public housing project between 127th and 135th Streets.

The years from 1950 to 1958 saw further expansion as the population grew (more by natural increase, 80%, than migration, 20%) and the South Side pushed eastwards and southwards as far as Lake Michigan into Kenwood and Hyde Park, then, skirting the University, into Woodlawn; westwards into Englewood, and directly southwards to join up with Lilydale, which extended to 97th Street. Outside Chicago the '50s also saw the creation of mainly black suburbs—Dixmoor, E. Chicago Heights, Phoenix and Robbins, Illinois. By 1960 E. Chicago Heights, for example, was 85.4% black and Robbins 98.7%.

The main expansion on the West Side was into Lawndale between Roosevelt Road and 22nd Street from Kedzie to Crawford, as a predominantly Jewish population moved northwards or to the suburbs. And it was on the dilapidated and overcrowded West Side that a new and angry music was reared.

King Cobra

The West Side's first record company was Eli Toscano's Abco label, which he started in partnership with Joe Brown from 2854 W. Roosevelt Road early in 1956. There was a fine release by Louis Myers (Abco 104), blowing harp in a close approximation of Little Walter, one by Morris Pejoe and a couple of 'city' blues from Arbee Stidham but nothing much happened until Brown dropped out and Toscano introduced his own Cobra label in August that year. It started with Otis Rush's *I Can't Quit You Baby* (Cobra 5000), which entered the charts in October and provided Cobra with their first and only Top Ten hit. It was yet another Willie Dixon song and Dixon was closely associated with the label as songwriter, A & R man and band-leader.

Rush, a quiet, handsome young man, had been playing guitar for only two years. Back home in Philadelphia, Mississippi, where he was born on 29 April 1934, he had tried to make the usual guitar out of baling wire, but he was playing harmonica by the time the family moved to Chicago in 1948. Working in the stockyards he met a boy, Mike Netton, who played drums and they tried to form a band. Then in 1954 he took up the guitar and one year later played his first club date for Bob Jones at the Alibi with 'Poor Bob' Woodfork, a guitarist from Arkansas, accompanying. With the success of his first record he was to become Cobra's most recorded bluesman. Records were his natural medium anyway, for he had learned his blues from records and the radio in the first place.

The great influence was another Mississippi guitarist, B. B. King, who had developed a completely original style which owed nothing to the Delta where he was born. King sang an open throated gospel-styled blues backed by polished 'city' musicians and used a guitar technique fashioned on fast, free, single-note runs combining influences as diverse as Django Reinhardt, Charley Christian and even Les Paul. But with the freedom of a jazz soloist

★ **HIS FIRST TEXAS TOUR** ★

OTIS RUSH
AND HIS ORCHESTRA

Latest Hits: "My Love Will Never Die" - "Violent Love" - "Love That Woman"

RHYTHM & BLUES AGENCY PH. NORMAL 7-4151 or 4152 **CHICAGO, ILL.**

B.B. played the blues. He had a string of hits through the '50s for RPM, the Modern subsidiary, and by 1956 it was his brew of blues and jazz that the younger West Side men were savouring and finding to their taste.

Rush was a fine guitarist using a style more ringing but less fleet and multi-noted than King's. There was a suspense and agonised tension to his music as he dragged out the notes, left them hanging and quickly followed with explosive clusters. His vocals are in much the same style; he tortures the words in his crying, sometimes falsetto voice with a frightening intensity, the band groaning and heaving in the background. Like all the new young bluesmen he was governed by the commercial dictates of the time, which required one blues side to be coupled with a rock 'n' roll novelty or dire ballad for release, and it speaks volumes for Rush as an artist that of his eight records for Cobra five songs at least were outstanding—a consistency achieved by few of his contemporaries. *Groaning The Blues* (Cobra 5010), a Dixon number, is one of the most violent and expressive performances of a modern singer while *My Love Will Never Die* (Cobra 5005), also credited to Dixon, is a beautiful blues in minor. Of his own songs *Checking On My Baby* (Cobra 5027) was another near-classic performance, marred only by the ugly riffing sax, while on *Double Trouble* (Cobra 5030), the modern blues masterpiece, again in minor, he approaches the harrowing poetic terror of a Robert Johnson:

> I lay wake at nights, false love, just so troubled
> It's hard to keep a job, laid off, having double trouble
> Hey hey yeah they say you can make it if you try
> Yeah some of this generation is millionairees
> It's hard for me to keep decent clothes to wear.

The West Siders had taken King's style to heart, made the guitar more prominent, and with a small R & B band with sax instead of brass set the blues on the road to the '60s. There were still experiments. The early Rush sides had Shakey Horton on harmonica but he was so unobtrusive that he sounded like a second sax. Usually Harold Ashby played tenor, Lafayette Leake or Little Brother Montgomery played piano while the drummer was Odie Payne and the omnipresent Dixon played bass.

But more than anything the guitar was different. Guitarist Jimmy Dawkins gives a fascinating explanation of how the busy West Side guitar style arose:

> It was the thing that we couldn't get the money to have a full band. There's a thing with most of the West Side boys. What we're doing is playing with a bass, drums and guitar, but we're *thinking* of a horn or two horns and when we throw those heavy chords that's what we're doing. It's a creative thing. It makes us get this heavy sound as we call it substituting for a full band . . . we just weren't able to hire and we had to fill it up some kind of way. And we'd rather play with three pieces because it makes us work harder.

Another development, more harmful to subtlety and swing, was the use of the electric bass. Otis Rush had a guitarist, Willie D. Warren from Greenwood, Mississippi, whom legend credits with being the first electric bass player. He would use his guitar just like a bass, playing only on the low strings of the instrument. Then the first Fender basses appeared on the scene and very soon every band was using them.

Otis was soon joined on Cobra by another young Mississippian who played in the intense West Side manner. Magic Sam was born Sam Maghett in Grenada, Mississippi, on 14 February 1937 and like Rush learned his blues from the records of Muddy and Little Walter. When he was 13 the family moved to Chicago and he grew up in the neighbourhood of 27th and Calumet with childhood friends Syl Johnson and Mack Thompson. He was 19 when he started professionally and his first gig was in his uncle Shakey Jake's band with Mack Thompson at the Wagon Wheel, Madison and California. Thompson remembers they made an audition dub of *All Your Love* and hawked it round the record companies until finally Toscano showed interest. After the session they had to think of a professional name instead of the one he was using, Good Rocking Sam,

Cobra Records' publicity picture of Magic Sam, 1957/8.

which was already in use by another artist. Toscano wanted to call him Sad Sam but Mack objected that 'This is old time.' Similarly with Singing Sam. This new, confident breed of bluesmen wanted something up to date. Then Mack came up with Magic Sam from an approximation of Maghett Sam and that was it. Sam eloquently underlined the new attitude: 'I don't want to be Sad Sam, Poor Sam, Black Sam, Dark Sam or what have you.' So Magic Sam it was and his new name was very quickly established with his first record *All Your Love* (Cobra 5013) in 1957. It was a fine slow blues and the forerunner of many versions of the same tune. While his tremolo guitar was distinctive enough, as a creator Sam was very limited and he constantly returned to the theme on record, using it with slight variations for the slow blues side of each of his Cobra records, *Everything Gonna Be Alright* (5021), *All Night Long* (5025) and *Easy Baby* (5029). However, he was tremendously popular in Chicago and the records sold well until the army interrupted his career and he was drafted in 1959. Out again seven months later, after one month of service and six months in jail for desertion, Sam found it hard to pick up the pieces of his musical career.

Cobra had moved offices to 3346 W. Roosevelt by the time they launched their last subsidiary, Artistic, in August 1958. Artistic introduced the last of their trinity of young West Side guitarists, George 'Buddy' Guy. Buddy was born in Lettsworth, Louisiana, on 30 July 1936 and unlike the others had been playing semi-professionally for a few years before he arrived in Chicago. He'd learned his blues from the records of Hopkins and Hooker and T-Bone Walker on the radio. Then came the usual boyhood experiments with a home-made guitar at the age of 13, until his father bought him a $3 instrument four years later. His first real guitar was bought for him by a stranger, one Mitchell, who needed a guitarist to back his singing. This Buddy did and at week-ends they played around Baton Rouge until, as mysteriously as he came, Mitchell vanished. Buddy still had the guitar of course, and while working in a filling-station to support his mother he practised and played locally awaiting his chance. It looked as if it had come when Big Poppa (the 270lb John Tilley), the most popular artist in the locality, arrived in Baton Rouge without his guitar-player and hired Buddy. But Buddy was so nervous he lost the job. Six months later Big Poppa returned and gave the boy another try. This time Buddy's friends got him so drunk that he overcame his stagefright. From then on Buddy joined Tilley's band and had an opportunity to play with all the name artists in the area, men like Lightning Slim, Lazy Lester and Slim Harpo. In 1956 a friend returning from Chicago wanted him to go back with him but Guy decided to wait a year until he was 21. When he did make the trip it was tough finding a job but eventually he was hired by sax player Rufus Foreman who was resident at Theresa's on Indiana. But before Buddy joined them the Foreman band lost the job and Buddy still wasn't playing anywhere. After another period of kicking his heels they were hired by Sinclair, manager of the Big Squeeze club on the West Side, and the band, with Rufus (tenor sax), Baby Face Willette (piano), Hal Tidwell (drums) and Buddy on guitar and handling the vocals, played there for four or five months before returning to Theresa's.

Buddy's career was really boosted when he met Otis Rush and Magic Sam at a 'Battle of the Blues' organised at the Blue Flame, 55th and State Street. From there Sam took him to Toscano and a recording contract and, most important of all, to Willie Dixon. By the time of his first records, *Sit And Cry* (Artistic 1501) and *This Is The End* (1503), his style was already formed; the high screaming voice breaking on the top notes, cutting like a scalpel through an open nerve and soaring over the squeezed strings of his B. B. King-like guitar. The frenetic energy of his singing and playing was matched only by his exciting stage show and in action Guy put on the kind of unrestrained exhibition that had the audience up yelling on their feet while Buddy was crawling down on his knees. More than anything his blues were an extrovert expression of black pride, symbolising the coming of age and rapidly growing confidence of his people, though the excitement and violence contrasted strangely with his quiet and unassuming manner offstage.

'A Crap Shootin' Fool'

Also on Artistic was a record by Magic Sam's uncle and manager, Shakey Jake. James D. Harris was born in Ellis or Earle, Arkansas, on 12 April 1921 and came to Chicago at the age of seven. Before he became a musician he'd been a professional gambler for 15 years and his stage-name was a relic of his past:

> The boys used to holler 'Shake 'em Jake, shake the dice!' and so I would give them a little click . . . never did shake them, just hittin' them together and the boys used to argue, 'Shake 'em Jake', and so they just started to callin' me Shakey Jake.

After a disgruntled loser had shot him in the side Jake decided on music as a less dangerous occupation. He started organising bands and while they played to the audience out front Jake would be in the back shooting dice with the tavern owner! The band didn't make very much but Jake got along very well with his gambling income. Eventually he learned the harp but on his first record, *Call Me If You Need Me* (Artistic 1502), he only sang, assisted by Sam's stinging guitar. The session was done free but Jake didn't mind—he won $700 shooting craps with Eli Toscano. Jake adds, 'Eli was a crap shootin' fool!'

Artistic's first artists: top left and bottom, *Buddy Guy;* top right, *Shakey Jake, from the original Artistic publicity photograph for* Call Me If You Me/Shake Your Moneymaker.

The rest of Toscano's artists told similar stories but they didn't fare so well. Sam was young, anxious to get started in the business, and didn't worry about the money from the records; Otis ruefully recalls that his records made a lot of money but Toscano would gamble it all away.

Toscano recorded other bluesmen as well. There was an eccentric pop blues *Row Your Boat* (Artistic 1500) from Charles Clark with superb accompaniment from a group including Sonny Boy Williamson, but as well as the aggressive and self-confident music of the West Siders there were a few records by the older singers. Shakey Horton had one on Cobra as did Sunnyland Slim and Little Willie Foster. Foster was playing harp in Floyd Jones's band at Vi's Lounge, 14th and Ashland, at the time and Floyd wrote one of the songs, *Crying The Blues* (Cobra 5011). Old-fashioned though it was by 1957, the lyrics were a sharp reply to the introverted self-indulgence of the songs and music of the young West Side men:

> Crowds of children screamin' and cryin', peoples kept
>   on passing by (x2)
> They out in the zero weather and nobody hear them cry.

Foster's wailing harp and Lazy Bill's solid, thumping piano were the last echoes of the dying classic style.

When Cobra's operations ceased prematurely with the gangland murder of Toscano in 1959—his body was dragged out of Lake Michigan—Dixon took Rush and Guy to Chess. Otis contributed another modern blues masterpiece in *So Many Roads So Many Trains* (Chess 1751), a quite ordinary song which Rush's performance invests with an impact and force beyond description, Guy, whose strained, aggressive singing sometimes conveys the haunting fear and violence that marked Robert Johnson's work, also had an impressive debut on Chess with the excellent *First Time I Met The Blues* (Chess 1753)—actually a Little Brother Montgomery song from 1936. His portrayal of nameless terror invites comparison with Johnson:

> The first time I met the blues, people, you know I was walkin',
>   I was walkin' down through the woods,
> Yea-ees the first time, the first time I met the blues don't you
>   know I was walkin', I was walkin' down through the woods;
> Yea-ees you stopped by my house first blues—don't you know
>   you got me, you got me all the harm that you could.
>
> The blues got after me people you know they ran me from
>   tree to tree,
> Yea-ees the blues got after me, don't you know you ran me,
>   ran me from tree to tree;
> Yea-ees you shoulda heard me beggin' blues, aiee, blues
>   don't murder me.

Guy's outgoing stage act made him more popular than Rush, who had only one more release on Chess while Guy recorded fairly steadily as a name artist and as a house musician until well into the '60s. Otis then signed with Duke Records, which released only one of his records and hamstrung him for the duration of his contract.

Blues From London

Magic Sam, on returning from his brief stint in the army, finally signed to record with Mel London's Chief label. Mel London was the archetypal R & B record man with a string of labels to his credit—or rather his debit, for as each one failed another would rise Phoenix-like from the ashes. Chief started in early 1957 with a calypso offering by London himself but settled down to a steady fare of R & B and rock 'n' roll. The main artists were Junior Wells, whose ten records accounted for about a quarter of the label's total output, Magic Sam, Lillian Offitt and Earl Hooker. Wells's releases were mediocre except when he joined forces with Earl Hooker and Sam's four records were indifferent too. Lillian Offitt was an R & B singer from Nashville but she made one excellent blues, *Will My Man Be Home Tonight* (Chief 7012), which was one of London's best sellers. It was a strong melody, Lillian's acid-sweet voice fitted perfectly this tale of domestic woe and Earl Hooker's slide accompaniment was superb. But the low-spot was an awful gimmicky crying passage and a child's voice comforting, 'Don't cry, mommy'. With a family like that no wonder the man didn't stay home.

Chief's only other good sellers were Junior Wells's *Messing With The Kid* (7021) and, with Earl Hooker, *Blues In D Natural* (7016), and there was a minor rock 'n' roll hit by one Tobin Matthews, but without doubt the finest blues items on the label were those by Elmore James and one other Wells-Hooker instrumental, the brilliant *Calling All Blues* (7020). Chief folded in 1961 to be replaced by the short and sharp Profile label. The only two blues issues, by Junior Wells of course, were nice: *Come On In This House* (4011) and *Prison Bars All Around Me* (4013), a new version of his old States song *So All Alone*. Undaunted by the Profile disaster Mel bounced back with his new company, Age, and new artists. Earl Hooker still had some issues but the new star was Ricky Allen, who was very popular locally and enjoyed three of Age's four best sellers; the other was by Big Moose (John Walker), but the only real blues among the 20-odd issues was Hooker's *Blue Guitar* (Age 29106), actually the instrumental track of Muddy's *You Shook Me*.

Earl, a cousin of John Lee Hooker, was born in Clarksdale, Mississippi, on 15 January 1930, but was brought up mostly in Chicago. In 1945 he learned to play guitar under the tutelage of Robert Nighthawk and it's Nighthawk that his brilliantly smooth slide technique recalls. He joined Ike Turner's band in Memphis in 1949 and toured extensively, cutting his first record, Nighthawk's *Sweet Little Angel*, for Henry Stone's obscure Rockin' label of Miami, Florida. Earl didn't have a good voice and

Theresa's Lounge, 48th and Indiana, and Theresa's takeaway matchbook, a perennial blues souvenir.

from then on he concentrated on instrumentals, recording for King and then for the small Chicago companies. Despite being dogged by ill-health throughout his career and frequently hospitalised with tuberculosis, Earl achieved the reputation of being the finest guitarist in Chicago.

Earl's band was used to back R & B singer Bobby Saxton on his big-selling record for Bea & Baby. The label was owned by Cadillac Baby, a fascinating character. He was born Narvel Eatmon in Cayuga, Mississippi, about three miles from Edwards and near Vicksburg, in 1914. From an early age he was steeped in the blues of the area; local artists like the Chatman brothers and Walter Jacobs (Vincson) made a special impression on him. After work on the W.P.A. he hitch-hiked to Chicago in 1935, where he found a job as a night-watchman and janitor. By 1947 he'd bought the car that was to provide him with a name in keeping with his flamboyant personality. As a natural showman he logically decided to move into the club business and in the early '50s he took over the old DeLisa's premises and opened up his Cadillac Baby's Show Lounge at 4708 S. Dearborn. He was generous with his musicians and always ready with a

TRI-STATE INN
2576 JENNINGS - GARY, IND.
BLUE MONDAY   EVERY MONDAY NITE

EARL HOOKER

Latest Recordings:
"Heard and Heavy"
"Dynamite"

AND HIS ROADMASTERS

★ **FEATURING** ★
BOBBY SAXTON
"Trying to Make a Living"
— AND —
HAROLD TIDWELL
"Linda Lou" - "Sweet Sue"
ALSO MISS LINDA LOU

NJOY ALL KINDS OF FINE FOOD AT OUR NEW
BUILT-IN SNACK BAR!

★ ★   DONATION 50c   ★ ★

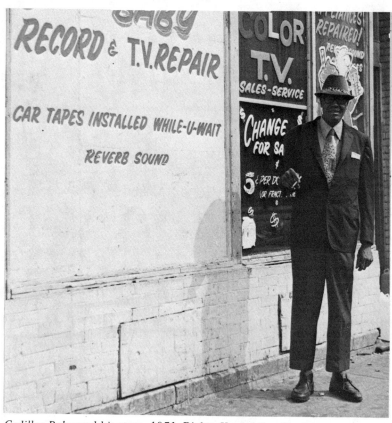

Cadillac Baby and his store, 1971. Right: *Hound Dog Taylor.*

helping hand and when he started the Bea & Baby label (named for himself and his wife, Bea) in the late '50s the artists returned the favours by recording for him. There were records by Eddie Boyd and Sunnyland Slim but the two big sellers were commercial items, *Trying To Make A Living* (Bea & Baby 106) by Bobby Saxton and Detroit Junior's *Money Tree* (111). There were several records by Little Mack and Hound Dog Taylor had a nice one, *My Baby's Coming Home* (112). Baby used a variety of labels including Miss and Keyhole and Hound Dog's record was reissued on Marjette and Key.

Little Mack (Simmons) from Twist, Arkansas, where he was born in 1933, was an average singer and harp-player. He arrived in Chicago in 1951 and learned harp from Little Walter but his main influences were the records of Junior Parker and B. B. King. His own group was formed in 1952 with Eddie King (guitar), Bob Anderson (bass) and Robert Whitehead (drums), and he held it together for about 10 years.

Hound Dog's record was the most interesting. He played slide guitar very much like Elmore James, in keeping with his Mississippi origins. Theodore Roosevelt Taylor was born in Greenville on 14 April 1916 (or possibly in Natchez on 12 April 1915). First he tried the piano and then made a cigar-box guitar, to be replaced by the real thing, ordered from Sears Roebuck. He was 19 by then and learned to play by watching the musicians in Tchula, where he was then living. His big influence was Elmore James but he names Lightnin' Hopkins and Sonny Boy (Rice Miller) as other sources of inspiration, and in fact he played with Sonny Boy on the King Biscuit programme. After some trouble in Mississippi he left to come to his sister in Chicago. He played with Johnny Williams at Stormy's and there were plans to record them, which fell through. Later Hound Dog was signed up by DJ and manager Big Bill Hill.

Cadillac Baby even had some unissued sides by Sleepy John Estes and Hammie Nixon but with the decline of the early '60s the label's activity ceased. It was a difficult period all round for Baby as the club had to close when the street was torn down for the project housing. He reopened at 624 E. 47th Street but not for long. In 1965 came his last move to 4405 S. State Street, where he now runs a chaotic store.

Most of the artists on the small labels did the rounds and Hooker, Hound Dog, Little Mack and Detroit Jr cropped up on Carl Jones's group of labels. Carl Morris Jones was a singer who was born in Waxahatchie, Texas, in 1917. In the '30s he'd toured with the Carolina Cotton Pickers and then he moved to Chicago in 1937. He recorded with groups for Richard M. Jones at Mercury in 1942 and then gradually picked up experience of the business by recording other artists for the company. Finally with encouragement from Richard M. he started his C.J. label about 1959 from 4803 S. Indiana, next door to Theresa's famous tavern. Ike Perkins was the A & R man and, with odd sessions by Little Mack, Slim Willis, Detroit Jr, Hound Dog and Homesick James, releases were spread haphazardly over C.J. and companion labels Colt and Firma. Homesick recorded two Memphis Minnie numbers (Colt 632) in his typical style while the others recorded mainly originals—Little Mack had a nice blues in the Muddy Waters style, *My Walking Blues* (C.J. 606). It's interesting that these South Side labels had no artists playing in the then 'new' Chicago manner of Rush or Guy.

Other companies that popped up briefly were Vi Muszynski's Bandera and Rev. H. H. Harrington's Atomic H. Bandera had one record by the ex-Parrot singer Dusty Brown and one issue by the young Chicagoan Jimmy Lee Robinson. He was born in the city on 30 April 1931 and although his mother encouraged him to play piano he was more interested in the guitar. About 13 years old, and with his first week's pay from washing dishes, he bought an old $8 guitar and got the Maxwell Street singer Blind Percy to teach him the chords. He started out on Maxwell and then graduated to club dates with Eddie Taylor around 1949. Soon afterwards he married but after some trouble with his father-in-law he 'had to do a little time.' On coming out in 1952 he met Freddy King, a guitarist from Longview, Texas, and they decided to put together a group to play a club date that the optimistic Freddy had lined up. Jimmy's guitar was in pawn and he didn't have an amplifier, but Freddy didn't worry. As he said, 'I haven't got an amplifier. I haven't even got a guitar.' Somehow they made the gig, redeeming Jimmy's guitar, borrowing another and sharing an amplifier. This was the beginning of their regular group. Adding a drummer, Sonny Scott, as the 'Every Hour Blues Boys' they played clubs like Cadillac Baby's for a year or so until they both joined harmonica-player Little Sonny Cooper's band. Later Jimmy and Freddy went different ways, Jimmy to join Elmore James and Freddy on to a recording contract and subsequent fame.

Freddy King was born on 30 September 1934 and had been playing guitar since he was ten. Influenced at first by T-Bone Walker and then by B. B. King, he played in the harsh new style. After John Burton bought out Al Benson's Bronzeville company he recorded Freddy for his new El-Bee label, which didn't last long. But it did bring Freddy to the attention of King Records and in 1960 he signed with their Federal subsidiary, achieving great success with *Have You Ever Loved A Woman* (Federal 12384) and, biggest of all, *Hideaway* (12401). His huge number of single releases through the '60s with a band and style similar to B.B.'s readily testifies to his great popularity.

No such luck for Jimmy Lee, though, who left Elmore to go on the road with Little Walter for about four years until the band broke up when Walter was shot in the leg. Next he joined Magic Sam's group, which included Shakey Jake, Johnnie Jones and drummer George Beasley, until his recording for Bandera. *All My Life* (Bandera 2506) was a nice semi-pop blues with an unusual melody and a tough little band of Tall Paul Hankins (piano), Eddie Clearwater (Harrington) (bass) and Buddy Rogers (drums). But Bandera met with the fate of most small Chicago companies and folded after about ten issues. As Vi Muszynski explains bitterly, 'After spending or investing a fortune in the record business as well as the best years of my life I found it doesn't pay for a small outfit to try getting established.'

Atomic H was even shorter-lived, with only a few known issues, including one by Homesick James (as Jick and his Trio), until its owner, Rev. Houston H. Harrington, revived the label with new issues appearing in the '70s. One early release was by Harrington's nephew, Eddie Clearwater, who also recorded for Federal playing in a passable imitation of Chuck Berry. Atomic H had two items by Morris Pejoe but the most interesting issue was by what was virtually the Muddy Waters Junior Band under the name of Jo Jo Williams. As one would expect, *All Pretty Wimmens* (Atomic H unnumbered) was in an older style and a fine blues to boot.

Jo Jo and Mojo

Joseph 'Jo Jo' Williams was born in Coahoma County, near Clarksdale, Mississippi, in 1920. His father was a railroad man and in 1923 the family moved to Walls near Memphis and Jo Jo grew up there and in and out of Memphis. It was at the Princess Theatre on Beale Street that Jo Jo developed a taste for the music and he started to play guitar there about 1942. At the Mississippi country suppers he had seen Son House and Willie Brown but when he arrived in Chicago it was the modern sound of Jimmy Reed that most influenced him. He had his own band in Argo, Illinois, with Lazy Bill and Earl Dranes and then he joined harp-player Mojo Buford in the Muddy Waters Junior Band.

George Buford was younger than Jo Jo; he was born in Hernando, Mississippi, on 10 November 1929. At the age of nine he was singing in a spiritual group, the M & O Gospel Singers, but later in his teens he was listening to the records of Louis Jordan. In 1944 he came to Memphis where he heard B. B. King and Joe Hill Louis on WDIA. After his divorce he left for Chicago in 1953 and got together with guitarist David Members and his nephew Sam Burton, a drummer, to form a group. They played at

MO-JO BRAND
SOUTHERN
JOHN the CONQUERER
ROOT

VALMOR PRODUCTS CO.

NOT FOR INTERNAL USE

Atomic H's Jo Jo Williams.

Walter's Show Lounge, 47th and Lake Park, and then at a club at 51st and Preston. Then came the meeting with Jo Jo. Otis Spann heard the band one night and on his recommendation Muddy sent them to a gig at the Jamboree, where they proved popular enough for Muddy to take them under his wing as his Junior Band. Then came the recording for Harrington at a studio out in Cicero, the group consisting of Jo Jo, Buford; Lazy Bill, Members and Burton. When Cotton left Muddy in 1960 Buford, after no little coaxing from Spann (who also played harp), replaced him. Jo Jo formed his own band for a while with guitarist Abraham 'Little Smokey' Smothers (from Lexington, Mississippi), pianist Alex Randall and a drummer, until he too joined Muddy to play bass-guitar when the band was on tour. Finally in 1962 Williams and Buford left to move to Minneapolis. Jo Jo put it aptly when he said, 'I always liked the music but I got into it professionally a little late.'

There were compelling social reasons for the blues' lean years in and after the late '50s. As the postwar migrants settled down to urban life there was an undoubted reaction to the 'cotton-field' nostalgia that the blues was supposed to represent. This had always been so. Even in the boom years when Muddy and the others were justly proud of their part in taking the blues into smooth clubs like the Pershing, Eddie's or 44 Club, where no blues band had ever played before, this rediscovery of their roots was but a passing fad for most of the black populace. In later years they were not to welcome any such reminders. The singers themselves are always on the defensive and not a little hurt by this attitude and everyone will tell a story of the man who puts down the old-hat blues with derision but is later discovered, shamefaced, at the front of the queue for a Muddy or Little Walter show. Jimmy Rogers says:

> Some of them they come out with it and some of them will try to hide it. You play a club has nothin' but jazz, you see a lot of your blues-lovers there and after hours you go down in the dumps where the blues is really jumpin' there you look and see the same people.

Increasing prosperity played the main part in this reluctance of most blacks to admit being touched by their past. Also, of course, that past was often too embarassing or painful and was best forgotten. For although unemployment remained higher through the late '50s and the whole of the '60s than in the frantically busy years just after the war, blacks had made steady if not spectacular economic progress; for example, the average male black wage had risen from 41% of the equivalent white wage in 1939 to 60% by 1960. And if the blues had lost some meaning for this new and relatively successful urban population it certainly had little relevance for their city-raised children, who were to form the largest proportion of the record-buying public. Cadillac Baby's complaint that 'these young people don't know nothin' about no blues, they don't feel it, they've had too good a way to go' is no less true for its being part of the older generation's traditional attitude to the young, echoed the world over.

As the rock 'n' roll boom turned the heads of the record producers towards a lucrative young pop market the few blues records made were not easy to promote. With the blues' popularity confined to a mainly older, black, lower working class, a market not assiduously courted by the advertisers, airplay was consequently more difficult to obtain. Jimmy Lee, talking about his Bandera records, explained: 'It takes an awful lot of money to get a hit and I was even paying out of my own pocket to get the stuff played on the radio.' Cadillac Baby echoes the sentiments when talking of the DJs: 'We don't get the cooperation today. That's why so many small companies has went out of business.' It was all very different from the day when Len Chess could walk into a radio station down South holding a pile of records, which were torn out of his hands and put straight on the turntable.

The importance of the early DJs cannot be overestimated. Al Benson is generally reckoned to be the father of Chicago's black radio but the first black DJ was Jack L. Cooper of WSBC in Cicero and later WHFC. Other early DJs were Eddie Honesty at WJOB in Hammond, Indiana, and McKie Fitzhugh, who was broadcasting on WOPA in 1954.

But while the '60s reduction in blues programming on the black stations was probably at first due to financial considerations it's certain that the policy was enforced by a militant black establishment, which was attempting to raise 'standards' and viewed with distaste anything which, it imagined, smacked of slavery or 'Uncle Tomism'. Just as radio exposure was a major factor in the growth of Chicago's blues, so the lack of airplay, more than any great amelioration in living conditions, will finally kill the style.

Bluesmen had always seen the recording business as secondary to public performances. It was a good thing and very necessary to have records out and their names on the labels but few ever expected, and with good reason, to get rich through a big hit. Records were for publicity and if a hit record ensured steady work in clubs or on the road, all well and good; any royalties would then be the icing on the cake. So the change in policy of the radio stations meant a serious loss of earning power through fewer jobs. While this hit the major artists hard they had at least made *their* names. But it was catastrophic for the unknown new artists who would never be able to make it nationally.

Even work in the clubs was beginning to be scarce since the recession of '54, and unemployment among musicians was so high that Petrillo was asking Eisenhower to intercede and reduce the level of the Entertainments Tax. The heyday of the big tavern owners like the Jewish brothers Boobie and Mitt, who had a string of clubs including the Zanzibar, the Rock Bottom and the 1015, was drawing to a close and in this sad period of declining interest in the blues, club-owners or DJs who swam against the tide, like Johnny Pepper or Big Bill Hill, are especially interesting. Big Bill Hill, well named at 6′ 2″ and 250 lb, was born in England, Arkansas, on 6 April 1914. He arrived in Chicago in 1932 during the Depression but eventually found a job in a steel mill. He worked steadily and saved his money to try and break into the radio business but being black and without experience he had to start by using his savings to buy time to advertise for sponsors! His only asset, he claimed, was 'the biggest mouth in Chicago.'

In 1949 he did get a break with a small station, WLDY at Elmwood Park, Illinois, and then with WCRW. His big break came in 1955 with a spot on WOPA. He had been acting as MC for shows at Sylvio's and the Blue Flame and his first broadcast for WOPA was live from Sylvio's. People thought he was crazy to try and feature the blues but the live broadcasts were a great success. At his peak of popularity he was riding high and diversifying into other fields with subsidiary interests in a dry-cleaner's and in artist management through his Colt Booking Agency. But it was not to last. In 1963 he opened the Copa Cobana on West Roosevelt, still featuring live broadcasts, but the club was never successful and he had to close down three years later.

'I Just Wanted To Be In The Public Eye'

Johnny Pepper, who came from Little Rock, Arkansas, was a young man of about 26 when he opened his lounge at 503 E. 43rd Street in 1956. He'd studied electronics and had been working for Ford's when he decided, with no experience at all, to go into the tavern business. 'I just

The new Pepper's at 1321 S. Michigan opened in Spring 1971, introducing blues in the Loop.

wanted to be in the public eye,' he explains. With a loan from the credit union at Ford's for the liquor licence, no cash register, no cooler and no stock, he opened. Johnny explains, 'I'd buy like a couple of bottles from the cut-rate liquor store, leave a customer and run out the back-door and get a couple more.' But he did at least have a band, Shakey Jake's. The four-foot bandstand was so small that only three musicians could get on it at the same time. From Pepper's memories of his opening night the size of the bandstand didn't worry Jake. 'He got drunk. And the customers come, they said, "Where's the band?" Well he had lay down in front of the doorway on the sidewalk. I said, "You just stepped over your musician".'

The band would play for $10 or $12 a night and presumably Pepper started off with a blues band because they were cheap to hire. Certainly he didn't intend having a blues club 'because there at that particular time there wasn't much demand for blues.' Or that's how it seemed but Johnny soon found out that blues was what his particular customers wanted. 'I hired one jazz band and I like to went out of business, 'cause everyone stopped coming.' Pepper was a shrewd businessman though. For instance Otis Rush would play on a Tuesday night and with nothing much happening around town Pepper would make it a 25-cent night. It was a quarter to enter and a quarter for all drinks but he'd still take enough on the door to pay the band their $90 and have a little over. With the drinks it was, in all, a $500 night. Other clubs had similar policies. The Zanzibar, which could pack in about 300 people, charged 90 cents for admission but the first drink cost only a dime. With an eye to all the gimmicks Pepper would also organise amateur talent competitions which were hugely popular. By 1959 the club was going strong with top name artists like Muddy, Wolf, Magic Sam, Junior Wells and Otis Rush, and with the bands and talent shows Pepper was able to make the blues play.

'The Beat Have Changed'

But success stories were all too rare by this time.

The older artists had died or retired. Memphis Minnie was sick and in a nursing home in Memphis, Broonzy died in 1959, Washboard Sam and Tampa Red had retired, Walter Davis was working as a telephonist in St Louis and Jazz Gillum and Bumble Bee Slim had dropped out of sight. Of the new names only the major artists were still working but those who had never made it had all but dropped out of sight. Shines and Pryor had given up the music in disgust, Johnny Williams had entered the church, and Moody Jones had become pastor of a Sanctified church as early as 1955. Horton was working casually in the neighbourhood bars of Indiana Avenue and J. B. Hutto was playing house-parties round 39th Street until the area became too rough. J.B. lost his guitar when a woman broke it over her husband's head, and he quit music for the quieter life of an undertaker.

Win Stracke, Brother John Sellers, Little Walter and Sunnyland Slim, 16 August 1958, commemorating Big Bill Broonzy, who had died the previous day.

Johnny Temple had his last group, the Rolling Four, in 1956, and they played mostly pop songs at the Club Hollywood downtown. Spires had retired from music, Nighthawk had gone back to Helena, Nix had left town, and even those singers who wouldn't give up, like Floyd Jones, Johnny Young or Eddie Taylor, all had day jobs. In Floyd's words, 'the beat have changed.'

While nearly all the small record companies had closed their doors or were operating only intermittently, one new label, USA, appeared on the scene. The owner was Paul Glass of All State Record Distributors, 1448 S. Michigan Avenue, but the irrepressible Mel London was also connected with the company in some way. USA had some local hits with two of Willie Mabon's double entendre items. *Just Got Some* (USA 735) a follow-up to his successful *Got To Have Some* on Formal, Don Tally's label—and *I'm The Fixer* (741), but the best thing about them was Mabon's always beautiful piano work. As well as some nice blues from J. B. Lenoir (744) and California-based T. V. Slim (739) there was Homesick James's version of Robert Johnson's *Crossroads* (746), which, improbably, was quite a local success. Most of the blues A & R men seem to have produced sessions for USA: London, Dixon and Ike Perkins were all associated with the company. It was Perkins who produced the Detroit Jr (Emery Williams Jr) date, which resulted in a lovely, relaxed piano blues, *The Way I Feel* (814), the like of which had not been heard in Chicago for many years.

Elmore

There was, however, one major singer who, despite health problems, had continued working through the '60s, whose music had bent in the prevailing wind of change but was still as fresh and exciting and up-to-date as it was in the early '50s. This was Elmore James.

Recent research by Wardlow and Leadbitter shows him to have been born Elmore Brooks, son of Leola Brooks, a 15-year-old farmhand, on 27 January 1918 at Richland, Mississippi. His father's name is not known, but it seems likely from family resemblances that it was in fact Joe Willie 'Frost' James, with whom his mother soon afterwards set up home on various plantations near the small Holmes County communities of Lexington, Goodman, Durant and Pickens, off Highway 51. Little is known about his early years but they couldn't have been very different from any of his peers'. By the age of 12 he had his 'strings upon the wall', later graduating to a 'lil ole two, three string box made out of a ole lard can.' He is remembered by a distant cousin at Goodman playing a cheap guitar and singing *Dust My Broom* and *Smokestack Lightning* for Saturday night dances at Franklin. Apart from mandolinist/guitarist Fred Chambers, Elmore was the only guitarist round Goodman at that time, but he wasn't using a slide then.

Elmore James.

In 1937 his mother and father moved to Belzoni in the Delta, settling first on the Turner Brothers' plantation, but moving from farm to farm in a vain attempt to wrest some kind of living out of the vicious sharecropping system. At one plantation, the Kincaid, they adopted an orphan, Robert Earl Holsten, and later Robert was to play rhythm guitar behind Elmore on the plantation and sometimes in the jukes of Belzoni. It was this period in Belzoni that was to have the greatest influence in shaping Elmore's music, for by now he was 19 years old, with a taste for moonshine whiskey and women but none for work on the farm, the music was becoming the most important thing in his life. He married a local girl, Josephine Harris, bought his first real guitar, a $20 National, and started rambling, his constant companions Robert Johnson and Rice Miller. It was Johnson who inspired Elmore to use a slide and, with a metal pipe across the strings. Elmore gradually developed his style. But from all accounts he was a slow learner. Eddie Taylor, who was five years younger than Elmore, saw him at Belzoni and says, 'I used to hear him play and see him play. But I didn't pay no attention too much because I didn't like his style.' Elmore didn't have too much time to pick up Robert's style, though, for on 16 August 1938 Johnson died in Greenwood.

Elmore and Rice Miller were very close and by 1939, while Elmore was working on the Daybreak plantation, Sonny Boy, who was hanging round Greenville, would often come into Belzoni to play. Although Elmore preferred to play alone or with his half-brother Robert, he had formed a band including Precious White on sax, Tutney Moore on trumpet, Robert on rhythm guitar and 'Frock' O'Dell on drums, to play dances. Robert remembers they played the Harlem Theatres in Belzoni and Hollandale, the Midnight Grill in Tchula, Peacock Inn in Belzoni and Big Boy Cray's juke near Goodman. Their busiest season was in the winter when there was 'no work to do, cotton all picked.'

This was when Elmore used to take off without saying a word and be gone for a couple of weeks at a time. Possibly his trips were to Helena, where Sonny Boy was broadcasting his King Biscuit Show, but soon Elmore was to take a much longer trip and he wouldn't see his home again for a couple of years. He was drafted into the Navy in July 1943 and, after active service in Guam and an honourable discharge, he returned to Belzoni in November 1945 to find his parents had split up and gone North to Chicago, while his brother was living in Canton, where he had a radio business.

He stayed in Canton for a year and it was then, as a young man in his 28th year, that his heart condition was detected and he went into hospital in Jackson. That same year he resumed his association with Rice Miller on trips to Helena and in 1947 he was back in Belzoni working on the Silver Creek plantation and trying his hand at marriage again.

Bit by bit he was picking up the threads of his musical career, which received an added impetus when Rice joined him in Belzoni to do a radio show advertising Talaho patent medicine for the O. J. Turner Drug Store. Elmore made odd appearances on the programme, which was recorded at Turner's store and beamed from WAZF in Yazoo City or WJPJ in Greenville. With the success of the programme Sonny Boy took up a better offer from Hadacol, another patent medicine firm, and in 1949 he moved to West Memphis to advertise on KWEM. Elmore then teamed up with Willie Love in Greenville where they broadcast over WDVM. After a short stay in West Memphis, where he learned of Sonny Boy's contract with the Diamond Record Company of Jackson, Elmore was back in Canton to be on hand for Sonny Boy's record sessions. On 5 January 1951 Elmore, in company with Willie Love and Joe Willie Wilkins, accompanied Sonny Boy on the *Eyesight To The Blind* session for Trumpet. Although he made further trips to record with Sonny Boy he refused to record himself. Elmore was always rather shy and very nervous but for someone who had been so keen to get on record it was ironic that when his chance came he suffered from stage-fright. No, he wouldn't record *Dust My Broom*, no, they couldn't persuade him. And then something curious happened. While Elmore was rehearsing the number, but without his knowledge, Trumpet recorded it. It seemed the obvious thing to do and probably his accompanists, Sonny Boy and 'Frock', knew about it but Elmore was very upset. Lillian McMurry is, unusually for her, less than forthcoming about Elmore and even attempted to play down the success of the record, although it entered the R & B charts on 5 April 1952 and reached the Top Ten! Elmore never recorded again for Trumpet and the reverse of the record, though credited to him, is actually by another artist, Bobo Thomas. *Dust My Broom* (Trumpet 146) was a superb country blues, very close to Robert Johnson's original, and the forerunner of many successful versions of the song, as Elmore used and reused the theme time and time again.

But at first he stayed round Canton living off the royalties and adamantly refusing to cut a follow-up. There were other offers from Modern and Chess but Elmore ignored all blandishments until Joe Bihari succeeded in persuading him to go to Chicago and record. There Elmore lived with his uncle Mac Willie James at 4714 S. Evans (Wolf was lodging there too), played his first club date with Kansas City Red at Chuck's, Damen and Madison, and recorded for the Biharis about October 1952.

The sides appeared on Lester Bihari's Memphis-based subsidiary Meteor, and were immediately successful. *I Believe* (Meteor 5000) was a glorious version of the *Broom* theme with Johnnie Jones's band accompanying. As well as Elmore's superlative slide there was Johnnie's brilliant piano and J.T. Brown's vibrant, buzzing sax, and the interplay between them was as if they had played together all their lives. Even before the record was in the

charts Elmore and the same group recorded for Chess on 17 January 1953 and yet another version of the song was issued, *She Just Wont Do Right* (Checker 777). These Chicago versions had a lovely, relaxed swing,

Elmore and unknown girlfriend.

unhurried and graceful but still immensely forceful. The Bihari session featured Elmore's guitar more prominently while on the Checker J.T.'s jaunty sax was more to the fore. Elmore had a contract with the Biharis and the Checker issue may have been withdrawn. Anyway, in November he was back again with a session for release on Flair. These early Flair sides with the Johnnie Jones band were all of an astonishingly high standard. with *Hawaiian Boogie* (Flair 1011), a storming slide instrumental, and *Make A Little Love* (Flair 1014) outstanding. But recording Elmore must have been a daunting prospect; takes sometimes ran into double figures and on *Wild About You Baby* (Modern 983) reached a record 22!

Elmore soon tired of Chicago and returned to Canton and his friends, playing locally at the Club Bizarre or with Willie Love in Greenville. Again his heart complaint was troubling him and he preferred to be near Jackson and the hospital. The Biharis were still recording him—when they found him; for with Ike Turner they would have to hunt Elmore all over town. The sessions in Jackson and in Canton at the Club Bizarre were hastily organised and badly recorded. Ike Turner was the only readily identifiable member of the groups and he played a fine piano introduction to *Hand In Hand* (Flair 1031) while Elmore contributed one of his best slide solos on *Please Find My Baby* (Flair 1022). The *Cash Box* review of 20 March 1954 was almost as exciting as the music; *Hand In Hand* was an 'OK job with lots of emotion' but on *Make My Dreams Come True* 'James rides herd on this moving beat and comes up with a sock side. Could make a strong dent in the market.'

That year, with manager Otis Ealey, Elmore was living in Atlanta with a new 'wife', Janice, whom he'd met in Jackson, but after a quarrel with her he took off for Chicago, with Ealey still looking after his bookings. Elmore was certainly dusting his broom.

Despite the good reviews in *Cash Box* and the receptive state of the market at that time Elmore's record sales were slipping, and scratch sessions in Hollywood with the turgid Maxwell Davis band did nothing to restore them. This was musically the poorest period of Elmore's career and in 1955 Modern dropped him, Elmore signing off appropriately with *Goodbye Baby* (Flair 1079), for which a vocal group was added—another sign of the times.

'Everybody Be In There'

Back in Chicago he again encountered his distant cousin Homesick James. While Elmore, still with Johnnie Jones's band, was working at Sylvio's, Homesick was nearby at the Johnson Lounge with Big Bill Broonzy. They had discovered their kinship when Homesick used to visit a relation, L. J Grant, in Canton and it was Elmore's uncle Mac who reintroduced them in Chicago. From then on Homesick intermittently played bass-guitar with Elmore, each joining the other's band when he wasn't working.

Homesick, Elmore and drummer Robert Plunkin, playing at Thelma's, possibly c. *1960.*

Homesick was lodging with Johnnie Jones and his wife Letha at 1636 S. Springfield and most of the time he and Johnnie would sit round drinking and playing records, usually Tampa's, Maceo's and Big Bill's, Johnnie came from Jackson, Mississippi, where he was born about 1924, son of George Jones and Mary Crusoe. He'd been in Chicago since the late '40s, having travelled up with Baby Face Leroy, and spent much of his time learning from Big Maceo. After Maceo's stroke Johnnie took over as Tampa's regular pianist and recorded frequently with him. Then came Johnnie's magnificent Aristocrat session with Muddy Waters but he didn't record again under his own name until Elmore's first Flair date when, with the band, he cut a rocking, if innocuous, version of the Dozens, *Sweet Little Woman* (Flair 1010). He even had a session for Atlantic in 1954 recording a Peetie Wheatstraw song, *Doin' The Best I Can* (Atlantic 1045), but with J. T. Brown below his best form and Elmore playing acoustic guitar it was disappointing. By contrast *Chicago Blues*, recently issued for the first time, is superb. Johnnie was another heavy drinker and wild character. He was also very popular. With pure admiration in his voice Johnny Shines says, 'He was *terrible!*' and Homesick laughs too when remembering how Elmore and Johnnie used to argue. 'Elmore and Johnnie used to just have a fight every night. That was the whole point. If they didn't get in no argument there wouldn't be no band, y'know. After they get to, y' know, yakkin' each other then the band would get lively. Everybody be in there—whole big party, yessir!'

The band toured regularly at this time. One night at Bougemont Grove, St Louis, playing to 5000 people, a fight started in which several were

killed. Also on the bill was a terrified Etta James and a very young Tina Turner. But there were the lighter moments. The rhythm section backed Etta in her spot and as Johnnie Jones rarely toured with them the driver Big Jim Gregory would fill in on piano. Jim could only just play the chords but Etta kept asking him to solo. Finally, when the night came that Jim was really going to have to play piano, he vanished and never took the stage again! Another night they stopped off at a grocery store for some cold cuts and while the rest of the band were buying at the counter drummer Willie Nix was busy stuffing cans of every description in to his coat. Big Jim marched him up to the lady owner and a crestfallen Nix was made to empty his pockets. They were all annoyed at the foolhardy Nix as a black band had to be very careful on tour of the South for obvious reasons. Homesick recounts one potentially dangerous incident which, trivial and amusing though it was, serves as an eloquent reminder of the times. Homesick and Elmore were in the back of the station-wagon drinking when they pulled into a gas-station. As he filled up the white pump-attendant, staring at the band's motif which was painted across the side of the van, said, 'That Broom-Dusters sure looks funny.' Homesick, thinking it was one of the band mimicking the white accent, poked his head up and asked, 'Who the hell said that?' When he saw the pump-attendant he quickly ducked down and didn't dare raise his head again until they were 20 miles out of town.

Through 1956 Elmore played regularly at Sylvio's with occasional dates at other West Side clubs like the Key Largo, Charlie's Lounge and Club

Left: *Boyd Atkins, S.P. Leary, Magic Sam, Letha and Johnnie Jones, Georgia Maghett (Sam's wife), Odell Campbell, at the Joneses' house at 18th and Michigan, 1959.* Above: *Johnnie Jones.*

Alex; then in 1957, just out of hospital after his second heart attack, he landed his next recording contract, with Mel London. The first session for Chief was easily the best. There was more variation, two of the numbers were new and only one side, *Coming Home* (Chief 7001), employed the *Broom* theme. But even then, what a side it was! With Elmore's impassioned singing and equally fierce bottleneck guitar, backed up by the second and rhythm guitars of Homesick and Eddie Taylor (all three playing through the same amplifier), it was tremendously noisy and exciting. On the reverse, *The Twelve Year Old Boy*, the excellent, modern lead guitar was played by Wayne Bennett, with bass punctuation from Elmore and the others. If Mel London really did write this unusual song then it was further evidence of his abilities but he also claimed credit for *It Hurts Me Too* (7004), the old Tampa Red hit from 1949, when it was titled *When Things Go Wrong*. The good lyrics and strong melody were typical of Tampa's later, wistful, pop blues. In Elmore's hands, though, it was an anguished cry; this was the first indication of his special ability to interpret other artists' songs and make them peculiarly his own. In all the Chief session was a very impressive comeback to the recording scene but, apart from their reissue by VJ soon after, little else happened. Other sessions for Chief with Eddie Taylor playing the lead were more ordinary.

Elmore made one brief trip to Jackson in 1958 and even worked as a DJ on WRBC but he was soon back in Chicago. His health was deteriorating and he was thinner and looking far older than his 40 years. But he was still very popular in the clubs and there was renewed interest from the record companies. Bobby Robinson of Fire Records in New York had wanted to record Elmore ever since he'd heard *I Believe* and sessions were arranged. Then in April 1960 Chess tried again with Elmore. The one issue, *The Sun Is Shining* (Chess 1756), was another great blues with accompaniment by Homesick and Eddie Taylor, and it was interesting to see how Elmore's music had moved closer to that of the West Side men. It was completely modern and up-to-the-minute blues but it also avoided all the pitfalls of the new school. With the same kind of declamatory vocal and tough band, but with Elmore's slide instead of the already overworked King-styled guitar, and untouched by rock 'n' roll or ballad influences, his music easily straddled the two styles. But his second Chess venture was as abortive as the first and he skipped out on his contract to continue recording for Fire. Sessions followed thick and fast; there were instrumentals like *Bobby's Rock* (Fire 1011), traditional Mississippi Delta themes like *Rollin' And Tumblin'* (1023) and originals like the more than usually imaginative *The Sky Is Crying* (1016).

But, in trouble with the union for non-payment of dues, his membership lapsed on 1 April 1961. Elmore was blacklisted in Chicago and in 1962 once more he returned to Jackson. Homesick joined him for a while and they lived with Johnny Temple at his house at 905 Annbank Street, doing very little. But the inactivity, though it suited Elmore, got on Homesick's nerves and he went back to Chicago. Certainly Elmore's heart trouble didn't allow him to work much, for by now he was very sick. But he still ignored the doctors' warnings about his heavy drinking. His records must have sold well for there were still sessions, usually in New York, for Robinson. As well as his own songs there were fresh versions of standards like *Look On Yonder Wall* (Fire 504), cut in New Orleans with Sam Myers on harp, *Mean Mistreating Mama* (Enjoy 2020), with its great piano breaks, and even a fine version of Memphis Slim's hackneyed *Every Day I Have The Blues* (Enjoy 2027). Bobby Robinson, from Union, South Carolina, had a great love for the blues and recorded Elmore sympathetically. Even during the Jackson period, when he furnished him with a New York band including brass and saxes, Elmore's guitar was kept well to the fore and the horns were never obtrusive.

'Believe My Time Ain't Long'

Though Elmore was in exile in Jackson he wasn't forgotten in Chicago, where Big Bill Hill was working to straighten out Elmore's problems with the union. This he succeeded in doing and in May 1963 Big Bill sent for him to open at his new Copa Cobana Club. Elmore arrived on Sunday and that night he and Homesick and drummer Cascell Burrows worked at Hill's place. Later they all stopped by Sylvio's to hear Wolf. On Monday and Tuesday nights they worked at the Copa Cobana and on Wednesday Elmore went down to the Union Hall to get a contract to start properly on the Friday. Elmore was living with Homesick and his family at 1503 N. Wieland and Homesick takes up the story of that Friday night:

> I laid down for a while so he say, 'Wake up, old dude. Get up.' I had a little dog, a cocker spaniel—Elmore called him 'Black Night' —y'know I wouldn't go through the words that he say. He used a kind of bad word but anyway he wakened me up. After that we ate. Then he went and taken a shower. Then he come back and went in the room to change his clothes. He was right off the room where my wife was and I asked him, 'Do you want me to bring you the tablets or something?' So he mumbled something. So my wife went to the door and she looked in there and he was just laying out on the bed, y'know, on his back. One hand across his chest. She ran to get me, y'know, I wasn't fully dressed, say, 'Come here, come on James. Something wrong with Elmore.' This was around about 7.30 in the evening and this was May 24th 1963. My daughter tried to give him artificial respiration but she wasn't able to succeed, and wasn't nobody, because his time just had to come like that.

So died one of the best loved of all the bluesmen. Elmore was shy and nervous, drank heavily and would pull stunts, like pawning his friends' belongings, or going on the road with his band and leaving them and running off with the money. But there never seemed to be any hard feelings, for, as Homesick says, 'All musicians will do *that*!' He adds, 'That was my brother, just like a brother I would say,' and Eddie Taylor confirms: 'Elmore wasn't hard to get along with, boy, he was real nice.'

Elmore is survived by several 'wives': Janice is a cashier at a 24 Hours store in Chicago, and there's Mickey, who was his first wife in Chicago, Mary Lee, Martha, Mildred and Mattie Mae. He had three or four children and recently a son, probably Josephine's, about 27 years old, appeared in Chicago playing guitar like Elmore.

Elmore's position in the Chicago scene is important, for, while Muddy updated Mississippi's blues for an early postwar audience, Elmore followed through the logical development and modernised them for all time. The starkness of the Delta blues is always present in his work; the ferocious and anguished vocals, the impassioned bottleneck guitar and the powerful surging rhythms remain as fresh today as they ever did. The proof of this, if needed, is contained in an ironic postscript—the posthumous success of *It Hurts Me Too* (Enjoy 2015), released by Robinson just a few months after his death.

The greatest decline of the blues was during the '60s. Chess, then at 2120 S. Michigan, virtually abdicated from blues recording and VJ, with offices at 1149 S. Michigan and then 2129 S. Michigan, was forced into bankruptcy in 1964. This time the huge gap left in the recording scene was not plugged by any thrusting young independents for, in contrast to the late '40s, the demand did not appear to exist. The only eager new companies on the scene were led by collectors, Pete Welding of Testament and Bob Koester of Delmark, who set about documenting· Chicago's forgotten bluesmen with LP releases slanted at a white collectors' market. Possibly Delmark's recordings of Junior Wells and the West Side men, Magic Sam, Luther Allison, Mighty Joe Young and Jimmy 'Fast Fingers' Dawkins, have reached the small and perhaps growing number of blacks in the universities but these ventures, though laudable, have not rekindled any blaze of interest or reinstated the artists with their own audience.

There were odd commercial releases, some very odd, still aimed at that natural market. From the ailing VJ company came a 1964 session by Eddie Taylor with a top-heavy band of Reed, Hubert Sumlin, Johnnie Jones, a bass-guitarist, and Earl Phillips, and *Do You Want Me to Cry* (Vivid 104) showed that Eddie's music hadn't changed since the early '50s. Taylor as well as Sumlin and Johnnie Jones participated in another strange session organised and produced by drummer Willie Williams. Four instrumentals were cut and Williams hawked the tapes around the companies, with no success. Eventually DJ 'Open the Door' Richard took them, dubbed an unknown vocalist over one track, and the resulting *Rough Dried Woman* by 'Big Mac' was issued by Stan Lewis on his Jewel subsidiary, Ronn.

Al Benson reappeared briefly in 1966 with a new label, Crash, which reintroduced Magic Sam. *Out Of Bad Luck* (Crash 425) was excellent, even if it was Sam's one tune again, and Benson's other label The Blues had an issue each by Big Moose Walker, Earl Hooker's organist and pianist, and Shakey Jake. There were new singers too, but most were sadly derivative, like Jimmy Reed imitators G. L. Crockett, on Jack Daniels' 4 Brothers label, and Prez Kenneth (Kidd) on Biscayne, a label run by DJ Bill Tyson; or B. B. King imitator Little Oscar on Palos. J. L. Smith recorded for guitarist and cab-driver Freddy Young's Friendly Five and F-M while Little Mack popped up recently with a fine *Mother In Law Blues* for Cadillac Baby, reissued on Puros and Dud-Sound. Willie Dixon of course was the guiding light behind a host of new small companies. For Dud-Sound and T.D.S., owned by guitarist Johnny Twist and cab-driver Oscar L. Coleman (Bo-Dudley), Dixon organised sessions at Harvey, Illinois. Slide guitarist

Koko Taylor with Mighty Joe Young and the Touch of Souls.

Johnny Littlejohn cut an excellent version of Dixon's *29 Ways* (T.D.S. 4713) and an even better version of *Broken Hearted Blues* as *Bloody Tears* on Weis 3437. Bo Dud's *Shotgun Rider* (F-M 745) was pleasant enough but Freddy Roulette's steel guitar solo was the most exciting new sound to come out of Chicago in years.

Also via Dixon came Chess's last Top Ten blues hit, Koko Taylor's version of *Wang Dang Doodle* (Checker 1135). Koko, born Cora Walton in Memphis on 28 September 1938, occupies an interesting niche in blues history, as she must certainly be the very last of the female blues singers. With a tough, growling singing voice that contrasts strongly with her quiet and sweet offstage manner and peaceful domestic life with her husband Bob and 15-year-old daughter, Koko brings the long line of swaggering, hell-raising blueswomen to a demure close. Most of the Dixon songs she has recorded since have been unsuited to her rather inflexible voice and nothing much has happened for her since her big hit. However, she still tours, and a second Chess LP, with Mighty Joe Young's band, has recently been released.

Much has been made of the apparent dearth of blues in Chicago today, but a glance at the lists, in the Chicago magazine *Living Blues*, of over 20 black clubs which regularly feature bluesmen (or near-bluesmen) hardly supports such pessimism. But the main argument concerns the quality of the music and it is true that the sound of Chicago's blues has changed, as most of the younger men play in a pastiche of the B. B. King style, with its inherent limitations, while those older singers who still play in the early '50s style obviously do so with less dexterity than they had 20 years ago. Talking to the singers themselves reveals the polarisation clearly, for the younger bluesmen barely conceal their contempt for the music of, say, Muddy and Jimmy Rogers, while the older ones, equally disparaging, say, 'Anybody can squeeze a string' or describe today's music as 'holler and jump-up'. Time hasn't been kind to the bluesmen, either, and the list of obituaries grows ominously longer. Baby Face Leroy is dead (although no trace of his death can be found in Cook County's records); Elmore is dead; J. B. Lenoir was killed in a car crash; Little Walter died in his sleep,

apparently after a street brawl: Johnnie Jones died in a hospital, as did Otis Spann. Sonny Boy died in Helena, as did Robert Nighthawk. Willie Foster is crippled after a shooting incident, Reed and Wolf are often sick. Death has also thinned the ranks of the younger singers, robbing us of two blues talents of the greatest promise. Both Earl Hooker and Magic Sam died on the eve of commercial success, an irony particularly reserved for bluesmen. Muddy Waters, still the King, has slowly recovered from a serious car accident and, with a band including guitarists Sammy Lawhorn and James 'Pee Wee' Madison, pianist Joe Willie 'Pinetop' Perkins and drummer Little Willie Smith, is still impressive. With no recent singles issued, Muddy's work is mainly on the college circuit or in Europe, but at home he still plays a few clubs like the White Rose, 153rd and Vincennes, in Phoenix. This was J. B. Lenoir's old haunt in the mid-'50s and many of the patrons still retain their affection for the older blues styles. The young couples will dance, whatever the music, but the older ones, the women especially, shout out requests for Muddy's old numbers. Muddy, with the dignity of a delegate to the United Nations, remains the elder statesman of Chicago's blues.

Today's blues in the small bars still draws strength from the slide guitar style, whose shrill whine rings loud and clear from the taverns. Homesick James, J. B. Hutto, Hound Dog Taylor and David 'Honeyboy' Edwards have always played with a slide. But a newer name is Johnny Littlejohn (John Funchess) from Lake, Mississippi, who, although a part of the Gary scene in the early '50s, when he played with John Brim as well as with Reed and Taylor, had to wait until 1965 to get on record. In 1970 Littlejohn teamed up with Jimmy Rogers, who was keen to return to a musical career after a clothing store in which he had an interest was burned down during the riots. Rogers still plays and sings immaculately in the classic style and for a time it seemed that they were the most exciting prospect on Chicago's music scene. But after a fire destroyed the house on West Washington where they both lived, they split up and Jimmy moved to Los Angeles for a time. He is now back in Chicago though.

With the Myers brothers still playing and Eddie Taylor as good as ever, as well as the many good young guitarists like Luther Allison, Jimmy Dawkins and Mighty Joe Young, it would be premature to write an obituary for the blues in Chicago. But the situation among the pianists is

Representing today's Chicago blues, left to right: *David 'Honeyboy' Edwards; Pee Wee Madison, guitarist with Muddy Waters; slide guitarist Johnny Littlejohn; Jimmy 'Fast Fingers' Dawkins; harp-player Carey Bell; and Pinetop Perkins, Muddy Waters' pianist.*

not so happy. Sunnyland is still around and Pinetop Perkins is a welcome addition to Chicago's scene, but Spann and Johnnie Jones are dead and Henry Gray has moved back to Louisiana. Nor are there many bright prospects among the young harmonica-players. Wells is still playing, but, apart from Carey Bell, who is quickly proving a worthy follower of Little Walter, Chicago is no longer the blues harmonica town.

Without a strong record-company pushing, Chicago is no longer *the* blues recording centre either. The scant rewards from blues releases have meant that recording the music has reverted to the small operators, and even there the ranks are thinning. Jimmy Bracken was back in operation with a new label, Ra-Bra, but sadly he died before it could bear any fruits. Similarly with Rev. H. H. Harrington, who died in 1972 after his brief comeback on the record scene.

The final chapter of the Chess story was written in the '70s. Leonard died on 16 October 1969 and Chess was bought out by GRT. Phil left to run the radio station WVON and Marshall Chess, Leonard's son, was the only remaining member of the family involved in the Chess record operation. Before he, too, eventually left he produced a few freaky sessions submerging Muddy and Wolf in the electronic quagmire inhabited by the white rock groups. Wolf was endearingly succinct about it all; 'dog shit' was how he described it.

Ralph Bass heads what little remains of Chess's Chicago operation. Controlled by GRT in New York, the studios are reduced to cutting backing tracks. Bass is the only connection with the great days and he is trying, in a race against time, to document the vast storehouse of material. With a tiny staff and office after office empty, the Chess building at 321 E. 21st is a sorry sight.

The feeling that the blues are marking time in the city is inescapable; as the older artists die or retire the young ones, hampered by the dictates of changed social and economic pressures, seem unable to make a significant breakthrough to give a cohesion and form to a new style of Chicago blues.

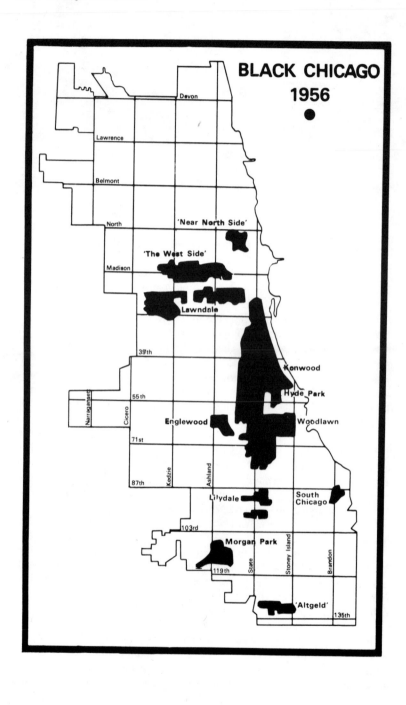

BLACK CHICAGO
1956

Devon

Lawrence

Belmont

North

'Near North Side'

'The West Side'

Madison

Lawndale

39th

55th

Narraganset

Cicero

Kenwood

Hyde Park

Woodlawn

Englewood

71st

Kedzie

Ashland

87th

Lilydale

South Chicago

103rd

Morgan Park

119th

State

Stoney Island

Brandon

'Altgeld'

135th

Postscript / Why Chicago?

At a time when blacks were leaving the South in their thousands to swell the urban populations of the North and West it's interesting that two only of the host areas, Chicago and California, should develop a discrete regional postwar style. What was so special about these areas?

Chicago, for example, with a Non-White proportion of 14.1% by 1950, was not markedly different from the other 11 Northern cities of over 100,000 population with black concentrations as high (or higher). If migration, which relocated a huge new audience, isolated by the segregation of the cities into a compact market, was the only factor in the renaissance of the blues, then other large cities should have been capable of supporting a local blues scene and, moreover, a regional style should have sprung up in the last of the great attraction centres, the Northeast to which migration was heaviest of all.

Clearly the greatest encouragement to the growth of a local style, given a black population large in number and proportion, was the existence of a 'race' recording industry, and Chicago in this respect obviously enjoyed advantages over Cleveland, say, or Pittsburgh. But so too did New York. Los Angeles was an exception; there a new 'race' record industry, built up from scratch, could grow and prosper in happy isolation, not hampered as other cities were by their close proximity to Chicago or New York. But the puzzling fact that the migrants to New York or Newark were unable to establish a modern urban style suggests that the 'quality' of migration, that is the musical tradition of the migrants, was as important as the quantity.

California's blues were a marriage of the Texas guitar with the urban jump blues of the '40s, while Chicago's purer and more traditional style was the offspring of the Mississippi blues. The modern Delta style took root in Chicago because of the vast influx of Mississippi migrants during the '40s—out of the total net migration to Chicago for these years it's probable that one half came from Mississippi alone.

An idea of how the backgrounds of Chicago's black population changed from 1930-50 must be gleaned from the Illinois census figures, as the 1950 statistics for Chicago are not available. But on the assumption that the make-up of Chicago's black population does not differ widely from that of Illinois, Table 11 attempts to relate these backgrounds to the regional theory of blues, by grouping together states with a roughly similar blues tradition. The groupings are arbitrary for this rather dubious exercise; thus Tennessee is included in the 'Delta' states to take in the Memphis-born, while Louisiana could be split between the Delta and Texas groups, as could Arkansas. But bearing in mind the cavalier approximations and the imperfections of the regional theory itself the figures suggest the superiority of certain styles in certain areas.

Table 11   *Birth States of Illinois Negroes (1930-1950)*

	1930	% Total	1950	% Total
'Delta'				
Mississippi	50,851		136,960	
Tennessee	34,844		47,605	
Arkansas	16,425		44,150	
	102,120	(31%)	228,715	(35%)
'South Eastern'				
Alabama	24,958		42,555	
Georgia	24,902		30,475	
S. Carolina	5,533		6,920	
N. Carolina	2,760		3,795	
Florida	1,888		3,470	
	60,041	(18%)	87,215	(13%)
'Texas'				
Louisiana	19,867		29,385	
Texas	6,669		10,390	
Oklahoma	2,315		4,115	
	28,851	(9%)	43,890	(7%)

Note: The figures for 1950 refer to Non-Whites. (Source: US Census)

For California for 1950 the proportions are: Texas 37%, the Delta 12% and for the South Eastern states only 5%; the figures tend to confirm what is in fact observed, namely, the supremacy of the Delta style in Chicago and that of Texas in California. But this glib presentation of migration statistics overlooks the anomaly of New York. Table 11a carries out the same analysis for New York state;

Table 11a   *Birth States of New York Negroes (1930-1950)*

	1930	% Total	1950	% Total
'Delta'	5,636	(1%)	19,955	(2%)
'South Eastern'	114,224	(34%)	319,455	(39%)
'Texas'	5,064	(1%)	13,755	(2%)

This suggests even more strongly that the South Eastern style should have been dominant in New York. That no such thing happened on the East Coast may have several reasons, and the first of them may be that the figures are meaningless anyway! But it is more likely that New York and the East Coast are exceptions, their apparent distaste for blues of any kind having been previously noted. It could have been that the migrants to the East Coast cities were less gifted exponents of their traditional style, but this doesn't seem very probable, when one considers those that did record. Or perhaps the singers were a very small proportion of the migrant body but this doesn't seem to be the answer either, for only one artist's

Two faces of Chicago, a generation apart. Left, *a South Side scene, 1948.* Right, *a project on S. State, 1972.*

success would have been necessary to trigger off the musical explosion, as Muddy Waters's was in Chicago.

The most reasonable explanation must be a musical one: that the very nature of the South Eastern style, with its gentle picked melodies, inhibited its modernisation, which in the case of Mississippi was effected by heavy amplification and adaptation to a band style. It seems certain that the Delta blues, harsh, rhythmic and aggressive, were more in tune with the feelings and aspirations of the new generation of urban dwellers, who, though mindful of their past, had set their sights firmly on the future. This seems to be borne out by the popularity of the Chicago artists throughout the country (apart from New York and Philadelphia) during the heyday of the style.

It would make for a neater explanation if it could be shown that the migrants to Chicago brought with them a ravenous and unsatisfied appetite for the old country blues but the only, admittedly sketchy, evidence is that this was not so. In his fascinating research into Library of Congress material Tony Russell uncovered a listing of the records on the Clarksdale jukeboxes of September 1941 and out of 108 listings from five jukes—Messenger's Cafe, the Chicken Shack, the Dipsie Doodle, Lucky's and the New Africa—only about 20 were strictly blues. The most popular artists, found on every box, were Count Basie, Fats Waller, Lil Green, Louis Jordan and Walter Davis. Overall there were two records by Big Bill, one each by Jazz Gillum, Washboard Sam, Sonny Boy Williamson and Peetie Wheatstraw and—the only items which could be considered country blues—one by Blind Boy Fuller (*Good Feeling Blues*) and the sole example of the local tradition, Tommy McClennan's *Whiskey Head Man.*

The only comparison that can be made is with the most popular records in Chicago's Bronzeville, on the eve of war three years earlier, where the story is the same. Out of 15 listed records only five were blues, four of them by Big Bill and one by Leroy's Buddy. Seemingly the patrons of the Clarksdale jukes and the Chicago bars had very similar tastes. One would have expected a much higher representation of blues on the Clarksdale boxes, let alone country blues, and common sense resists the argument that the major companies had so lost touch with their market that the black patrons were grudgingly punching the boxes for music that was less to their liking, simply because that was all that was available.

The conclusion is inescapable: migration brought to Chicago a population nurtured in country traditions rather than one with an emphatic taste for the country blues, and the rise of the postwar Delta blues was a complete if accidental musical revolution, as a new, exciting music was fashioned from a much earlier tradition by amateur bluesmen who grew up playing in the old local styles.

Will it ever happen again? If the preceding analysis is correct it is impossible that a pure blues form will ever rise again in a similar manner. The migration factor will become decreasingly significant in the future, as the city populations have already grown far too big for the balance to be tipped by any new influx, however great it may be. But, more important, there are no regional styles left to be transplanted to the cities, for records, radio and TV have smoothed out their idiosyncrasies and variations, and every subsidiary blues style is now spread evenly through the South. Whilst the old styles linger on, those young blacks who are still serving an apprenticeship in the blues turn almost exclusively to the records of Muddy Waters, Jimmy Reed and, especially, B. B. King for their inspiration. From now on any change in the direction of the blues will be through the super-eminence of a new blues hero—a new B. B. King, for instance—and the trend is almost certain to be towards larger and more jazz-influenced groups.

The rise of the Chicago blues happened at the time it did because every factor was favourable. Those same factors will never apply again.

Sources

ARNOLD, Billy Boy. 'In Search of Sonny'. *Melody Maker,* 20 and 27 November 1971.
BOCOCK, Mike. 'Chuck Berry', in *Nothing But The Blues* (q.v.).
BRUYNOGHE, Yannick. *Big Bill Blues.* Cassell & Co., Ltd., London, 1955.
CAYTON, Horace, and DRAKE, St. Clair. 'Bronzeville Life in 1946'. *Holiday,* 1947.,
. *Black Metropolis.* Harcourt, Brace, New York, 1945.
CHARTERS, Samuel. *The Bluesmen.* Oak Publications, New York, 1967.
DAWKINS, Jimmy. 'Earl Hooker'. *Blues Unlimited* 59 (January 1969).
. 'Morris Pejoe'. *Blues Unlimited* 67 (November 1969).
DEMETRE, Jacques. 'Willie Dixon', in *Nothing But The Blues* (q.v.).
DUNCAN, Otis Dudley, and DUNCAN, Beverley. *The Negro Population of Chicago.* University of
    Chicago Press, Chicago, 1957.
HOLT, John. 'Jimmy Reed'. *R&B Monthly* 12 (January 1965).
KOESTER, Bob. 'Lester Melrose: An Appreciation'. *American Folk Music Occasional* 2 (1970).
LEADBITTER, Mike. 'Little Walter', in *Nothing But The Blues* (q.v.).
. 'Freddy King', in *Nothing But The Blues* (q.v.).
. *Nothing But The Blues.* Hanover Books, London, 1971.
. 'Turning Point For Chess'. *Jazz & Blues,* June/July 1971.
. 'Lazy Bill Called Me Homesick'. *Blues Unlimited* 84 (September 1971), 85 (October 1971),
    86 (November 1971).
, and WARDLOW, Gayle Dean. 'Canton Mississippi Breakdown'. *Blues Unlimited* 91 (May
    1972).
LEISER, Willy. 'Down In The Alley'. *Blues Unlimited* 100 (April 1973).
. [Willie Mabon interview.] *Blues Unlimited* 101 (May 1973).
OLIVER, Paul. 'Muddy Waters', in *Nothing But The Blues* (q.v.).
. *Conversation With The Blues.* Cassell & Co., Ltd., London, 1965.
. 'Remembering Sonny Boy'. *American Folk Music Occasional* 2 (1970).
O'NEAL, Jim. 'Pepper's Lounge'. *Living Blues* 5 (Summer 1971).
. 'Cadillac Baby'. *Living Blues* 6 (Autumn 1971).
. 'Dusty Brown'. *Blues Unlimited* 84 (September 1971).
, and IGLAUER, Bruce. 'Remembering Magic Sam'. *Living Blues* 1 (Spring 1970).
, and O'NEAL, Amy. 'Chicago Blues Radio: Big Bill Hill'. *Living Blues* 7 (Winter 1971-72).
PATERSON, Neil. 'Magic Sam'. *Blues Unlimited* 7 (December 1963).
. 'Little Mac', in *Nothing But The Blues* (q.v.).
. 'Buddy Guy', in *Nothing But The Blues* (q.v.).
. 'John Brim', in *Nothing But The Blues* (q.v.).
. 'Otis Rush', in *Nothing But The Blues* (q.v.).
ROWE, Mike. 'Freddy Below', in *Nothing But The Blues* (q.v.).
. 'J.B. Hutto', in *Nothing But The Blues* (q.v.).
. 'Johnny Shines', in *Nothing But The Blues* (q.v.).
. 'Floyd Jones', in *Nothing But The Blues* (q.v.).
. 'Eddie Taylor', in *Nothing But The Blues* (q.v.).
. [Unpublished interviews with Johnny Shines, Shakey Horton, Homesick James and Muddy
    Waters.]
, and SCOTT, Frank. [Unpublished interviews with Eddie Taylor and Jimmy Rogers.]
RUSSELL, Tony. 'Clarksdale Piccolo Blues'. *Jazz & Blues,* November 1971..
. 'Musicians Talking: Johnny Williams'. *Jazz & Blues,* December 1971 and January 1972.
. [Unpublished interviews with Floyd Jones and Moody Jones.]
SCOTT, Frank. 'Al Smith'. *R&B Monthly* 15 (April 1965).
SHURMAN, Dick. 'Billy Boy Arnold', in *Nothing But The Blues* (q.v.).
SLAVEN, Neil. 'Jimmy Lee Robinson'. *R&B Monthly* 23 (December 1965)
SMITH, Francis. 'The Death Of Sonny Boy Williamson', in *Nothing But The Blues* (q.v.).
SPEAR, Allan H. *Black Chicago.* University of Chicago Press, Chicago, 1967.
STOLPER, Darryl. 'It Was Very Rewarding'. *Blues Unlimited* 88 (January 1972).
TILLMAN, Keith. 'Bring It To Jerome'. *Blues Unlimited* 63 (June 1969).
TITON, Jeff. 'Calling All Cows'. *Blues Unlimited* 60 (March 1969), 61 (April 1969), 62 (May
    1969), 63 (June 1969).
. 'All Pretty Wimmens'. *Blues Unlimited* 64 (July 1969), 65 (September 1969).
. 'Mojo Buford'. *Blues Unlimited* 76 (October 1970), 77 (November 1970), 78 (December
    1970).
VERNON, Mike. 'Eddie Boyd'. *R&B Monthly* 24 (January-February 1966).

WELDING, Pete. 'Muddy Waters'. *Down Beat,* 8 October 1964.
. 'Howling Wolf'. *Down Beat,* 14 December 1967.
. 'Johnny Young', in *Nothing But The Blues* (q.v.).
. 'Big Boy Spires', in *Nothing But The Blues* (q.v.).

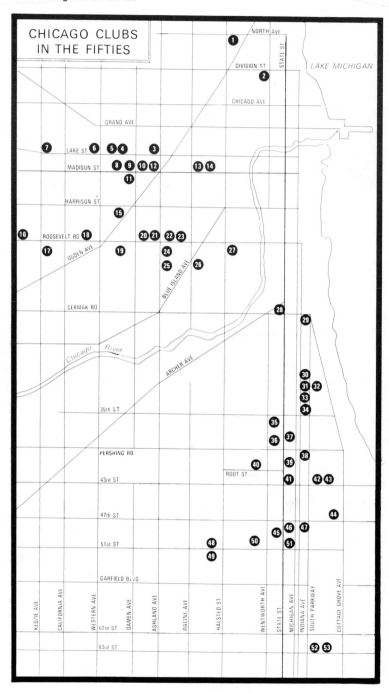

CHICAGO CLUBS
IN THE FIFTIES

Key

1 COTTON CLUB, Clybourn & Halsted; 2 SQUARE DEAL CLUB, 230 W. Division;
3 unknown name, 1601 W. Lake; 4 JOHNSON LOUNGE, 2200 W. Lake;
5 SYLVIO'S, 2254 W. Lake; 6 GATEWOOD'S TAVERN, W. Lake & N. Artesian;
7 CASBAH LOUNGE, 1181 W. Roosevelt; 8 PURPLE CAT, 2113 W. Madison;
9 CHUCK'S, Damen & Madison; 10 GLOBETROTTER LOUNGE, Damen &
Madison; 11 RED'S LOUNGE, Damen & Madison; 12 LOVER'S LOUNGE, Paulina
& Madison; 13 unknown name, 1145 W. Madison; 14 1015 CLUB, 1015 W.
Madison; 15 MASON & DAVE'S, Polk & Ogden; 16 COPA CABANA, 3358(?) W.
Roosevelt; 17 JAKE'S TAVERN, 13th & Kedzie; 18 CONGO LOUNGE,
Roosevelt & Washtenaw; 19 ROCK BOTTOM, Hoyne & Washburne; 20 CHARLIE'S
LOUNGE, 1811 W. Roosevelt; 21 DAVE'S TAVERN, 1806 W. Roosevelt; 22 1410
CLUB, 1410 W. Roosevelt; 23 TAY MAY, 1400 W. Roosevelt; 24 CLUB
ZANZIBAR, 13th & Ashland; 25 VI'S LOUNGE, 14th & Ashland; 26 TRIANGLE
INN, 14th, Racine & Blue Island; 27 unknown name, O'Brien; 28 HOT, Cermak &
State; 29 CARLISLE'S, 339 Cottage Grove; 30 FLAME CLUB, 3020 S. Indiana;
31 TEMPO TAP, 31st & Indiana; 32 PLANTATION, 328 E. 31st St; 33 TUXEDO
LOUNGE, 3119 Indiana; 34 SMITTY'S CORNER, 35th & Indiana; 35 DU DROP
LOUNGE, 3609 Wentworth; 36 CLUB ALIBI, 3726 Wentworth; 37 TICK TOCK,
37th & State; 38 CLUB CLAREMONT, 39th & Indiana; 39 BROOKMONT HOTEL,
40th & Indiana; 40 STORMY'S INN, Root & Princeton; 41 COSY INN, 43rd &
State; 42 PEPPER'S, 503 E. 43rd St; 43 WHITE ELEPHANT (DON'S DEN), 528 E.
43rd St; 44 708 CLUB, 708 E. 47th St; 45 CADILLAC BABY'S, 49th & Dearborn;
46 unknown name, 48th & State; 47 THERESA'S, 48th & Indiana; 48 SQUARE'S,
931 W. 51st St; 49 ADA'S LOUNGE, 5114 Peoria; 50 CASTLE ROCK, 50th &
Princeton; 51 BARRELHOUSE, 51st & Michigan; 52 520 CLUB, 520 E. 63rd St;
53 620 CLUB, 620 E. 63rd St.

Chicago R & B Hits 1945-59

Compiled from *Billboard* and *Cash Box* National R & B Charts (excluding Mercury entries). From
1950 onwards, items marked with one asterisk are *Billboard* Top Ten entries; those marked with
two asterisks are *Billboard* Number 1 hits. Artists' names are capitalised when they are blues-singers
hitherto discussed. Labels are abbreviated as follows: Ab (Abner), Ar (Aristocrat), Bb (Bluebird),
Cb (Cobra), Ch (Chess), Cha (Chance), Ckr (Checker), Met (Meteor), Mi (Miracle), Par (Parrot), Pre
(Premium), St (States), Tpt (Trumpet), Un (United), Vi (Victor), VJ (Vee-Jay), 4B (Four
Brothers).

1945   BIG BOY CRUDUP, *Keep Your Arms Around Me* (Bb); BIG BOY CRUDUP, *Rock Me
Mama* (Bb).

1946   ROOSEVELT SYKES, *The Honeydripper* (Bb); ROOSEVELT SYKES, *Sunny Road*
(Vi); BIG BOY CRUDUP, *So Glad You're Mine* (Vi).

1947   Gladys Palmer, *Fool That I Am* (Mi).

1948   Sonny Thompson, *Long Gone* (Mi); MEMPHIS SLIM, *Messin' Around* (Mi); Arbee
Stidham, *My Heart Belongs To You* (Vi): Sonny Thompson, *Late Freight* (Mi); SONNY BOY
WILLIAMSON, *Better Cut That Out* (Vi).

1949   MEMPHIS SLIM, *Frisco Bay* (Mi); Eddie Chamblee, *Blue Dreams* (Mi); Eddie
Chamblee, *Back Street* (Mi); MEMPHIS SLIM, *Blue And Lonesome* (Mi); Sonny Thompson, *Still
Gone* (Mi); TAMPA RED, *When Things Go Wrong* (Vi); MEMPHIS SLIM, *Angel Child* (Mi);
NIGHTHAWKS, *Annie Lee Blues* (Ar).

1950   Gene Ammons, *My Foolish Heart* (Ch); MUDDY WATERS, *Rollin' Stone* (Ch).

1951   MEMPHIS SLIM, *Mother Earth* (Pre); MUDDY WATERS, *Louisiana Blues* (Ch);
MUDDY WATERS, *Long Distance Call* (Ch); Jackie Brenston, **Rocket 88** (Ch); MUDDY
WATERS, *Honey Bee* (Ch); Lynn Hope, *Tenderly* (Pre); John Godfrey, *Hey Little Girl* (Ch);
TAMPA RED, *Pretty Baby Blues* (Vi); BIG BOY CRUDUP, *I'm Gonna Dig Myself A Hole* (Vi);
Tab Smith, **Because Of You** (Un); HOWLING WOLF, *How Many More Years* (Ch); MUDDY
WATERS, *Still A Fool* (Ch).

1952   Roscoe Gordon, **Booted* (Ch); MUDDY WATERS, *She Moves Me* (Ch); Jimmy Forrest, ***Night Train* (Un); (ELMORE JAMES, *Dust My Broom* (Tpt); Four Blazers, *Mary Jo* (Un); LITTLE WALTER, ***Juke* (Ckr); EDDIE BOYD, ***Five Long Years* (J.O.B.); Four Blazers, *Please Send Her Back To Me* (Un); Joe Williams, *Everyday I Have The Blues* (Ckr); WILLIE MABON, ***I Don't Know* (Ch); LITTLE WALTER, *Sad Hours* (Ckr); Jimmy Forrest, *Hey Mrs. Jones* (Un).

1953   LITTLE WALTER, *Mean Old World* (Ckr); Danny Overbea, *Train Train Train* (Ckr); EDDIE BOYD, *24 Hours* (Ch); Sax Kari, *That's Your Little Red Wagon* (St); WILLIE MABON, ***I'm Mad* (Ch); LITTLE WALTER, *Tell Me Mama* (Ckr); EDDIE BOYD, *Third Degree* (Ch); Spaniels, *Baby It's You* (Cha); LITTLE WALTER, *Blues With A Feeling* (Ckr); MEMPHIS SLIM, *The Comeback* (Un); MUDDY WATERS, *Mad Love* (Ch); Four Blazers, *Perfect Woman* (Un); (ELMORE JAMES, *I Believe* (Met)).

1954   LITTLE WALTER, *You're So Fine* (Ckr); MUDDY WATERS, *Hoochie Coochie Man* (Ch); LITTLE WALTER, *Oh Baby* (Ckr); Spaniels, *Goodnight Sweetheart* (VJ); MUDDY WATERS, *Just Make Love To Me* (Ch); MUDDY WATERS, *I'm Ready* (Ch); LITTLE WALTER, *You Better Watch Yourself* (Ckr); Lowell Fulson, *Reconsider Baby* (Ckr); Moonglows, *Sincerely* (Ch); WILLIE MABON, *Poison Ivy* (Ch); LITTLE WALTER, *Last Night* (Ckr).

1955   JIMMY REED, *You Don't Have To Go* (VJ); LITTLE WALTER, ***My Babe* (Ckr); Moonglows, *Most Of All* (Ch); Danderliers, *Chop Chop Boom* (St); Bo Diddley, *Bo Diddley* (Ckr); Lowell Fulson, *Loving You* (Ckr); HOWLING WOLF, *Who Will Be Next* (Ch); LITTLE WALTER, *Roller Coaster* (Ckr); J.B. LENORE, *Mama Talk To Your Daughter* (Par); Bo Diddley, *Diddley Daddy* (Ckr); MUDDY WATERS, *Mannish Boy* (Ch); Chuck Berry, ***Maybelline* (Ch); WILLIE DIXON, *Walking The Blues* (Ckr); El Doradoes, *At My Front Door* (VJ); Spaniels, *Painted Picture* (VJ); SONNY BOY WILLIAMSON, *Don't Start Me To Talkin'* (Ckr); Chuck Berry, *Thirty Days* (Ch); Priscilla Bowman, ***Hands Off* (VJ); MUDDY WATERS, *Sugar Sweet* (Ch).

1956   JIMMY REED, *I Don't Go For That* (VJ); El Doradoes, *I'll Be Forever Loving You* (VJ); JIMMY REED, *Ain't That Loving You Baby* (VJ); Flamingos, *I'll Be Home* (Ckr); Chuck Berry, *No Money Down* (Ch); HOWLING WOLF, *Smokestack Lightning* (Ch); LITTLE WALTER, *Who* (Ckr); MUDDY WATERS, *Forty Days And Forty Nights* (Ch); Moonglows, *We Got Together* (Ch); Flamingos, *Kiss From Your Lips* (Ckr); JIMMY REED, *Can't Stand To See You Go* (VJ); Chuck Berry, *Roll Over Beethoven* (Ch); Magnificents, *Up On The Mountain* (VJ); MUDDY WATERS, *Don't Go No Farther* (Ch); Moonglows, *See Saw* (Ch); JIMMY REED, *I Love You Baby* (VJ); Chuck Berry, *Too Much Monkey Business* (Ch); OTIS RUSH, *I Can't Quit You Baby* (Ch); Dells, *Oh What A Night* (VJ); HOWLING WOLF, *I Asked For Water* (Ch); SONNY BOY WILLIAMSON, *Keep It To Yourself* (Ckr); JIMMY REED, *You Got Me Dizzy* (VJ).

1957   JIMMY ROGERS, *Walking By Myself* (Ch); JIMMY REED, *Honey Where You Going* (VJ); Chuck Berry, ***School Day* (Ch); JIMMY REED, *Sun Is Shining* (VJ); Moonglows, *Please Send Me Someone To Love* (Ch); Spaniels, *Everyone's Laughing* (VJ); JIMMY REED, *Honest I Do* (VJ); Chuck Berry, *Rock And Roll Music* (Ch); Gene Allison, *You Can Make It If You Try* (VJ); Tune Weavers, *Happy Birthday Baby* (Ckr).

1958   Chuck Berry, ***Sweet Little Sixteen* (Ch); Jimmy McCracklin, *The Walk* (Ckr); Gene Allison, *Have Faith* (VJ); Chuck Berry, *Johnny B. Goode* (Ch); Chuck Berry, *Beautiful Delilah* (Ch); Jerry Butler, *For Your Precious Love* (Ab); JIMMY REED, *Down In Virginia* (VJ); Chuck Berry, *Carol* (Ch); Moonglows, *Ten Commandments Of Love* (Ch); Chuck Berry, *Sweet Little Rock And Roller* (Ch); LITTLE WALTER, *Key To The Highway* (Ckr); JIMMY REED, *I'm Gonna Get My Baby* (VJ); MUDDY WATERS, *Close To You* (Ch); Gene Allison, *Everything Will Be All Right* (VJ); Wade Flemons, *Here I Stand* (VJ); John Lee Hooker, *I Love You Honey* (VJ); Chuck Berry, *Run Rudolph Run* (Ch); Bobby Day, *Over And Over* (Ch); Dee Clark, *Nobody But You* (Ab).

1959   JIMMY REED, *I Told You Baby* (VJ); Bo Diddley, *I'm Sorry* (Ckr); Bo Diddley, *Crackin' Up* (Ckr); Bo Diddley, *Say Man* (Ckr); LITTLE WALTER, *Everything's Gonna Be Alright* (Ckr); Bo Diddley, *Say Man Back Again* (Ckr); Chuck Berry, *Almost Grown* (Ch); Dee Clark, *Just Keep It Up* (Ab); Dee Clark, *Hey Little Girl* (Ab); Chuck Berry, *Back In The USA* (Ch); Chuck Berry, *Anthony Boy* (Ch).

CHICAGO "TOP TEN" BLUES HITS ONLY 1960-67

1960   JIMMY REED, *Baby What You Want Me To Do* (VJ).

1961   JIMMY REED, *Bright Lights Big City* (VJ).

1965   G.L. CROCKETT, *I'm The Man Down There* (4B).

1966   KOKO TAYLOR, *Wang Dang Doodle* (Ckr).

Record Listing

BILLY BOY ARNOLD (1955-57) *I Wish You Would/I Was Fooled/My Heart Is Crying/Prisoner's Plea/You Got Me Wrong* (Buddah BDS 7511).

BIG MACEO (1941-49) *Chicago Breakdown/I Got The Blues/County Jail Blues/Why Should I Hang Around/Texas Stomp/Anytime For You/Maceo's 32-20/ Since You Been Gone/Worried Life Blues/Winter Time Blues/Big Road Blues/Broke And Hungry Blues/Detroit Jump/I Lost My Little Woman/Texas Blues/Tuff Luck Blues* (RCA 730.577); *Big City Blues* (Blues Classics BC-12); *Just Tell Me Baby* (Specialty SNTF5015).

BLUE SMITTY (1952) *Crying/Sad Story* (Chess LP411).

EDDIE BOYD (1952-53) *Twenty Four Hours/Third Degree* (Chess LP1446); *Five Long Years* (Blues Classics BC-8).

JOHN BRIM (1950-56) *Gary Stomp/Drinking Woman/Going Down The Line/Mean Man* (Boogie Disease BD101/2); *Humming Blues/Trouble In The Morning* (Muskadine LP100); *Ice Cream Man/You Got Me/Rattlesnake/Be Careful/Tough Times* (Chess LP1537).

BIG BILL BROONZY (1932-53) *Big Bill's Blues/You Do Me Any Old Way/Trucking Little Woman/Bull Cow Blues/Southern Flood Blues/New Shake 'Em On Down/Night Time Is The Right Time/Trouble And Lying Woman/Baby I Done Got Wise/Just A Dream/Oh Yes/Medicine Man Blues/ Looking Up At Down/When I Been Drinking/All By Myself/Night Watchman Blues* (Epic EE22017, CBS-Realm 52648); *Jacqueline/ Little City Woman/Lonesome/Romance Without Finance* (Chess 6641 047). (Also two LPs of primarily early [1928-32] material: Yazoo L-1011, L-1035.)

OTHUM BROWN (1948) *Ora Nelle Blues* (Muskadine LP100).

MOJO BUFORD (1963) *Mojo Woman/Steal My Chickens/Standing On The Corner/Somebody Knockin'/Tell Me Whatcha Gonna Do/Twin City Blues/Chicago Four Blues/Mojo Woman No. 2* (Vernon VS19).

DOCTOR CLAYTON (1942-46) *My Own Blues/Moonshine Women Blues/Pearl Harbour Blues/Ain't No Business We Can Do/I Need My Baby/Ain't Gonna Drink No More/Root Doctor Blues/Copper Colored Mama* (RCA-International INT1176)

BIG BOY CRUDUP (1941-54) *If I Get Lucky/Mean Old 'Frisco Blues/Rock Me Mamma/Keep Your Arms Around Me/Cool Disposition/She's Gone/So Glad You're Mine/Ethel Mae/That's All Right/Lonesome World To Me/Shout Sister Shout/My Baby Left Me/I'm Gonna Dig Myself A Hole/Mr So And So/Keep On Drinkin'/If You Ever Been To Georgia* (RCA LPV-573, RD-8224).

WALTER DAVIS (1930-40) *M&O Blues/Ashes In My Whiskey/Think You Need A Shot/Sweet Sixteen/Moonlight Is My Spread/Don't You Want To Go/L&N Blues/The Only Woman/That Stuff You Sell Ain't No Good/Root Man Blues/Just Want To Talk Awhile/Minute Man Blues/ New Come Back Baby/Let Me In Your Saddle/Howling Wind Blues* (RCA-International INT1085); *Why Should I Be Blue/Santa Claus/Jacksonville–Part 2/Call Your Name/Please Don't Mistreat Me/I Can Tell By The Way You Smell/Can't See Your Face* (Yazoo L-1025).

FORREST CITY JOE (1948) *Memory Of Sonny Boy/Sawdust Bottom* (Chess 6641 047).

BABY FACE LEROY FOSTER (1948-50) *Locked Out Boogie/Shady Grove Blues* (Chess 6641 047); *Boll Weevil/Rollin' And Tumblin'–Parts 1 and 2* (Blues Classics BC-8); *Red Headed Woman* (Muskadine LP100); *Take A Little Walk With Me* (Boogie Disease BD101/2).

LITTLE WILLIE FOSTER (1953-57) *Falling Rain Blues* (Blues Classics BC-8); *Little Girl/Crying The Blues* (Boogie Disease BD101/2).

JAZZ GILLUM (1938-42) *You're Laughing Now/I'm Gonna Get It/Let Her Go/She Won't Treat Me Kind/I'll Get Along Somehow/Got To Reap What You Sow/Key Hole Blues/Riley Springs Blues/I Got Somebody Else/It Looks Bad For You/Me And My Buddy/It's All Over Now/One Letter Home/You Drink Too Much Whiskey/Outskirts Of Town/Woke Up Cold In Hand* (RCA-International INT1177).

BUDDY GUY (1960-64) *Watch Yourself/Stone Crazy/I Found A True Love/First Time I Met The Blues/Let Me Love You Baby/No Lie/I Got A Strange Feeling/My Time After Awhile/Ten Years Ago/Broken Hearted Blues* (Chess LP409).

JOHN LEE HENLEY (1952) *Knockin' On Lula Mae's Door/Rhythm Rockin' Boogie* (Boogie Disease BD101/2).

EARL HOOKER (1953-69) *Chicken/Wild Moments* (Blue Flame BLP101); *Tanya/Blues In D Natural/Blue Guitar* (Red Lightnin' RL005); *The Hook/New Sweet Black Angel/Going On Down The Line/Original Sweet Black Angel/Guitar Rag/Earl's Boogie-Woogie/ Improvisations On Dust My Broom/Improvisations On Frosty* (Arhoolie 1066).

BIG WALTER HORTON (1951-54) *Hard Hearted Woman* (Blues Classics BC-8); *Cotton Patch Hotfoot/Blues In The Morning/Little Boy Blue/Walter's*

Blues/Black Gal/Hard Hearted Woman/Jumpin' Blues/So Long Woman (Polydor 2383 200).

▸ HOWLIN' WOLF (1951-61)   *Passing By Blues/I'm The Wolf/The Sun Is Rising/My Friends* (Kent KST9002); *Riding In The Moonlight/Dog Me Around/Worried About My Baby/Brownskin Woman/Crying At Daybreak/House Rockin' Boogie/Moanin' At Midnight/Backslide Boogie/Twistin' And Turnin'/Keep What You Got* (United 717, Ember EMB3370); *Forty Four/Evil/Smokestack Lightning/ Somebody In My House/How Many More Years/I'm Leaving You/All Night Long/Moanin' For My Baby/Baby How Long/No Place To Go/ I Asked For Water/Moanin' At Midnight* (Chess LP1450); *Shake For Me/The Red Rooster/You'll Be Mine/Who's Been Talkin'/Wang-Dang-Doodle/Little Baby/Spoonful/Going Down Slow/Down In The Bottom/Back Door Man/Howlin' For My Baby/Tell Me* (Chess LP1469); *Just My Kind/I've Got A Woman/Work For Your Money/I'll Be Around/You Can't Be Beat/You Gonna Wreck My Life/ I Love My Baby/Neighbors/I'm The Wolf/Rocking Daddy/Who Will Be Next?/I Have A Little Girl* (Chess LP1512).

J.B. HUTTO (1954)   *Dim Lights/Things Are So Slow* (Blues Classics BC-8); *Lovin' You/Pet Cream Man/Now She's Gone* (Muskadine LP100); *Combination Boogie* (Boogie Disease BD101/2).

ELMORE JAMES (1951-62)   *Dust My Broom* (Blues Classics BC-6); *Whose Muddy Shoes/Madison Blues/I See My Baby/My Best Friend/ The Sun Is Shining/Talk To Me Baby/Dust My Broom/Tool Bag Boogie/Call It Stormy Monday* (Chess LP1537); *Wild About You Baby/I Held My Baby Last Night/Long Tall Woman/Where Can My Baby Be/I Believe/Sinful Woman/Canton, Mississippi Breakdown/1839 Blues/Please Find My Baby/So Mean To Me/Hand In Hand/Rock My Baby Right* (Kent KST9001, United Artists UAS 29109);*Coming Home/Take Me Where You Go/Cry For Me Baby/Elmore's Contribution To Jazz/Knocking At Your Door/It Hurts Me Too/The 12 Year Old Boy* (Cobblestone LP9001); *It Hurts Me Too/Everyday I Have The Blues/Dust My Broom/Shake Your Moneymaker/Bleeding Heart/Pickin' The Blues/She's Got To Go/Talk To Me Baby/I Believe/Sunnyland Train/Stranger Blues/12 Year Old Boy/My Baby's Gone/Find My Kinda Woman/Up Jumped Elmore/Anna Lee/I've Got A Right To Love My Baby/Mean Mistreatin' Mama/ Look On Yonder Wall* (Trip LP8007).

● FLOYD JONES (1947-54)   *Dark Road/Stockyard Blues* (Blues Classics BC-8); *On The Road Again/Keep What You Got* (Muskadine LP100); *Skinny Woman/Big World/Floyd's Blues/Any Old Lonesome Day* (Boogie Disease BD101/2); *Playhouse/You Can't Live Long/ Dark Road* (Chess LP411); *Ain't Times Hard/Schooldays On My Mind/Any Old Lonesome Day* (Buddah BDS7511).

LITTLE JOHNNIE JONES (1949-54)   *Big Town Playboy/Shelby County Blues* (Chess 6641 047); *Chicago Blues/Hoy, Hoy, Hoy/Wait Baby/Up The Line (Doin' The Best I Can)* (Atlantic SD7227, WEA-Atlantic K40404).

J.B. LENOIR (1951-56)   *Natural Man/Don't Dog Your Woman/Let Me Die With The One I Love/Carrie Lee/Mama What About Your Daughter/If I Give My Love To You/Five Years/Don't Touch My Head/I've Been Down So Long/What Have I Done/Eisenhower Blues/Korea Blues/Everybody Wants To Know/I'm In Korea* (Chess LP410).

▸ LITTLE WALTER (1947-61)   *I Just Keep Loving Her/Moonshine Baby/Bad Acting Woman* (Muskadine LP100); *Blue Baby* (Boogie Disease BD101/2); *Muskadine* (Blues Classics BC-8); *My Babe/Sad Hours/You're So Fine/Last Night/Blues With A Feeling/Can't Hold Out Much Longer/Juke/Mean Old World/Off The Wall/You Better Watch Yourself/Blue Lights/Tell Me Mamma* (Chess LP1428); *Nobody But You/My Baby's Sweeter/Roller Coaster/As Long As I Have You/Oh Baby/Take Me Back/Everything's Going To Be Alright/Mellow Down Easy/I Hate To See You Go/I Got To Find My Baby/Everybody Needs Somebody/Blue Midnight/I Had My Fun/Key To The Highway/Blue And Lonesome* (Chess LP1535).

JOHNNY LITTLEJOHN (1968)   *What In The World You Goin' To Do/Treat Me Wrong/Catfish Blues/Kiddeo/Slidin' Home/Dream/Reelin' And Rockin'/ Been Around The World/Shake Your Moneymaker* (Arhoolie F1043).

LAZY BILL LUCAS (1954)   *She Got Me Walkin'/I Had A Dream* (Boogie Disease BD101/2).

● MAGIC SAM (1957-58)   *Everything Gonna Be Alright/Look Whatcha Done/All My Whole Life/Love Me With A Feeling/All Your Love/Call Me If You Need Me/Roll Your Money Maker/Easy Baby/Magic Rocker/Love Me This Way/21 Days In Jail/All Night Long* (Blue Horizon 7-63223).

● MEMPHIS MINNIE (1950-54)   *Down Home Girl/Night Watchman Blues/Why Did I Make You Cry/Kid Man Blues* (Biograph BLP12035); *Broken Heart/Me And My Chauffeur* (Chess 6641 047); *Kissing In The Dark/World Of Trouble* (Boogie Disease BD101/2). (Also two LPs of earlier material: Blues Classics BC-1, BC-13.)

RICE MILLER (SONNY BOY WILLIAMSON "NO. 2") (1951-60)   *Do It If You Wanna/Cool Cool Blues/Come On Back Home/Stop Crying/Eyesight To The Blind/West Memphis Blues/I Cross My Heart/Crazy About You Baby/Nine Below Zero/Mighty Long Time/She Brought Life Back To The Dead/Stop Now/Mr. Down Child/Sonny Boy's Christmas Blues/Pontiac Blues/Too Close Together* (Blues Classics BC-9); *Don't Start Me To Talkin'/I Don't Know/All My Love In Vain/The Key/Keep It To Yourself/Dissatisfied/Fattening Frogs For Snakes/Wake Up Baby/Your Funeral And My Trial/Ninety Nine/Cross My Heart/Let Me Explain* (Chess LP1437); *She Got Next To Me/Santa Claus/Little Village/Lonesome Cabin/I Can't Do Without You/Temperature 110/Unseen Eye/Keep Your Hands Out Of My Pocket/Open Road/This Old Life* (Chess LP1536).

MUDDY WATERS (1946-53)   *Hard Day Blues/Jitterbug Blues/Burying Ground Blues* (Testament T-2207); *Gypsy Woman/Little Anna Mae/I Can't Be Satisfied/I Feel Like Going Home/You're Gonna Miss Me/Rollin' Stone/Louisiana Blues/Evans Shuffle/Long Distance Call/Honey Bee/Howlin' Wolf/She Moves Me/My Fault/Still A Fool/They Call Me Muddy Waters/All Night Long/Please Have Mercy/Who's Gonna Be Your Sweet Man* (Chess 6641 047); *Sad Letter/Gonna Need My Help/Whiskey Blues/Down South Blues/Train Fare Blues/Kind-hearted Woman/Appealing Blues/Early Morning Blues/Too Young To Know/She's All Right/My Life Is Ruined/Honey Bee* (Chess LP1511). (For 1941-42 Library of Congress recordings: Testament T-2210.)

ROBERT NIGHTHAWK (1949-53)   *Sweet Black Angel/Anna Lee/Return Mail Blues/Jackson Town Gal* (Chess 6641 047); *Kansas City Blues* (Blues Classics BC-8); *I Feel So Bad* (Boogie Disease BD101/2); *Crying Won't Help You/The Moon Is Rising* (Red Lightnin' RL005).

WILLIE NIX (1951-53)   *Lonesome Bedroom Blues* (Kent KST9002); *Nervous Wreck/All By Yourself/No More Love/Just Can't Stay* (Boogie Disease BD101/2).

SNOOKY PRYOR (1948-63)   *Boogie/Telephone Blues/Boogy Fool/Raisin' Sand/I'm Getting Tired/Going Back On The Road/Crosstown Blues/ I Want You For Myself/Cryin' Shame/Eighty Nine Ten/Someone To Love Me/Judgement Day/Uncle Sam Don't Take My Man/Boogie Twist* (Flyright LP100).

JIMMY REED (1953-)   [British and US reissues have taken quite different forms. In Britain there are several LPs on Joy, such as JOYS111, JOYS120 and JOYS127. In the US comparable coverage is provided by the double LP Kent KST-537.]

JIMMY ROGERS (1950-56)   *Ludella* (Biograph BLP12035); *That's All Right/Ludella/Goin' Away Baby/I Used To Have A Woman/Money Marbles And Chalk/Back Door Friend/The Last Time/Out On The Road/Act Like You Love Me/Blues All Day Long/Chicago Bound/ Sloppy Drunk/You're The One/Walking By Myself* (Chess 6641 047).

OTIS RUSH (1957-60)   *Double Trouble/Jump Sister Bessie/She's A Good 'Un* (two takes)/*Checking On My Baby/Sit Down Baby/ Love That Woman/Keep On Loving Me Baby* (two takes) *My Baby Is A Good 'Un/If You Were Mine/I Can't Quit You Baby/All Your Love/Groaning The Blues/It Takes Time/Violent Love/Three Times A Fool/My Love Will Never Die* (Blue Horizon 7-63222); *I Can't Stop/I'm Satisfied/All Your Love/So Close/You Know My Love/So Many Roads* (Chess LP1538).

JOHNNY SHINES (1946-53)   *Delta Pine Blues/Ride, Ride Mama/Evil Hearted Woman Blues/Tennessee Blues* (Testament T-2207); *So Glad I Found You/Joliet Blues* (Chess LP411); *Ramblin'* (Blues Classics BC-6); *Evening Sun/Brutal Hearted Woman* (Muskadine LP100); *Living In The White House* (Boogie Disease BD101/2).

LITTLE MACK SIMMONS (1959-60)   *Come Back/My Walking Blues* (Blue Flame BLP101);*Times Are Getting Tougher/Don't Come Back/Sky's Crying/ Hootchie Kootchie Man* (Bea & Baby CB-101).

OTIS SPANN (1960)   *The Hard Way/Take A Walk With Me/Otis In The Dark/Little Boy Blue/Country Boy/Beat Up Team/My Daily Wish/ Great Northern Stomp/I Got Ramblin' On My Mind No. 2/Worried Life Blues* (Barnaby KZ30246); *It Must Have Been The Devil/Otis' Blues/Going Down Slow/Half Ain't Been Told/Monkey Face Woman/This Is The Blues/Evil Ways/Come Day Go Day/Walking The Blues/ Bad Condition/My Home Is On The Delta* (Barnaby KZ31290). (Both LPs jointly with Robert Lockwood Jr.; latter also features St Louis Jimmy Oden.)

BIG BOY SPIRES (1952-53)   *One Of These Days/Murmur Low* (Chess LP 411); *Which Woman Do I Love* (Blues Classics BC-23).

SUNNYLAND SLIM (1947-60)   *Farewell Little Girl/Broke And Hungry/Illinois Central/Nappy Head Woman/Across The Hall Blues/Walking With The Blues/Sweet Lucy Blues/No Whiskey Blues* (RCA-International INT1176); *Johnson Machine Gun/Fly Right Little Girl/*(Chess 6641 047); *Going Back To Memphis* (Blues Classics BC-15); *Recession Blues/Everything's Gonna Be Alright* (Delmark DS624); *Too Late To Pray/House Rock* (Bea & Baby CB-101).

EDDIE TAYLOR (1954-64)   *You'll Always Have A Home/Do You Want Me To Cry/Big Town Playboy/Ride 'Em On Down/Bad Boy/I'm Sitting Here/Don't Knock At My Door* (Cobblestone LP9001); *I'm Gonna Love You/Looking For Trouble* (Buddah BDS7511).

HOUND DOG TAYLOR (1962)   *Christine/Alley Music* (Blue Flame BLP101). (Also a 1971 LP: Alligator LP4701.)

* WASHBOARD SAM (1935-53)   *Mama Don't Allow/Jesse James Blues/Mama Don't Allow No. 2/Big Woman/We Gonna Move/Back Door/Lowland Blues/ Out With The Wrong Woman/Save It For Me/I'm On My Way/Levee Camp Blues/Low Down Woman/I'm Going To St Louis/Lover's Lane Blues/Flying Crow Blues/Digging My Potatoes* (Blues Classics BC-10); *Life Is Just A Book/I'm Feeling Low Down/Brown And Yellow Woman Blues/Flying Crow Blues/I'm Not The Lad/Levee Camp Blues/She Belongs To The Devil/My Feet Jumped Salty/I've Been Treated Wrong/Let Me Play Your Vendor/Gonna Hit The Highway/Evil Blues/You Stole My Love/Get Down Brother/I Get The Blues At Bedtime/I Laid My Cards On The Table* (RCA LPV-577, RD-8274); *Shirt Tail/Diggin' My Potatoes/Minding My Own Business/Horseshoe Over My Door/By Myself/I'm A Lonely Man* (Chess 6641 047).

JUNIOR WELLS (1953-60)   *Hoodoo Man* (Blues Classics BC-8); *Tomorrow Night* (Boogie Disease BD101/2); *Calling All Blues* (Buddah BDS7511). (Also a *c.* 1970 LP: Delmark DS628.)

BIG JOE WILLIAMS (1935-47)   *Stepfather Blues/Baby Please Don't Go/Wild Cow Blues/I Know You Gonna Miss Me/Rootin' Ground Hog/Brother James/Won't Be In Hard Luck No More/Crawlin' King Snake/I'm Gettin' Wild About Her/Peach Orchard Mama/Meet Me Around The Corner/Please Don't Go/Highway 49/Someday Baby/Break 'Em On Down* (RCA-International INT1087); *King Biscuit Stomp/I'm A Highwayman/Don't You Leave Me Here/Banta Rooster Blues/P Vine Blues/Mellow Apples/House Lady Blues/Baby Please Don't Go/Stack Of Dollars/Break 'Em On Down/Wild Cow Moan/Rootin' Ground Hog/Somebody's Been Borrowing/I Won't Be In Hard Luck* (Blues Classics BC-21).

JO JO WILLIAMS (1959)   *All Pretty Women/Rock And Roll Can Save Your Soul* (Delmark DL624).

HOMESICK JAMES WILLIAMSON (1953-62)   *Homesick* (Blues Classics BC-8); *The Woman I Love* (Boogie Disease BD101/2); *Set A Date* (Blue Flame BLP101).

* (John Lee) SONNY BOY WILLIAMSON (1937-46)   *Groundhog Blues/Collector Man/Until My Love Come Down/You Give An Account/Western Union Man/Shotgun Blues/ Welfare Store/She Don't Love Me That Way/Black Panther Blues/Bad Luck Blues/My Black Name/Jivin' The Blues/My Little Machine/ Joe Louis And John Henry/Sloppy Drunk Blues/Check Up On My Baby* (Blues Classics BC-3); *Skinny Woman/T.B. Blues/Train Fare Blues/She Was A Dreamer/Big Apple Blues/You Got To Step Back/Shady Grove Blues/My Baby's Made A Change/Broken Heart Blues/Stop Breaking Down/GM&O Blues/Shake The Boogie/Hoodoo Hoodoo/Mean Old Highway* (Blues Classics BC-20); *Honey Bee Blues/Whiskey Headed Blues/Lord Oh Lord Blues/Shannon Street Blues/ You've Been Foolin' Around Downtown/Deep Down In The Ground/Number 5 Blues/Christmas Morning Blues/Susie Q/Bluebird Blues—Part 2/Little Girl Blues/ Low Down Ways/Goodbye Red/The Right Kind of Life/Insurance Man Blues/ Rainy Day Blues* (RCA-International INT1088).

JOHNNY YOUNG (1947-48)   *Money Taking Woman* (Blues Classics BC-8); *Let Me Ride Your Mule/My Baby Walked Out* (Boogie Disease BD101/2).

Index